Strategic Risk Leadership

This casebook extends *Strategic Risk Leadership: Engaging a World of Risk, Uncertainty and the Unknown*, bringing theory and practice grounded in the first book to life with an array of applicable, real-world examples.

The book enables critical thinking about the current state of risk management and ERM, demonstrating contemporary shortcomings and challenges from real-life cases drawn from a global selection of well-known organizations. It confronts modern risk management practices and discusses what leaders should do to deal with unpredictable environments. Providing a basis for developing more effective risk management approaches, the book identifies shortcomings of contemporary approaches to risk management and specifies how to deal with the major risks we face today, illuminated by a variety of comprehensive global examples. It also provides valuable insights on these approaches for managers and leaders in general—including risk executives and chief risk officers—as well as advanced risk management students. End-of-chapter cases illustrate both good and bad risk management approaches as useful inspiration for reflective risk leaders.

This book will be a hugely valuable resource for those studying or teaching risk management.

Torben Juul Andersen is Professor of Strategy and International Management at the Copenhagen Business School and Director of the Global Strategic Responsiveness Initiative. He has previously held executive positions at Citibank/Citicorp Investment Bank, SDS Securities, Unibank, and PHB Hagler-Bailly and is an Honorary Fellow at the Institute of Risk Management (IRM). Torben has authored numerous books and academic articles on strategy and risk management topics.

Peter C. Young holds the 3M Endowed Chair in International Business at the University of St. Thomas, Opus College of Business and is Director of the Risk Leadership Initiative. He was previously the E. W. Blanch Senior Chair in Risk Management. Peter has been a Visiting Professor at City University, London and Aoyama Gakuin University, Tokyo, as well as Distinguished Honorary Professor at Glasgow Caledonian University. Among many awards, he has received the ALARM-UK Lifetime Service award.

"Drawing on a rich array of cases, Torben Juul Andersen and Peter C. Young explore the many faces of risk leadership as a new object for scholarly and practical attention. They provide a compelling synthesis of leadership and risk management thinking grounded in settings as diverse as ocean racing, refugee crises and financial markets. Risk leadership is skillfully positioned as an emergent way of thinking rather than a job description. Not only does it require reflective, collaborative and capable practitioners but also wisdom, value commitment and courage in the face of uncertainty. *Strategic Risk Leadership: Context and Cases* is highly recommended. It is a pleasure to read and is packed with valuable insights for students, academics and the general business reader. It should be compulsory reading for Chief Risk Officers."

Michael Power, *London School of Economics and Political Science, UK*

"True risk leadership combines the judicious use of quantitative techniques with the sound application of qualitative judgment with proper account of the constraints imposed by dynamic, complex environments. This excellent book provides a conceptual framework and set of case studies to elucidate the characteristics of strong risk leadership. What makes this book especially important is that it is timely, coming at a time when risk management is both ubiquitous and poorly defined. Readers of this book will learn important lessons that will make them want to engage in effective risk management, and provide them with guidelines for leading initiatives for dealing with risk and uncertainty in their organizations."

Hersh Shefrin, *Santa Clara University, USA*

Strategic Risk Leadership

Context and Cases

Torben Juul Andersen and Peter C. Young

Routledge
Taylor & Francis Group

LONDON AND NEW YORK

First published 2022
by Routledge
2 Park Square, Milton Park, Abingdon, Oxon OX14 4RN

and by Routledge
605 Third Avenue, New York, NY 10158

Routledge is an imprint of the Taylor & Francis Group, an informa business

British Library Cataloguing-in-Publication Data
A catalogue record for this book is available from the British Library

Library of Congress Cataloging-in-Publication Data
Names: Andersen, Torben Juul, author. | Young, Peter C., author.
Title: Strategic risk leadership: context and cases/Torben Juul Andersen and Peter C. Young.
Description: New York, NY: Routledge, 2022. | Includes bibliographical references and index.
Identifiers: LCCN 2021014118 (print) | LCCN 2021014119 (ebook) |
ISBN 9780367709396 (hbk) | ISBN 9780367709389 (pbk) |
ISBN 9781003148579 (ebk)
Subjects: LCSH: Leadership. | Risk management.
Classification: LCC HD57.7.A525 2022 (print) | LCC HD57.7 (ebook) |
DDC 658.15/5–dc23
LC record available at https://lccn.loc.gov/2021014118
LC ebook record available at https://lccn.loc.gov/2021014119

ISBN: 978-0-367-70939-6 (hbk)
ISBN: 978-0-367-70938-9 (pbk)
ISBN: 978-1-003-14857-9 (ebk)

DOI: 10.4324/9781003148579

Typeset in Bembo
by Deanta Global Publishing Services, Chennai, India

Access the Support Material: www.routledge.com/9780367709389

Of course, my sincerest gratitude is extended to Torben. We have worked off and on for over ten years but working on these books has been an absolute tonic for me, and that has been completely a consequence of working with Torben. I have learned a lot from him. Our Preface cites individuals with direct contributions to our book. Beyond that select group I would add a general category for all-round, long-term inspiration. In that list, I would include Fiona Gilvey of Willis Towers Watson in London, Professor Lynn Drennan, formerly of Glasgow Caledonian University, Martin Fone, formerly of Charles Taylor Consulting, and Tim Wood of Tata Consultative Services. I doubt they are fully conscious of their influence on my thinking but…there you are…sometimes you are inspirational and you don't even know it!

Finally, and as always, I acknowledge the lifetime of support and love of my wife, Sian. Everything I do and have done has benefited from her presence. And we weathered COVID-19 quarantine together, which will go down in the annals of the Young family as a major accomplishment. Here, however, I want to add my daughters, Hannah and Mallory. They are well and fully grown and on their own, but they are never far from my thoughts and their intelligence, humor (they are pretty funny), thoughtfulness has definitely made life worth living. All my love to the three of you.

Peter C. Young
Minneapolis, March 2021

I have been blessed with inspirational mentors and colleagues in business and academia—many of whom I am fortunate to consider my friends. We all learn from people we admire as well as those we consider bad exemplars—that is, and should be, the name of the game—obviously, I am the only one not to ever make mistakes. No, seriously—thanks for many good insights and learnings over the years—yet all the errors can and should be ascribed to the authors. Thanks to Peter, for impeccable and fruitful collaboration—I appreciate it—and I am pleased with the outcome… and—not least—my thanks go to Mette, Christine, and Christian for their continued support and inspiration.

Torben Juul Andersen
Copenhagen, March 2021

Contents

Cases

Preface

If nothing else was learned in 2020 certainly it can be agreed that we inhabit a volatile world. Is this volatility a passing phase? There are many compelling reasons to believe it is not. But even if we were dealing with transitory phenomena, it is the world we inhabit *now* and we are obliged to find ways to cope with it. It must be said, however, that the intensely differing perspectives we have witnessed in the face of recent major crises bear witness to the fact that it is very difficult to think, act, and reach a consensus to meaningfully confront uncertainty. Furthermore, just to emphasize a point that will become relevant to this book, our leaders (business, political, religious) struggle to think and respond to uncertainty as well; the added dimension in their case being the *consequences* of their (in) actions are often broadly impactful and consequential. And, by the way, wrong choices and human errors are one thing; we should not forget to think about self-interested leaders willfully misleading us.

One important response that might arise to address our present circumstances is to value committing time and resources to improving our technical capacity for measuring and understanding the challenges we face—follow the science, to use the popular vernacular. However, a second response might be to learn how to function more thoughtfully when our capacity to measure is limited or is impossible. We suppose a third response might be to more clearly understand when we are dealing with risk and when we are dealing with uncertainty and to realize that different considerations and actions might be more relevant when dealing with one or the other. And, importantly, there likely are other lessons to be learned regarding good, bad, and non-existent leadership in uncertain conditions.

Risk and *uncertainty* are two words that occupy a central spot in this book. There is, in the field of risk management study and practice, a slowly growing recognition that we are only occasionally dealing with risk—that is, *measurable uncertainty*—and that uncertainty, complexity, and the unknown are more common preoccupations for risk managers. In our judgment, it is only the powerful counterweight of the field's history that has prevented wider recognition that this is the case. Simply put, the journey of risk management toward becoming a formalized practice has firmly embedded the idea that risk management is, essentially, a techno-scientific function primarily tasked with measuring risk and relying on the predictive power of this analysis to make decisions and take action. This idea in many respects is a very good thing—the advancement in the development of tools for critical analysis has been, and continues to be, profoundly important. That idea, however, has had a negative effect as well. It has crowded out or significantly devalued efforts to appreciate the presence of uncertain and emergent phenomena as the central risk management concerns they should be. Indeed, the prevailing view has even produced some support for the idea that it might be possible to characterize an organization's risk in a single number; a theoretically arguable but—in our view—perplexing interpretation of an organization's exposure to an uncertain environment.

This book builds on a journey begun in our previous work. In reflecting on how formal risk management deals with risk, uncertainty, and the unknown, a kind of repurposing emerged on how we think about and envision the deployment of risk management. It probably should be mentioned here that we do not particularly believe *risk management* is even the right descriptive term for what we have proposed. Maybe *uncertainty management* fits the bill, but we are not even clear in our minds about that. Anyway, time and custom have spoken so we will continue to use the term *risk management*.

What we find interesting about our repurposed view is that the placement of uncertainty and the unknown (include complexity here; we will explain later) as central elements of risk management allows a number of ideas or assumptions to come into a sharper or different focus. For example, and we think this is important, a central focus on risk commonly leads to the conclusion that preventing bad things from happening or improving the odds of good things happening are the main objectives of risk management; whereas a central focus on uncertainty and the unknown arguably leads to a greater sensitivity to the limits of our knowledge and the need to be alert to and to deal with surprises.

In other words, while preventing bad things and pursuing good things remain important functional or operational activities, the overarching purpose of risk management in an uncertain world is to seek *sustainable resilience*. *Sustainable*, that is, both in the sense of longevity and in the "green" sense of the word. And we use the word *resilient* to reflect ongoing efforts to develop organizations, societies, and indeed our planet in ways that are responsive to surprises, that are adaptive and innovative, that can bounce back (or forward) after events transpire, that keep options alive, and that lead us to a heightened awareness of the interconnectivity of things. It also suggests that we are open to admitting when we are wrong and are willing to change our minds and alter direction.

Our repurposing effort has yielded another different take on something that actually has been occurring in plain sight over the past 30 years. If any single sentence could characterize the trajectory of risk management during that period it would be this: *risk management has been moving in the direction of a more expansive, integrated, interconnected, and holistic view.* This is mainly true in the world of organizational management; largely characterized by the *Enterprise Risk Management (ERM)* concept. However, the integrating dynamic is larger than ERM and is visible in emergency/disaster recovery responses to highly impactful natural phenomena, in endeavors such as United Nations Development Program efforts or even NATO peacekeeping operations. Through these additional examples emerges another key idea-shift, which is the express appearance and importance of *collaboration* in all forms of risk management.

In the world of business particularly the integrating effort normally compels organizations to determine who is responsible for that integration. An organization-wide effort to join up risk management practices would seem to require an individual or group to oversee efforts to achieve consistency and efficiency. The Sarbanes–Oxley Act in the United States addressed this issue by placing expectations on executives and boards to take on this role, spurring a drive toward central control and responsibility, which in principle remains the case today. A further regulatory push after the 2008 financial crisis accelerated the emergence of a particular response: the appointment of a Chief Risk Officer (CRO) in many organizations. As this book will demonstrate, the arrival of the CRO has not been an unalloyed success, but the point remains that somehow a more integrated approach requires both strategic and operational attentiveness.

This leads to the introduction of a somewhat new terminology. Top executives and the CRO are expected to provide *risk leadership*. We are still in the early days of understanding what risk leadership entails, and—in fact—this book's primary intention is to pick up the thread of that line of inquiry. It is worth noting briefly that there is a reason for the late arrival of the risk leadership concept. Probably this is because the emergence of the CRO and Executive Team as—let us call them—*Risk Leaders* has been largely the result of external pressures or influences: new regulatory requirements, responses to a crisis situation, or external stakeholder pressures. Thus, careful *internal* reasoning as the basis for the development of the risk leadership idea and its purposes has lagged behind events. To put it differently, exogenous influences produced pressure to move with haste to the implementation of generalized risk leadership *practices* before time had been taken to think about what risk leadership *is* and what should be expected from it.

Consider this illustration. Looking at leadership in general, it is intriguing that major risk events are only rarely caused purely by mechanical failures, breaches of operating procedures, or failures to comply with specific risk management processes and practices. If the handling of operating systems fails, the underlying causes typically can be traced to the leadership approach adopted by the upper echelons of the organization; that is, by those that are supposed to govern the risk management processes. This suggests risk leadership thinking has not been sufficiently directed (if at all) to the role top leaders and managers *themselves* play as important sources of risk and uncertainty. The puzzle here is to note that most responses to such serious failures or scandals have been to impose more rules, processes, and oversight and not particularly to replace the top managers; but more about that as we proceed.

We see this book as an outgrowth of our earlier effort to examine and reimagine risk *management*. Within that repurposing arose a need to think critically about what risk *leadership*, and general leadership influences, might entail and how things can or should be practiced in an uncertain world. As the preceding paragraphs indicate, risk leadership might be part of a CRO's responsibility—expressly so, in fact—but, we argue, it is an expectation of all organizational leaders. And further, as we explore, the concept of risk leadership seems widely applicable; it is not just limited to organizational settings, nor, for that matter, is it limited to the top levels within the organizations themselves.

And so, here we arrive at an overview of this book.

The preceding paragraphs set out the foundations of the book's orientation, which are:

1. While we have developed useful capacities in assessing and addressing risks, we have had much less success in integrating ways to think about and address uncertainty, complexity, and the unknown. Certainly, this is the case in what we might call formal risk management practice.
2. The integrating dynamic in risk management study and practice, we believe, is sensible—and so there will continue to be a need for someone to oversee the development and ongoing performance of risk management efforts. However, we will observe that integration presents some challenges of its own and may have limits.
3. That "someone" may be a single individual or many people, but in any event, we will call them *risk leaders* and will argue that their role is to provide *risk leadership*. We should note here, however, that the case studies we include will rarely show

individuals who are consciously aware that they are performing risk leadership—such is the newness of the terminology.

4. While these leaders may seek data-driven support for the decisions they make, we are rather firmly committed to our view that leaders operate mainly in a world of uncertainties, complexity, and the unknown where they often, and subconsciously, are influenced by behavioral, psychological, and even cultural biases and potential ethical shortcomings that are hard to capture and address in formal risk management practices. And so we believe that central to the development of risk leadership is the need to develop ways to operate consciously and thoughtfully in an environment of uncertainty, complexity, and the unknown.

5. Let us not forget the previous mention of what could be called *collaborative risk management*. As major exposures like climate change and global pandemics affect everyone, they illustrate the need for collaborative solutions. Integration presumes collaborative effort, whether within a single organization (risk managers working with compliance officers and sustainability leaders), with organizational stakeholders (supply chain managers, distributors, customers, risk managers, financial institutions), or societal multi-organizational settings (public and private sector entities working with UNICEF to deliver food, clothing, education, and sanitation in developing countries). Since risk leaders are mainly concerned with uncertainties and surprises, it makes sense that a collaborating "sensibility" would be both a frame of mind as well as a viable strategy and tool toward achieving resilient and sustainable outcomes.

This, then, is the field of play for the book—with an objective to consider risk leadership as a meaningful response to our uncertain world. We do want to acknowledge that there already exists very helpful thinking about the tools and frameworks that these leaders might utilize. For example, the general field of Leadership study presents a number of useful insights that are highly relevant and provide an important anchoring into the extensive research that has been conducted around the topics of leaders and leadership. Notably, research in the areas of adaptive and complexity leadership appears to offer a particular gateway into that wider field of study. Also, the Risk Governance literature offers descriptive and prescriptive insights on the idea of integrative, collaborative risk management.

However, what we will be particularly keen to keep in mind is the leader (or where relevant, leaders) sitting in an office with all these tools, frameworks, and ideas available, but with an unclear view as to how to proceed. This motivates us to examine a few specific things in this book—particularly the question, "what does risk leadership entail?" Addressing this question will lead us to think about thinking, to reflect on human nature, to understand how values guide—or do not guide—our decision-making, and to consider the means by which individuals lead in response to uncertainties and the unknown. From this, we hope to shed light on both the *who* of risk leaders and the *what* of risk leadership.

Finally, we should note that much of what is written above is reflected in the choice of this book's structure. One particular way we could have proceeded is to trawl through scholarly risk management studies that have sought to describe and measure the performance and value of, particularly, ERM. And, in fact, commentary on that research appears in the book. However, we will attempt to argue that these, often quantitative and sophisticated, studies of risk management performance have encountered significant limitations or barriers. Consequently, they collectively offer a rather inconclusive view of the nature and impact of ERM. Beyond that, we are not even sure whether generally accepted methods of measuring ERM performance are directing us to look at the right things—which frankly may be part of the problem in assessing ERM's value-contribution. But we acknowledge that many concepts featured here are relatively new and there is a lot we just do not know at present, so the search for alternative performance measurements will become a feature of the book.

So, how can we proceed with limited reliance on theories and existing measures? We look for ourselves; the empirical method—as old as Aristotle. Admittedly, a case study-based, observational approach can be misused—cherry-picking those stories being only the most notorious abuse. We have been mindful of this in the assembly of cases and are comfortable that we have at least been conscious as to what each case might tell us—and what it cannot. The result is a set of case studies that highlight a range of issues we deem to be essential to understanding what risk leadership *is* perhaps more so than what it *does*. Decision-making and action-taking will appear here, of course, but the essential perspective is on equipping individuals to think critically about how they provide risk leadership. The cases presented offer both good and bad examples. Nevertheless, through this approach we are hopeful that readers will begin to see an emerging picture of, let us call this person, the *reflective risk leader.*

Foreword and acknowledgments

From the early days of writing *Strategic Risk Leadership: Engaging a World of Risk, Uncertainty and the Unknown*, in 2018, we had in mind two books—a book to set out a range of general ideas about risk management and leadership (released in early 2020), and then a second book intended to dig further into those ideas providing more substance to our thinking through the use of case study illustrations.

To a certain extent, our first book might be seen as a window on our thought processes rather than a summary of conclusions we had already identified before sitting down to write. We had a pretty clear idea of the issues we wanted to address but it was really through the writing process itself that we began to see the fuller picture (and implications) of what we were doing. In a way, that enhanced our enthusiasm for the second book—this book—because we developed greater clarity as to where our emerging ideas "needed to go"—meaning what further questions arose in the first book and how we needed to sort them out. One thing we confirmed with this book was our original thinking about case studies—a number of the issues we identified were not well-studied, not studied at all, or did not present consistent conclusive evidence of particular assumptions or views. Case studies proved to be a practical way to consider key points in the absence of more concrete and abundant data.

So, this second book came together for us as an undertaking with two distinct parts. First, as noted, we intended to include case studies and readers will find two to three case studies attached to each of the seven chapters. However, each chapter begins with a set-up, in effect, taking our views from the first book and exploring their implications. As just one example of this, the first book identified risk leadership (and Risk Leaders) as a subject worthy of further consideration, but one that was not connected in any meaningful way to the wider literature on general leadership. And so, this second book makes an effort to do that, and to identify further issues for study. It is no surprise to anyone that this is the way research works—but we still find the story behind how the two books evolved to be somewhat different from our past research experiences.

Individuals were noted in the front end of our first book as significant inspirations or supporters, and we still hold them as inspirational and supportive here. Owing to the process of case study development, several additional individuals proved to be absolutely essential to our present efforts. The fact that they all are good friends personally, as well as respected experts, only added to the pleasure of working with them. They are Major General (ret.) Tim Cross, whose experience in the Balkans, and his subsequent lecturing and consulting on the subject of leadership has been very influential in the development of our own thinking on the subject; Andrew Keeling, at one time responsible for risk at SABMiller, but who has a very distinguished and long career in other organizations, and is a very good friend and colleague; Aileen Guiney, the head of risk at Target Corporation, is the newest of our friends and colleagues but has been most helpful in many ways; Mustafa Omar of Shelter for Life was central to developing the LIFFT-Cashew case; and Kristine Raffel, currently responsible for risk at Vestas, a past writing partner, a source of numerous risk management insights, and an innovative thinker on the subject. Kristine, by the way, was formerly responsible for risk management at Copenhagen Airports and thus had contributory roles in two of the cases included in this book.

1 The journey from risk management to risk leadership

Leadership and risk leadership

To begin, it is important to establish what Risk Leadership mostly *is not*. It is not a distinct classification—it does not offer a unitary *theory* of leadership as might, say, Authentic or Transformational Leadership. Risk leadership mostly *is* an aspect of all leadership that has not received the attention it warrants. It also represents the briefest of job descriptions for individuals who might be referred to as *Risk Leaders*, though even in that context it would still feature as more a component than a category of leadership. For these reasons—there are essentially two distinct target audiences for this book:

- Individuals who assume senior positions with clearly designated responsibilities to lead on risk (Chief Risk Officers, CROs, are representative of this group)
- Any person at any organizational level or other social contexts who faces a challenge or opportunity to provide leadership that requires some level of knowledge and capability to respond to risk and uncertainty (this would include executives for whom risk management or risk leadership is a component of their overall responsibilities)

Two target audiences also point toward two lines of inquiry with the intention of eventually knitting them together—the underlying goal being to establish risk leadership as a subject meriting more serious study. The first line of inquiry is to develop linkages to relevant leadership studies relying on the scholarly (and some professional) leadership literature. The second line is to discern and analyze the leadership role and functions as described and embedded in the risk management literature. We first provide a very short overview of the leadership literature followed by a brief review of the Risk Leadership concept as it has emerged over the past decade.

Leadership

A review of the entirety of scholarly leadership research is beyond the scope and intentions of this book—leadership is a highly complex subject of study with seemingly inconsistent (or competing) views across a vast literature. Leadership is not only a complex subject; it may also mean different things at different times and to different constituents.[1]

Leadership research has also evolved over time through influences of broader changes in society and its values. For example, the inclusion of both gender and race are essential elements in any contemporary view of leadership, which was not so evident in the past.[2] Another development is the emergent focus on multi-directional leadership perspectives,

DOI: 10.4324/9781003148579-1

e.g., bottom-up, lateral, and top-down, that reflect more nuanced ways of thinking about power and decision structures in contrast to long-held assumptions.[3] These older assumptions include a view of the CEO (the Leader) and the executive team as being solely responsible for the formulation and enactment of a strategy to achieve intended objectives.[4] Current challenges to that view are shaped by a growing interest in complexity—which opens the door to new ways of thinking about leadership.

Despite the daunting effort to summarize Leadership studies, the first steps are misleadingly simple. For more than 2,500 years, the focus was on the leader himself (yes, "him"). Various studies continue to analyze leadership based on the observed traits of individual leaders.[5] Initially, these studies tended to be descriptive; seeking to uncover the divine attributes of the leaders—assuming that these were largely innate or inherited features—and, we note, the interest in these natural qualities has seen a certain resurgence.[6] This approach coincides with the "upper echelons theory" as a widely adopted perspective in management studies to explain how organizational outcomes associate with—or derive from—particular executive traits.[7] The early work on natural leadership traits eventually led to a search for attributes and skills as evidence of successful executive approaches that might be learned from conscious individual effort. This development extended the search for visible traits expressed in behaviors and actions taken by successful leaders.[8] The result has been a fruitful area of research, producing a *behavioral* view of effective leadership.

A critical recognition of the importance of context and circumstances for executive decision-making has challenged the simple association between leadership traits and specific outcomes.[9] This insight began a push toward a view of leadership as a contextualized *process* rather than "just" attributes and behaviors displayed by individual leaders. A common feature that emerged with process-oriented thinking was that leadership is not only a matter of a particular type of individual relying on specific traits to pursue the formulated organizational goals and objectives. Instead, leadership relies on a varying array of skills, knowledge, and attributes (and possibly some *luck*) when *responding* to and *interacting within* a specific environmental context. So, leadership would be different in different situations—a standardized set of traits and behaviors cannot be assumed to automatically work in any context.

In retrospect, it seems inevitable that consideration of contextual influences expanded to include the people who were to be led.[10] The slightly inelegant but widely adopted term *Followership* captures the idea that a leader must have followers. Thus emerged the idea that Leadership studies should acknowledge the interactions between the Leader, the Followers, and the Context triad to achieve a more comprehensive understanding of leadership. A widely used textbook captures the essence of this view by defining Leadership as: "a process whereby an individual influences a group of individuals to achieve a common goal."[11]

There are dozens of competing definitions, some more detailed, but this definition conveys in 15 words a recognition of the central presence of leaders, followers, and context—as well as the view that leadership is defined by the interactions between these elements. And it employs the concept of process and even hints at a moral foundation for leadership.

A few other points deserve highlighting—all will receive further attention throughout the book.

In the search for alignment between the Risk Leadership idea and general Leadership, a critical element to consider is that the term Risk Leadership plainly indicates that *risk* in some way is a defining feature of the concept. This requires elaboration, but it seems safe to assume that a risk leader or someone exercising risk leadership is recognized as possessing a distinct understanding of risk, as well as affiliated concepts like uncertainty, complexity, and the unknown. From this logical supposition, the challenge is to identify a point of entry into the wider field of Leadership study. In the search for parallel language and corresponding orientation, the specific characteristics of Complexity Leadership hold a promise to establish connective tissue.[12]

A second point to lift and carry forward is the distinction between Management and Leadership. It is unlikely that full agreement on the differences will ever occur, but in later sections of this book, it becomes necessary to draw a provisional line between risk managers/management and risk leaders/leadership. So, we note here:

- Most scholars agree that considerable overlap exists between management and leadership—any dispute mainly focuses on the degree of that overlap[13]
- A broad consensus argues that management serves to provide orderliness and consistency in (primarily) organizational settings[14]
- A generalized view suggests that leadership involves activities such as creating a vision, formulating strategy, thinking holistically, setting goals and aligning resources, and inspiring and empowering employees[15]

Small but soon-to-be-critical features (critical to this book) within Leadership studies are the concepts of *assigned* or *emergent* leadership.[16] Assigned leadership refers to an official leadership position (a CEO possesses assigned leadership), whereas another person might gain recognition as a leader through behaviors, capabilities, and actions; that is, they emerge as leaders without a formal designation. This will come to resonate with perhaps one of the most critical challenges reported by Risk Leaders. That is, the title CRO implies an assigned leadership status, but for reasons discussed later, we will need to be alert to detect the difference between *presumed* assigned leadership and *actual* assigned leadership. There is a reasonable chance that in many cases they do not align for CROs. Relatedly, leadership implies possession of influence and formal decision power whereas we will need to be attentive to a more textured view, seeing power as being developed or assembled over time. In this area of study, the ability to exert *expert* and *informational power* (here the term *risk competence* will be introduced) are likely to produce promising insights for risk leadership.[17]

The continuing search for leadership traits further relies on the identification of *personality factors*, of which conscientiousness, openness, extraversion, agreeableness, and neuroticism are representative of factors that contribute to a capacity to lead.[18] A leader's awareness of personal strengths and weaknesses with respect to these factors (sometimes referred to as *emotional intelligence*) is also found to be an influential individual trait.[19]

In the ensuing chapters, several leadership perspectives may be relevant including consideration of Complexity Leadership with insights from behavioral psychology, organizational culture, context-setting, Leadership Ethics, and Team and Collaborative Leadership all making appearances.

Risk leadership

A brief history of risk management

The earliest manifestation of risk management—as we tend to think of it today—was *insurance buying*, which became a more formally recognized function in the late 1940s.[20]

Due to this early orientation, over the ensuing 20 years, the risk management field became identified as primarily engaged in identifying and addressing potential *threats*, with a focus on risks (that is, *measurable* uncertainties) since insurance pricing requires a reasonable degree of measurability. The idea that risk also might be a source of *opportunities* to be exploited was not part of the early vocabulary and *uncertainty* was viewed as a second-ary—if even that—concern.[21]

Beginning in the late 1960s and continuing to the present day, insurance has remained influential, though in a different way. The insurance industry (particularly commercial property and casualty insurance) is subject to underwriting cycles that periodically feature intense price competition, which drives down prices eventually leading to excessive loss payouts. This contributes to a reactive hardening of markets, dramatic premium increases, or an outright disappearance of coverage. The resultant instability in insurance availability and affordability has been influential in pushing risk managers to consider alternatives to insurance. The emergence of conscious risk-retention strategies included self-insurance, alternative risk financing, captive insurance, and in recent years, risk-linked capital market tools.[22]

Self-financing options have had the ancillary effect of increasing interest in more ambi-tious risk control measures, for the obvious reason that in retaining the risks—rather than transferring them—the exposure to loss costs is more bearable if direct measures are taken to impact frequency and severity of potential losses. This growing focus on risk control revealed affinities between risk management and other loss prevention and reduction efforts, such as corporate safety and security, internal control systems and processes, business inter-ruption, and emergency response planning. Though never explicitly dictated, a view slowly emerged that these affiliated activities might also be considered risk management.[23]

Additionally, throughout the 1960s and 1970s, emerging operations management the-ories and practices began to expand and exert their influence. Total Quality Management (TQM), for example, introduced a more meticulous analysis of operating procedures and failures that caught the attention of both risk managers and insurance underwriters.

One of the most influential developments, undoubtedly, is the emergence of *financial risk management*.[24] Financial risk management arose in the financial services sector as an effort to deal with various types of credit risk, foreign exchange risk, interest rate risk, commodity price risk, and investment market risk. These were not new types of risk, of course, but their importance expanded due to a confluence of events including increas-ingly volatile (and vulnerable) global financial markets and economic turmoil following the OPEC oil crisis of 1974. In response, new instruments were developed to trade, transfer, and manage or hedge related financial exposures.

The development of financial risk management tools arose from a somewhat unique interaction between scholarship and business.[25] This interaction introduced more esoteric financial instruments, so-called *derivative* contracts, linked to methods such as the Black–Scholes option pricing model.[26] These tools might also be employed to invest and take risks, not just neutralize them; and this investment aspect of financial risk tools led to an early recognition that risk management might constitute the pursuit of *opportunities* and not just a reduction of *threats*.

The adoption of more innovative financial risk management tools came with an increasing degree of complexity and sophistication, which has proven to be a significant challenge for executives and boards. Combined with that complexity and the risk-taking (which is to say, investment) possibilities, organizational leaders had to address ever-increasing levels of risk/uncertainty that made it challenging—maybe impossible—for leaders to fully comprehend the net exposure produced by those instruments.[27] However, a final, and notable, consequence of this approach was that—through applications of such things as portfolio theory and Value-at-Risk (VaR) modeling—a foundation emerged for the idea of an organization-wide view of risk management.

Looking back on the evolution of risk management, it might be said that the story reveals the emergence of a number of *technical risk management* functions, first led by insurance-buying techniques and subsequently more sophisticated financial risk management methodologies, but also including affiliated managerial developments. The net effect was to expand the reach of individual risk management specialists into new and, sometimes, overlapping practice areas ultimately motivating both practitioners and scholars to reflect on the possible value of a more integrated approach to risk management.[28]

A seeming solution was found in corporate finance theory, where integrative risk management practices were argued to support better evaluations of risky business projects, improve risk-adjusted returns, and increase shareholder value by optimizing capital allocation. The aligned concept of risk appetite, to be outlined by top management, and enhanced risk controls like three-lines-of-defense practices further boosted the organization-wide risk management idea. [29]

On the practitioner side, adoption of more integrative risk management practices was, and remains, highly variable. Early experiences seem to suggest that any wide-ranging approach to risk management would have to be specific to the adopting organization, and indeed empirical evidence reveals that actual implementations do not align with a standardized template. Nevertheless, interest was high in developing a framework, eventually leading to the introduction of Enterprise Risk Management (ERM).[30]

The integrative idea of ERM was elaborated on by a number of standardized risk management frameworks. For example, the COSO framework (the most widely employed guidance in the United States) defined ERM as:

> a process, effected by an entity's board of directors, management and other personnel, applied in strategy-setting and across the enterprise, designed to identify potential events that may affect the entity, and manage risks to be within its risk appetite, to provide reasonable assurance regarding the achievement of entity objectives.[31]

In other words, ERM reflects a high-level—which is to say, top-down—governance (and strategy-making) perspective, with successful risk management outcomes linked to the ability to satisfy predetermined strategic objectives within defined risk limits signed off by the board of directors.

It is important to note that early on two weaknesses of this emerging holistic, integrated approach became evident. One was the lack of clarity determining how the process of integrating risk management actually occurs in an organization. Another entwined issue is the relatively limited consideration of *who* actually performs the integrating, organizing, and oversight. Some efforts have been made to address these weaknesses, and the ERM movement continues to dominate risk management thinking and practice. Virtually every developed country in the world now has some form of requirement or legal expectation for risk management to be practiced in ways similar to the ERM format.[32]

The emergence of risk leadership

Advocacy for the CRO position might be seen as heralding the introduction of a wider Risk Leadership idea, and there is some evidence for this.[33] However, the connectivity is not as firm as might be assumed.

While Doug Barlow[34] figures as the first Risk Manager, a post he held from 1963 to 1972 at Massey Ferguson, James Lam[35] is often credited as the first person to hold the CRO title, a position he assumed at GE Capital in 1993 and subsequently held with Fidelity Investments from 1995 to 1998. However, this formal executive risk position only began to receive more attention after major corporate scandals arose in the United States and Europe at the turn of the century, e.g., Enron, WorldCom, and Parmalat. These events triggered intense reviews of the governance, financial reporting, and internal control systems and processes, which resulted in specific and explicit executive risk management responsibilities set forward in the Sarbanes–Oxley Act[36] in the United States in 2002. SOX, as it is abbreviated, proved to have international impacts as well.

The aftermath of the global financial crisis 2007–2009, particularly the Lehman Brothers collapse in 2008, led to further scrutiny of the governance implications of risk management. The Basel Committee on Banking Supervision[37] ascribed the crisis to failed risk governance, skewed incentive structures, and overleverage in the financial industry. Hence, in 2010, the Committee proposed that banks should assign a CRO to head a risk compliance function with "authority, stature, independence, resources and access to the board."[38] The role of this executive function would include the identification, assessment, and monitoring of major risks on a firm-wide basis supported by an internal control system—all the hallmarks of ERM. It specifically mentioned that the "qualifications" of the "risk management personnel" should reflect sufficient experience, market knowledge, and "mastery of risk disciplines."

The Committee's updated guidelines in 2015 further specified the criteria of an executive risk position (CRO) as an individual with sufficient stature, independence, resources, and access to the board. The CRO should have the responsibility for overseeing the risk management systems, policies, processes, models, and reports so they fully support the strategic objectives and related risk-taking activities. These are not straightforward requirements and expectations to fulfill, and they open a question about the extent to which a single individual is able to combine independence with full responsibility for effectively managing all major exposures. Yet, the emphasis ascribed to the CRO position highlighted an emerging attempt to address "who" is responsible for integrating, organizing, and overseeing organization-wide risk management.[39]

The Basel Commission clearly provided a boost to the CRO idea. However, there were some issues in adoption and implementation. The CRO position was widely interpreted as a response to new regulatory requirements suggesting that CROs primarily should engage in compliance matters—and indeed, some CROs carry the dual title of Compliance and Risk Officer. Also, since the regulatory requirements—to a large extent—focused on financial institutions, the CRO idea was often perceived as specific to the financial sector. Nonetheless, the idea of an executive position to front the prescribed enterprise-wide risk management activities has gained general support. For example, the appointment of a CRO was included in the updated versions of OECD's Principles of Corporate Governance (2010, 2015).[40]

The CRO agenda promoted more concrete considerations about "who leads on organization-wide risk management." However, usage of the term *Risk Leadership* (and *Risk Leader*) seems more a decision of linguistic convenience than the result of a reflective consideration of how the CRO function could be described as engaging in risk leadership, nor was there evidence of efforts to link to broader thinking about general leadership. It does, however, seem to represent an effort to explain certain activities that did not quite fit a generally understood risk management framework. This story of the emerging terminology can be traced, at least indirectly, in recent reviews of the risk leadership idea.[41]

As this book attempts to clarify the meaning of Risk Leadership, it is useful here to stipulate the basis for validating the importance of the risk leadership idea. This will have to rest upon the following assertions:

1. The trajectory of development in the risk management field has reached a point where the conceptual and applied structure of risk management is inadequate to characterize many aspects of needed integrative efforts to address complexity, uncertainty, and the unknown.
2. External expectations imposed by regulators, legislatures, market requirements, and external interest groups have imposed integration as an enforceable expectation on organizations.
3. Risk and uncertainty are pervasive phenomena and the idea that they can be handled effectively in similar ways has been challenged by scholars and practitioners.
4. The consequence of Points 1, 2, and 3 is that integration requires top management engagement. And it is in this sense that the Executive Team holds general *risk leadership* responsibilities; indeed, they are *de facto* Risk Leaders. However, the breadth and detail of risk management involves specialized knowledge and express attentiveness. Many organizations have thus designated a top-level individual to assume more hands-on responsibility for these activities. CROs are illustrative of that and such individuals presumably are *Risk Leaders*. However …
5. Current thinking about risk management suggests that a space must exist to describe risk leadership occurring everywhere in an organization—or in other situations. Thus, it is important to anticipate and explain how risk leadership is not just the provenance of the CRO or top management. We orient our analysis toward top-level risk leadership in this book but this is primarily because that is where the action has been thus far. However, we are mindful to shape our comments to anticipate the application of risk leadership in many different contexts.
6. Although it needs to be shown, the term Risk Leadership suggests that there are particular aspects of risk, uncertainty, complexity, and the unknown that warrant a deeper understanding. This in no way argues that risk leadership is a new category of leadership, as previously noted. It is true that the Risk Leader might have express responsibilities, but it is more important to note that risk leadership is an *aspect* of leadership that has been under-recognized to date.

This final point offers a most serious challenge. That is, it might be that the invention of the *risk leadership* term and concept signifies a distinction without a difference. After all, we live in a world primarily characterized by uncertainty and therefore all leaders presumably consider, consciously or not, the presence and impact of uncertainty on decisions and actions. Why would it be necessary to construct a new area of leadership study and practice rather than just folding it into the more general debate? This, it must be conceded, is a fair point and any effort to give risk leadership shape, meaning, and value must detail its distinct differences while aligning with the wider field of leadership study to clarify its contributions.

Risk leadership: A working conceptualization

Our initial, and primary, focus is on organizational leadership. However, some of the most critical risk issues today are large-scale exposures that dominate the headlines, such as climate change, pandemics, migration, and political instability. In these contexts, organizations, governments, and, indeed, society in general must find ways to collaborate, because effective responses require something far beyond the application of traditional risk management tools within the organization itself. They require the creation of a joint vision, negotiation, cooperation, consensus building across involved parties, and decisions on sensible risk sharing/bearing arrangements. Arguably, these are actions of leadership. As will be seen, this collaborative dynamic does have parallels within single organizations. The integrating process with ERM relies on cross-silo collaboration and where, of course, collaboration is necessary for external stakeholders as well—typified by, say, global supply chain risk management. So, collaborative risk leadership appears relevant in and out of single organizational settings.

This book is an effort to provide a meaningful investigation of the risk leadership concept. To begin, then, consider the following provisional, working definition:

> Risk Leadership, consistent with all Leadership, anticipates a moral relationship between leaders, followers, and other stakeholders that recognizes and accounts for the presence of contextual factors. Key characteristics of that relationship are that it is trust-based, attuned to rights and responsibilities, and includes a recognition of the emotional dimension and a commitment to the common good. It differs from other Leadership concepts in the technical focus, which is to thoughtfully engage the challenges driven by the presence of complexity, risk, uncertainty, and the unknown.

We will elaborate on, challenge, and extend this initial risk leadership perspective as we progress through the ensuing chapters.

The cases

This chapter provides a short scene-setting review of the risk management story—how it started and developed; how Enterprise Risk Management entered the picture; and the consequent emergence of Chief Risk Officers/Risk Leaders as a new, heralded, but largely underexamined phenomenon. Throughout this book, there will be positive examples of "good and bad" risk leadership; but here we begin with three cases that collectively offer a kind of stair-step story of the emergence of risk leadership by first looking at the birth of formal modern expectations for risk management, followed by an early motive for its continued growth, and then followed by a warning shot across the bow of the aspirations that had formed over the journey.

Case 1.1: *Managing risks through regulation: The Sarbanes–Oxley Act*

Case overview

Fraudulent, reckless, self-dealing leadership and management in organizations of any type has a long and sordid history, but it was nevertheless something of a surprise to see a cluster of examples emerge at roughly the same time in the late 1990s and early 2000s. Perhaps this was not precisely a coincidence; it may have been a product of the booming economic, social, and political environments, and even the "spirit of the times" that led to this particular set of events. Three specific incidents, crises, or scandals: Enron,

WorldCom, and Tyco captured public and political attention, leading to a specific legislative response—the Sarbanes–Oxley Act of 2002.

In an end of year assessment by CNN/Money, December 2002, journalist Jake Ulick began his summary by stating,

> the deepest legacy of 2002, with its revelations of falsified corporate results and executive indictments, may (have caused) damage to investor confidence that could take years to restore. A money-making culture that turned Alan Greenspan, Abby Joseph Cohen and Jack Welch into financial heroes vanished this year, replaced by handcuffed chief financial officers, humbled equity analysts, and a stock market headed for a third year of declines.

The rollcall of dishonor included the aforementioned collapse of Enron, the bankruptcy of WorldCom, and charges filed against CEOs for essentially looting their respective firms in the cases of Tyco and Adelphia Communications (as noted, there were others). In conjunction with these dramatic events, stock analysts at big securities firms came under fire for apparently complicit stock research, reporting, and advisories; all evidence signaling a collaborative relationship in setting terms for trades in the market. The issue of regulator inattentiveness (and permissiveness) did not escape the attention of politicians in Washington DC either.

Alongside these stories, audit and consulting giant, Arthur Andersen (the audit and consulting firm that signed off on Enron's and WorldCom's books) was convicted of obstruction of justice—the penalties included a prohibition to audit public companies. Among the issues earning attention during the trial was the interconnectivity of audit and consulting practices within Arthur Andersen—in effect, revealing the practice of gaining ongoing management consulting relationships through "favorable" audits. Moral hazard had run amuck.

It was in this setting that the United States Congress stepped into the picture.

The Sarbanes–Oxley Act

The Senate Banking Committee's initial response was to hold hearings on the scandals and the general performance of financial markets; signaling an interest not only in specific illegal acts but in the context in which the scandals emerged. The hearings produced a surprising consensus across the political parties as to the essential problems, inadequate funds for the Securities and Exchange Commission, lack of auditor independence, stock analysts' conflicts of interest, meaningless disclosure provisions, inadequate oversight of accountants, and poor corporate governance practices. In addition to these core insights, the Committee found that the "Dotcom Bubble" was a specific contributing factor as were certain bank lending practices (which tended to overlook or devalue clients' risks). Excessive executive compensation was deemed to be an issue warranting further consideration as well.

The act was passed into law in July 2002. The Sarbanes–Oxley Act (abbreviated as SOX), by highlighting the problems in the audit and financial services worlds, prompted similar responses from countries around the world. Although not central to this case, between 2003 and 2007 comparable laws were passed in several countries, including Canada, Germany, South Africa, France, Australia, India, Japan, and Italy. As firms operating under the ambit of SOX (and these international responses) could attest, the new law was complex, complicated, and costly. Achieving compliance required addressing 11 key areas of compliance:

1. **Public Company Accounting Oversight Board (PCAOB)**

   Title I establishes the Public Company Accounting Oversight Board to provide independent oversight of public accounting firms.

2. **Auditor Independence**

   Title II establishes standards for external auditor independence to limit conflicts of interest. Among other things, it restricts auditing companies from providing non-audit services (e.g., consulting) for the same clients.

3. **Corporate Responsibility**

   Title III mandates that senior executives take individual responsibility for the accuracy and completeness of corporate financial reports. It defines the interaction of external auditors and corporate audit committees and specifies the responsibility of corporate officers for the accuracy and validity of corporate financial reports. It enumerates specific limits on the behaviors of corporate officers and describes specific forfeitures of benefits and civil penalties for non-compliance. For example, Section 302 requires that the company's "principal officers" certify and approve the integrity of their company financial reports quarterly.

4. **Enhanced Financial Disclosures**

   Title IV describes enhanced reporting requirements for financial transactions. It requires internal controls for assuring the accuracy of financial reports and disclosures, and mandates both audits and reports on those controls.

5. **Analyst Conflicts of Interest**

   Title V consists of only one section, which includes measures designed to help restore investor confidence in the reporting of securities analysts.

6. **Commission Resources and Authority**

   Title VI consists of four sections and defines practices to restore investor confidence in securities analysts.

7. **Studies and Reports**

   Title VII requires the SEC to perform various studies and report their findings.

8. **Corporate and Criminal Fraud Accountability**

   Title VIII, also known as the "Corporate and Criminal Fraud Accountability Act of 2002," describes specific criminal penalties for manipulation, destruction, or alteration of financial records or other interference with investigations, while providing certain protections for whistleblowers.

9. **White-Collar Crime Penalty Enhancement**

   Title IX, also known as the "White Collar Crime Penalty Enhancement Act of 2002." This section increases the criminal penalties associated with white-collar crimes and conspiracies.

10. **Corporate Tax Returns**

    Title X states that the Chief Executive Officer should sign the company tax return.

11. **Corporate Fraud Accountability**

    Title XI, also known as the "Corporate Fraud Accountability Act of 2002." It identifies corporate fraud and record tampering as criminal offenses and joins those offenses to specific penalties. It also revises sentencing guidelines and strengthens their penalties.

Assessing SOX

Not surprisingly, SOX and its various impacts have been the subject of considerable academic and professional examination and research. However, the sheer scope and complexity of the law have made it difficult to draw sharp conclusions about its ultimate effects. Broadly, the research can be categorized as assessing 1) costs of compliance, 2) impacts on the external audit and consultancy sector, 3) effects of the requirements on financial performance, and 4) the general efficacy of regulatory responses to the perceived problems. Title IV: Section 404, which requires firms to report on the adequacy of internal controls on financial reporting, has been a specific focus of attention for the risk management community. A short overview provides some detail on Section 404, but in doing so, shines a reflected light on the complicated nature of all other sections of SOX.

Section 404: Assessment of Internal Control has been, in some senses, one of the more controversial and contentious parts of SOX, and—as noted—it possibly is the section of SOX that has resonated most directly with risk management and risk leadership. In overview, it requires both management and external auditors to report on the adequacy of a company's internal controls of financial reporting. Among many complaints that have come from companies seeking to comply, Section 404 is frequently cited as one of the more costly and time-consuming requirements, especially as implementing, documenting, and testing controls were/are expected to be ongoing processes.

Under this section, management is required to produce a report on internal controls on an annual basis. The report is expected to affirm the responsibility of top management for establishing and maintaining an adequate internal control structure and procedures for financial reporting—including an assessment of that structure and process itself. This requirement has commonly meant that companies follow the Committee of Sponsoring Organizations of the Treadway Commission, representing five audit organizations (COSO), statement on internal control frameworks. Other guidance has been provided by the Public Company Accounting Oversight Board as well as the Securities and Exchange Commission. However, the key here is the requirement that both top management and the external auditor conduct a *top-down risk assessment*. This assessment, to be more precise, requires management's assessment and evidence gathering to be *risk-based*. Taken as a whole, Section 404 requires:

- Assessing both the design and operating effectiveness of selected internal controls related to significant accounts and relevant assertions, in the context of material misstatement risks
- Understanding the flow of transactions, including IT aspects, in sufficient detail to identify points at which a misstatement could arise
- Evaluating company-level (entity-level) controls, which correspond to the components of the COSO internal controls framework
- Performing a fraud risk assessment
- Evaluating controls designed to prevent or detect fraud, including management override of controls
- Evaluating controls over the period-end financial reporting process
- Scaling the assessment based on the size and complexity of the company
- Relying on management's work based on factors such as competency, objectivity, and risk

• Drawing conclusions on the adequacy of internal control over financial reporting

Title III: Corporate Responsibility yielded an associated impact, requiring principal officers to certify and approve the financial reports. This has come to be interpreted in a particular way within the risk management community. In effect, the CEO is *de facto* the Risk Manager of the firm, inasmuch as the basis on which the tasks above are assessed requires the organization leadership to first have clarified a policy or view about the objectives and benchmarking of risk management practices. From this interpretation has emerged concepts like *risk policy, risk appetite, risk tolerance*, and *three lines of defense*.

Owing to a lack of clarity in the particulars with SOX, COSO subsequently produced guidance on risk management. The articulation of these expectations, as set forward by the COSO document, served as a kind of connective tissue for linking SOX to broader developments in the risk management community—particularly Enterprise Risk Management (ERM). And, although never expressly stated in SOX (nor for that matter in COSO), this link-up acted as an early catalyst for the idea of the Chief Risk Officer, and the emergence of the risk leadership idea.

It is clear that the elevated status of risk management today is owed, in large part, to the Sarbanes–Oxley Act. However, this boost in prestige has not been singularly beneficial. Among the more prominent issues or problems with the SOX influence on modern risk management are:

1. The practical matter of external validation of risk management reporting has linked risk management more firmly to internal controls (auditors provide the external assessment). This is not just an issue of substance; it also is a matter of perception. To a significant degree, risk management has come to be seen as an internal control matter.
2. The emergence of CROs—prompted in part by SOX—has associated risk management with regulatory mandates. While SOX did have the effect of getting risk management on the executive and board agendas, it often produced the view that risk management was being imposed on organizational leadership from outside and was not seen as something driven by internal considerations.
3. Related to the internal control issue, the focus of risk management promoted an orientation toward measuring, documenting, introducing systems and process controls, and supporting institutional structures. There is some irony that the scandals that prompted SOX were mainly characterized by bad behavior on the part of individuals—commonly at top levels in the organization. While not automatically the intended outcome of SOX, the general shape of the response to these behavioral issues was to increase "policing" of the rank and file, rather than addressing top management behaviors directly.
4. In a more positive context, the required commitment of resources proved a boon to risk management practices—certainly at an operational level. Systems, processes, rules, oversight, data gathering, and top-level engagement are important operational aspects of risk management. So, while researchers continue to be challenged with assessing the overall effects of SOX, there is a general agreement that SOX and COSO have improved the technical qualities of risk management practices. Therefore, SOX and COSO work well for accomplishing what they set out to accomplish, which is no mean achievement. However, the question persists, is compliance with SOX/COSO the same thing as being effective in managing risk, uncertainty, and the unknown?

Reflections

Consideration of the influence of Sarbanes–Oxley on modern risk management is not only important as a concrete legal and regulatory requirement. Its contribution to how we think about risk management is significant. And, given the themes in this book, it probably is no surprise that many aspects of the book stand in direct contrast to the vision SOX has consciously or unconsciously imposed on current practices. However, even though there are numerous criticisms with this vision, it would be churlish not to acknowledge the value SOX/COSO (and include ISO 31000) have brought to the professionalization of risk management. Having noted that, three questions here merit further attention and discussion.

- There is something of a tautology in how scholars and practitioners view the value of risk management—and particularly ERM. Most research, for example, seeks to validate risk management based on the terms and conditions ERM sets for itself. However, alignment with the proclaimed goals and purposes of ERM does not particularly mean that ERM is fulfilling the role of effectively assessing and addressing risk, uncertainty, and the unknown. There is some support for skepticism on this point because research has proven inconclusive on ERM's value-adding contributions. Taken as a whole, the question here is whether ERM (as based on SOX/COSO) requires modification, radical overhaul, or is adequate and useful as it stands.
- One of the debates that seems fully unresolvable regarding regulation asks whether it is better to adopt a *rules-based* set of requirements or a *principles-based* set of requirements. While the argument is somewhat simplistic and imprecise, it is frequently suggested that COSO represents a rules-based approach while ISO 31000 is principles-based. From the standpoint of a Risk Leader, which is preferred, and why? Superficially, rules-based regulation explains exactly what a firm needs to do to comply, whereas principles-based regulation provides an "image" of compliance and directs firms to find their own way toward compliance.
- A somewhat more philosophical debate centers on legality vs. morality. Can we legislate morality? Here the public policy issues can take shape in terms of how we address risks while respecting concerns such as individual freedom and liberty, balancing costs and benefits, effectiveness of the measures taken, and other political and economic values and concerns. Simplistically, regulations *make* an organization do or not do something, whereas reliance on individual choice (it is argued) encourages an organization to *choose* to do or not do something. This is rarely an either-or proposition, but can we consider the criteria by which regulators choose one or the other? Interestingly, within an individual organization, the same question emerges in another form. Does the risk manager/leader achieve better outcomes by dictating the rules and practices of risk management, or is it more effective to provide space for individuals within organizations to devise responses to risks and uncertainties that they encounter?

Read more about it

Banerjee, S., Humphery-Jenner, M., and Nanda, V. (2015). Restraining overconfident CEOs through improved governance: Evidence from the Sarbanes–Oxley act. *The Review of Financial Studies*, 28(10), 2812–2858.

Singer, Z. and You, H. (2011). The effect of section 404 of the Sarbanes–Oxley act on earnings quality. *Journal of Accounting, Auditing, and Finance*. 26–3, 556–589.

Valenti, A. (2008). The Sarbanes–Oxley act of 2002: Has it brought about changes in the boards of large U. S. corporations? *Journal of Business Ethics*. 81, 401–412.

Zhang, X. (2007). Economic consequences of the Sarbanes–Oxley act of 2002. *Journal of Accounting and Economics*. 44(1–2), 74–115.

Case 1.2: Business development and risk management: The story of Lehman Brothers

Case overview

Lehman Brothers, once a prime international financial institution, filed for bankruptcy on September 15, 2008. It was said that Lehman's demise was caused by deregulation where financial markets stopped working due to a lack of confidence. Others, including Lehman CEO Richard Fuld, claimed that speculative "naked short selling" drove its collapse while some argued that its risk management failed. The turmoil during the 2007–2008 economic crisis threatened the stability of the global financial industry and developed economies went into a recession at the same time causing lost jobs and destroyed livelihoods. Several institutions were bailed out by the US Government including GM, AIG, Merrill Lynch, Bear Stearns, and Freddie Mac and Fannie Mae.

As a point of reference, the 2006 annual report from Lehman Brothers stated a commitment to "a culture of risk management at every level." This case looks into the accuracy of this statement and tries to assess why a company "committed to a culture of risk management" failed. This case discusses Lehman's exposures and the responses the company took to deal with emergent threats and opportunities in a changing market.

A brief history

Lehman Brothers dates back to its foundation in 1847 as a financial services firm trading commodities like cotton and coffee, gaining membership of the New York Stock Exchange in 1887. The company was acquired to form Shearson-American Express in 1984, it merged into Shearson Lehman Hutton in 1988, and was divested by American Express in 1994 as Lehman Brothers Holding in an initial public offering (IPO). The company was a primary US Treasury dealer and developed into a leading global financial services firm operating in capital markets, investment banking, and funds management. After the IPO, the company expanded and grew its revenues more than six times to exceed $19 billion by 2007. The company operated in major global markets with 60% of revenues from US markets, 25% in Europe, with other activities in Asia and emerging markets.

Lehman's long-term objective was to gain diversified growth and opened in many new locations in Doha, Dubai, Geneva, Istanbul, Lisbon, Moscow, Sao Paolo, and Shanghai to expand geographically and grow revenues. The company was recognized for business excellence and ranked #1 in several categories including fixed-income market share, trading, execution, and overall quality. Nevertheless, as noted, Lehman Brothers declared bankruptcy on September 15, 2008, after emergency takeover negotiations with Bank of America and Barclays failed.

Background

It is argued that effective risk management embodies a central risk oversight function and operating risk management procedures. Local risk awareness is necessary to ensure that day-to-day transactions are conducted in accordance with the risk policies while central coordination and monitoring are needed to establish objectives and set appropriate risk limits based on identification, assessment, and management of corporate exposures—an approach outlined in the enterprise risk management (ERM) frameworks.

Risk management at Lehman

By adopting ERM, a firm signals its attempt to identify all the major risks where local agents may report to a central risk function that in turn aggregates the risks into a corporate exposure for top management oversight. It is argued that integrative analysis of all risks provides a better overview of corporate exposures and allows better risk handling through downside risk prevention and enhancement of opportunities.

Financial exposures derive from volatile financial markets as well as credit, liquidity, and operational risks. Credit risk is the loss potential from failure to repay debt or honor an obligation. Liquidity risk is the potential inability to make daily payments due to a shortage of liquid funds. Market risk derives from financial losses (gains) on assets and liabilities caused by fluctuating foreign exchange rates, interest rates, and so on. According to Lehman, it "utilized a number of risk measurement tools" in the risk management process including sophisticated tools like VaR to integrate the exposure of many market events

Value-at-risk

VaR is a mathematical model that quantifies the expected portfolio loss over a given time period with a specified probability. It expresses risk in a single number across a complex portfolio of different assets and risks. VaR can be calculated frequently to assess the effect of trading activities and ease monitoring over time. Even if top managers and board members are unfamiliar with the detailed calculations, they can see exposures expressed in an aggregated number.

A VaR with say a 95% confidence interval indicates that the portfolio will not lose more than a certain amount ($124 million in the case of Lehman by 2007). So, 19 out of 20 days, the total loss will not exceed $124 million, but it does not say how much can be lost on the day the limit is exceeded. We note that the VaR more than doubled 2006–2007, increasing from $54 to $124 million (Exhibit 1). At the same time, assets increased by around 35%. This suggests that Lehman consciously increased its trading exposure. Whether this is excessive depends on the vulnerability to changes in market conditions. We note a leverage ratio of 30.7 times up from 26.2 times in 2006, implying that a 3.2% drop in the value of total assets will deplete the long-term capital of the company.

Mortgage-backed securities

Mortgage-backed securities are supported by cash flows from an assigned portfolio of mortgage loans, referred to as mortgage-pass through securities, constituting the largest segment of the US investment grade fixed-income market. This structure allows banks to

Exhibit 1 Selected Financial Data (Lehman Brothers Holding Inc.)

US$ million	As of or for the Year Ended November 30				
	2007	2006	2005	2004	2003
Consolidated Statement of Income					
Total revenues	$ 59,003	$ 46,709	$ 32,420	$ 21,250	$ 17,287
Interest expense	39,746	29,126	17,790	9,674	8,640
Net revenues	19,257	17,583	14,630	11,576	8,647
Non-interest expenses:					
Compensation and benefits	9,494	8,669	7,213	5,730	4,318
Non-personnel expenses	3,750	3,009	2,588	2,309	1,716
Real estate reconfiguration charge	—	—	—	19	77
Total non-interest expenses	13,244	11,678	9,801	8,058	6,111
Income before taxes and cumulative effect of accounting change	6,013	5,905	4,829	3,518	2,536
Provision for income taxes	1,821	1,945	1,569	1,125	765
Dividends on trust preferred securities	—	—	—	24	72
Income before cumulative effect of accounting change	4,192	3,960	3,260	2,369	1,699
Cumulative effect of accounting change	—	47	—	—	—
Net income	$ 4,192	$ 4,007	$ 3,260	$ 2,369	$ 1,699
Net income applicable to common stock	$ 4,125	$ 3,941	$ 3,191	$ 2,297	$ 1,649
Consolidated Statement of Financial Condition					
Total assets	$ 691,063	$ 503,545	$ 410,063	$ 357,168	$ 312,061
Net assets	372,959	268,936	211,424	175,221	163,182
Mortgage and asset-backed securities	$ 89,106	$ 57,726	—	—	—
Long-term borrowings	123,50	81,178	53,899	49,365	35,885

Total stockholders' equity	22,490	19,191	16,794	14,920	13,174
Tangible equity capital	23,103	18,567	15,564	12,636	10,681
Total long-term capital	145,640	100,359	70,693	64,285	50,369
VaR (value-at-risk)	$ 124	$ 54	–	–	–
Earnings per share:					
Basic	$ 7.63	$ 7.26	$ 5.74	$ 4.18	$ 3.36
Diluted	$ 7.26	$ 6.81	$ 5.43	$ 3.95	$ 3.17
Weighted average common shares outstanding:					
Basic	540.6	543.0	556.3	549.4	491.3
Diluted	568.3	578.4	587.2	581.5	519.7
Dividends declared and paid per common share	$ 0.60	$ 0.48	$ 0.40	$ 0.32	$ 0.24
Book value per common share	$ 39.44	$ 33.87	$ 28.75	$ 24.66	$ 22.09
Selected Data					
Leverage ratio	30.7x	26.2x	24.4x	23.9x	23.7x
Net leverage ratio	16.1x	14.5x	13.6x	13.9x	15.3x
Employees	28,556	25,936	22,919	19,579	16,188
Assets under management (in US$ Billions)	$ 282	$ 225	$ 175	$ 137	$ 120
Financial Ratios					
Compensation and benefits/net revenues	49.3%	49.3%	49.3%	49.5%	49.9%
Pre-tax margin	31.2%	33.6%	33.0%	30.4%	29.3%
Return on average common stockholders' equity	20.8%	23.4%	21.6%	17.9%	18.2%
Return on average tangible common stockholders' equity	25.7%	29.1%	27.8%	24.7%	19.2%

originate mortgage loans, repackage them, and sell them to investors, i.e., the banks can generate loans without retaining the underlying credit and liquidity risks. If the mortgage borrowers fail to repay their debt, the credit risk is with the holders of the mortgage-backed securities. From 2006, Lehman increased its inventory of mortgage-backed securities from $57.7 to $89.1 billion in 2007 (Exhibit 1).

Liquidity

VaR assumes that instruments in the portfolio be traded when needed, but this is not always possible when markets are distressed. To mitigate the liquidity risks, Lehman adopted a policy to maintain liquid assets to cover one year in a stressed environment. Lehman had a liquid pool of $34 billion in February 2008 increasing to $45 billion by May 2008. However, the ability to price mortgage-backed securities became increasingly difficult. The market valuations relied on rising housing prices where few considered a bearish real estate market.

Regulation: Naked shorts

The prevalence of naked shorts arguably caused tremendous harm to the Lehman stock. In naked shorts, investors sell stock they do not own without guaranteed delivery. In regular shorting, the shares are borrowed before they are sold short. Naked shorts flooded the market with non-existing shares and depressed the Lehman stock. A sold stock without delivery is "failed." The SEC established guidelines in 2005 to prevent "failed" trades but did not impose any sanctions. Short sellers were required to close out positions when the number of "fails" exceeded 10,000 shares for 13 days in a row. The SEC did not investigate who "failed" the trades, leaving companies exposed to blatant speculation from naked short sellers.

On September 9, 2008, there were over one million "fails" on Lehman stock. On September 10, there were 5.8 million, September 11, 22.6 million, and September 12, 32.8 million "fails." On September 17, two days after Lehman's collapse, the number of "fails" reached 49.7 million, corresponding to 23% of all outstanding stocks. This obvious market manipulation exposed Lehman to regulatory risk caused by poor enforcement of illegal market practices.

Internal operations

Potential losses arising from human mistakes and technology failures in processes represent operational exposures. Lehman does not appear to have significant problems with theft, fraud, or system failures related to trading, underwriting, or settlements. The company seemed to have taken steps to strengthen financial and data processing systems stating that "we have substantially upgraded and expanded the capabilities of our data processing systems and other operating technology" while showing awareness of the need to continue to upgrade.

Strategic risks

Lehman had several potential strategic risks including new technologies, industry paradigm shifts, competitor moves, brand erosion, project failure, and so on. For example, new market entrants in online broking affected the earnings of traditional brokerage firms. The quality of human capital is another important risk in a financial institution that affects the ability to respond to changing market conditions. Looking at headlines from prior financial crises, for example, "a fallen star" referring to Nick Leeson at Barings Bank and "Bernie Madoff's Ponzi scheme," pinpoint the importance of acts and behaviors among key people. That is, the quality and stature of the people seem to be an important risk factor reflected in the organizational culture they embrace.

Lehman's late responses

The analysis may suggest that Lehman was taking on more risk at a time when the booming housing market had peaked and financial markets had begun to deteriorate. The financial leverage of the company and its exposures to trading portfolios and mortgage-backed securities increased from 2006 to 2008 in seemingly conscious decisions to optimize shareholder returns. With hindsight, it may appear like top management excelled in a waning market and thereby failed to prepare for a potential crisis when there were signs that market sentiments were changing. CEO Dick Fuld stated that "our global franchise and brand have never been stronger, and our record results for the year reflect the continued diversified growth of our businesses."[iii]

Lehman's first quarter 2008 results reported net income of $489 million presenting a decrease of 57% from first-quarter 2007. Lehman's second-quarter 2008 results swung to a loss of $2.8 billion down from a gain of $1.3 billion in first-quarter 2007. Not until this time did Lehman start to seriously consider its financial position and according to Dick Fuld "have begun to take the necessary steps to restore the credibility in our great franchise and ensure that this quarter's unacceptable performance is not repeated." The company began to reduce exposures dropping leverage from 31.7 to 24.3 times while lowering its non-investment grade inventory and increasing long-term capital in a $4 billion issue of convertible preferred stock. [iv]

Cognitive bias and ethics

So, what happened behind the scenes as the economic scenario changed? What can explain why the company waited to reduce its exposures until mid-2008? It seems clear that top management and the board failed to respond immediately to red flags observed in the market. Lawrence McDonald, head of convertible securities trading claimed that "Lehman was heading directly into the biggest subprime iceberg ever seen, but unlike the captain of the Titanic, CEO Dick Fuld and his No 2, Joe Gregory, didn't try to swerve."[v]

Why was top management unable to react to the changing conditions? It seems like a product of its own past doings. In June 2005, Michael Gelband, Lehman's global head of fixed income, argued that aggressive mortgage lenders had created a market that was sure to falter. This diverged from the official view of top management, so he stepped down in May 2007 after disputes with Dick Fuld. Alex Kirk, head of credit products, left in February 2007 after disputes with top management. Madelyn Antoncic, Lehman's risk expert was excluded from important meetings and eventually fired after expressing bearish market views in 2006. There was a pattern of getting rid of people with dissenting views with a few powerful people at the top with no inclination to listen to professional people hired to manage corporate risks.

Walter Gerasimowicz, a Lehman investment strategist said that "it makes me rather sad to see this organization brought to its knees as the result of what I'll call a lack of control, poor management of internal risk and ultimate self-interest."[vi] McDonald affirmed that Lehman collapsed because of blindness and lack of direction from its CEO and the board of directors. It seems like the leadership had developed a cognitive bias anchored by years of increasing earnings that made them overestimate the ability of the CEO discarding any concerns expressed by the risk leaders and turning a 'blind eye' to reported exposures. As a reflection of this, CEO Dick Fuld received a $22 million bonus in March 2008, a few months before Lehman's final collapse, for the stellar performance in 2007.[vii]

One reason Lehman did not retreat from increasing bets in early 2007 when the mortgage market began to unravel is that a prudent risk culture must be anchored within the organizational behavior of people with a strong commitment from top management and the board. This was obviously not the case at Lehman. So, one reason for Lehman's collapse was a weak or absent risk management culture, with disconnects between the day-to-day operational managers and top management, which made the company unable to react in time.

Reflections

Lehman Brothers is far from the only company to profess adherence to risk management standards and practices only to later discover that this was, simply, not true. At least three insights can prompt a deeper discussion and consideration of key points in the chapter.

- The Lehman Brothers story poses a highly visible example—at least on the surface—of not "walking the talk." Adherence to ERM was proclaimed publicly and was featured, presumably, to demonstrate leading-edge thinking and management. We might consider this an example of *espoused policies* versus *policies in action*—a risk management concern that manifests itself in other forms in this book. How do we diagnose this particular case of saying one thing but doing another? Is this a failure of ERM or are other factors in play here? Finally, what might this tell us about ERM when a complete collapse of an organization happens on ERM's "watch"?
- This chapter lays out the ERM story; what it is, what it intends to achieve, what its value is to an organization. Focusing on a diagnosis of ERM (and less on the particulars of this case), do we have a sense of whether ERM is either missing or misunderstanding something about its role? In asking this, we must be cognizant that there are things that may be completely unanticipatable—no system, no person is perfect—so the critique here is not to compare real-world situations with perfection. However, one would clearly have to wonder how a highly touted ERM program did not have any anticipation of or solution for the problems that befell Lehman Brothers.
- Later in the book, specific questions are raised and answers are sought to matters that feature in this case study. Observations will be forthcoming, so here the subject for discussion is mainly speculative. What can we say about the performance of the organization's top leadership? We doubt the answer can be "the leaders performed excellently." What seems to be the fundamental diagnosis for the leaders' performance? Bad or evil intentions; incompetence; evidence of basic human nature; systems bound to fail?

Notes to case

[i] Lehman quarterly reports and preannouncement of third-quarter report.
[ii] Based on data from Wall Street's naked swindled, *Rolling Stone*, Issue 1089, and *Bloomberg* reports.
[iii] Management comments to Lehman's 2007 financial results on December 13, 2007.
[iv] Figures from Lehman's second-quarter results.
[v] Interview in *Business Week*, August 3, 2009.
[vi] *Bloomberg* interview, September 15, 2008.
[vii] McDonald, L. G. and Robinson, P. 2009.

Read more about it

Malloy, M. P. (2010). *Anatomy of a Meltdown: A Dual Financial Biography of the Subprime Mortgage Crisis.* Wolters Kluwer Law & Business, Alphenaan den Rijn, Netherlands.

McDonald, L. G. and Robinson, P. (2009). *A Colossal Failure of Common Sense: The Inside Story of the Collapse of Lehman Brothers.* Deckle Edge, New York, NY.

Vicky, W. (2011). *The Devil's Casino: Friendship, Betrayal, and the High Stakes Games Played Inside Lehman Brothers.* Wiley, Hoboken, NJ.

Case 1.3: LEGO Systems A/S: Developing a state-of-the-art strategic risk management approach

Case overview

The strategic risk management unit at the LEGO Group was considered a highly successful state-of-the-art adoption of enterprise risk management practices, notably because it was also applied to consider large and important strategic exposures.

As is the case in many other organizations, the initial risk management activities at the LEGO Group amounted to insurance buying of covers for disruptive casualties and damages to productive assets with quality control, safety, and financial and legal risks handled in the respective operating and functional entities. However, beginning around 2005, strategic risk management started in earnest, as a new senior management team noted that enterprise risk management might be helpful in assessing major threats in a competitive environment and taking a fresh look at things with the aim of turning around company performance. This positive inducement from top management supported the formation of a persistent and focused effort that evolved into a small, but very effective, strategic risk management unit at headquarters. Over time, the unit developed its own unique approach to deal with corporate risks and opportunities.

The turnaround was remarkably successful, and the LEGO Group experienced consistent growth of top- and bottom-lines for more than a decade until 2017 when positive trends diverged and dipped. This adversity led to a relatively dramatic one-time adjustment of the managerial and administrative structures, which effectively eliminated the strategic risk management function as it had operated over the preceding decade.

A brief history

The beginning of the LEGO Group was at the carpenter workshop of Ole Kirk Christiansen in the village of Billund, where he started to make wooden toys in 1932.

The business was incorporated as LEGO in 1934. LEGO is derived from the Danish words "leg godt," which means "play well" in English. The company started the production of plastic toys in 1947, which eventually became the famous interlocking bricks that remain a centerpiece of the company's successful products. The motto of the LEGO Group is: "only the best is good enough," which refers to the emphasis on high quality and not cutting corners to give customers the best value. The motto was formed by Christiansen early on to imprint on all employees the directive to never skimp on quality, which remains a core value in the company today.

Godtfred, the third son of Ole Kirk Christiansen, became part of the senior management at LEGO in 1954. He advanced the idea of creating a toy system around the bricks as the basis for creative play. To advance this proposition, the locking capacity of the brick was enhanced and developed into its modern form, which was patented in 1958. Godtfred Kirk Christiansen acted as the CEO of the LEGO Group from 1957 until 1979. The Duplo product line was introduced in 1969 to attract younger children to the LEGO play concept and the first LEGO minifigures were introduced in 1978. After Godtfred's death in 1995, his son Kjeld Kirk Kristiansen took the helm as CEO.

Recent history

The success of the LEGO Group is supported by a strong and unique market concept in the toy industry that has led to its strong global brand—actually overtaking Ferrari as the world's most recognized brand in 2015. Yet, an excessive belief in the LEGO brand and the possibilities for wider business expansion led to an extended use beyond the initial core toy products slowly diluting the deployed resources. By the early 2000s, the company had expanded into theme parks, book publishing, children's apparel, and specialized toys in increasingly unrelated or weakly linked business activities. The strategy overextended the resources beyond the core competencies of the company, slowing revenue growth and cash generation.

Jørgen Vig Knudstorp was appointed CEO of the LEGO Group in 2004, having worked with the company since 2001, to turn things around and revitalize the business. Knudstorp sparked a tremendously successful rebound under his tenure, and the net income of the LEGO Group went from loss to stellar profits with a 600% increase in turnover from DKK6.3 billion in 2004 to DKK37.9 billion by 2016. Part of this success was the result of refocusing on product offerings around the quality of the basic bricks, which, in turn, served as the foundation for developing hugely popular building sets. For more than a decade, the LEGO Group posted annual growth figures on both the top and bottom-line in excess of 10% in a global toy market growing by less than 2% per annum. As a natural consequence, the LEGO Group eventually overtook both Hasbro and Mattel as the world's largest toy manufacturer. In late 2016, the company announced the resignation of Knudstorp as CEO to instead assume the role as Chairman of the Board for the LEGO Group.

As part of the turnaround at the LEGO Group, the company experimented with (and ultimately developed) a unique strategic risk management function. According to Hans Læssøe, then Head of Strategic Risk Management at LEGO, the CFO approached him in February 2006 and said: "We need some strategic risk management, don't you think?" Hans Læssøe had never heard about this concept before, but as a 25-year veteran employee at LEGO with an engineering background, he proved to be a fit for the job. He reported back that he thought it was a fair proposition, and he was ready to start developing the concept. In the beginning, he was given a day a week to start working on this, with a promise that senior management would support expanding his engagement and time committed, if needed.

Læssøe organized his work by pursuing three fundamental questions: What can hit you? How important is it? What are you going to do about it? These issues reflect the basic elements of the generic risk management model that underpins all the formal ERM frameworks as a testament to the hands-on approach adopted in the beginning rather than attempting to implement a highly formalized ERM framework. The effort had a distinct focus on strategic risks, recognizing that other functions in the organization managed insurance contracts for productive assets and buildings, health and safety conditions, financial exposures, and so on. Formally being part of the Finance Department, Læssøe's engagement to develop the possibilities offered by ERM reflected the dire economic circumstances at the time as well as a recognition that the company needed something new to move the organization in the right direction and establish a stronger economic footing.

The effort led to the formation of a small strategic risk management function for the LEGO Group in 2007 supporting the executive team in their struggles to reverse the declining sales and increase the net cash generation. This effort introduced a set of strategic risk management practices that seemed to work very well for the company. The Executive Committee used it as a way to challenge its strategic thinking and test the robustness of strategic initiatives and major investments. A simple scenario-planning framework engaged high-level executives in open discussions and was eventually adopted to assess all investment projects above a certain size, thereby helping decision-makers consider potential threats and opportunities. This was complemented by a conventional risk management approach to identify major enterprise risks, establishing a risk register of about 100 risks, which were updated, assessed, and mitigated on an ongoing basis.

Strategic risk management

Strategic risk management as it evolved at the LEGO Group from late 2006 eventually turned into a distinct four-step process of risk identification, risk simulations, scenario discussions, and project risk assessments. In outline, this process was:

1. Identify major risk factors in line with traditional risk management considering different types of risk, e.g., hazards, financial risk, operational risks, and strategic risks based on periodic reporting from business units aggregated into corporate exposure. To remain efficient, fewer than 100 risks were registered and monitored for ongoing mitigation efforts with responsibilities and risk ownership delegated to line managers.
2. Perform Monte Carlo simulations to assess the potential of extreme outcomes considering different events and stress testing scenarios in view of possible market volatility and abrupt changes in the business environment. This supported the budgeting process, internal accounting, and financial reporting assessing possible financial consequences on major investments as support for strategic decisions.
3. Challenge top management and the board, as well as engaged management teams, conducting scenario discussions in Prepare for Uncertainty (PfU) exercises. Initially applied to senior management during the turnaround phase to assess the viability and resilience of strategic choices. Later this was also applied by selective management teams to assess project investments in discussions of relevant scenarios.

4. Consider risks and opportunities of major business projects in an Active Risk and Opportunity Planning (AROP) process to effectively impose advanced risk management assessment on new investments made in business operations.

Risk identification

The strategic risk management function was formed to ensure the LEGO Group had processes in place to address potential effects of major strategic risk events identified and described in combined bottom-up and top-down processes. The responsibility for related risk mitigation activities was allocated to executives in the relevant business units. Risk ownership implies responsibility for strategic objectives and the activities pursued by business units to achieve them, which must be anchored with line-management. The risk management function leads and supports top- and line-management in the application of systematic analytical practices and processes to deal with pending risks and opportunities as they emerge. The risk function is not a profit center but serves to support management to achieve their objectives and realize their budgeted performance targets.

Risk simulations

The Monte Carlo simulations were added to the process in 2008 as Hans Læssøe (holding an MSc Engineering degree in nuclear power safety) started experimenting with various budget simulations based on assumed outcomes of identified key risk factors. This helped business controllers assess the effects of market volatility, for example, quantifying the impact of sales volatility creating new insights by use of quantification techniques to challenge general beliefs and overcome intuitive biases. It was also applied to analyze aggregated credit exposures as input in discussions about buying credit risk insurance. The simulations consolidated the risk effects into an integrated corporate exposure to assess effects from various risk factors and their assumed outcomes considering the aggregated impact on corporate performance. It provided the means to calculate worst-case scenario losses compared with the budgeted performance numbers that could serve as a basis to discuss risk appetite and acceptable risk levels with senior management and the board.

Risk scenario discussions

PfU was a systematic approach to define and test the effects of a few distinct but possible future business scenarios and potential effects on the stated strategic objectives considering various trends in the global economy that could require rapid risk responses. It consisted of a simplified process to generate four strategic scenarios through engaged discussions, for example, with the top management team or selective groups of knowledgeable managers focusing on defined scenarios based on megatrends described in, say, the annual risk reports from the World Economic Forum. The process might entail engaged discussions with senior management before setting the strategy as a means of considering the implications of possible world economic scenarios rather than "just" extrapolating existing conditions five years into the future. It would provide opportunities to revisit the viability and resilience of major strategic initiatives to see how emergent risks and opportunities might affect strategic outcomes and then adopting a prioritized set of actions.

Risk in business implementation

Active Risk and Opportunity Planning (AROP) was applied to assess the risk profile of major business projects above a given size, or level of complexity, with explicit considerations of how to deal with potentially significant risks and opportunities. The process would consider risks imposed on the project from changes to the outside economic conditions as well as consider internal risks related to project effects on the full corporate business system. The process would determine an agreed scaling of risk levels through analyses and discussions to reach consensus and develop specific action plans for dealing with potential exposures and provide timely responses. This also entailed follow-up reporting with accountability among those involved with ongoing reassessments of needed mitigation efforts and supportive risk reporting.

Later developments

With the mounting success of the revitalized organization, the need for strategic risk management became less obvious as time went by—the argument being, why do we need to be challenged as before, when we actually are so successful? The expansive growth increasingly depended on global access beyond traditional markets in Western Europe and North America. So, demands to make the organization more international and attract qualified executives and young talented employees became a priority. As a consequence, the company introduced a more extensive global governance structure with overseas headquarter locations beyond the original confines of Billund, the small Danish town where the LEGO headquarters was located

However, the LEGO Group reported an unexpected drop in profits down 3% for the first half of 2017—the slowest for more than ten years. As a consequence, the company decided to cut 1,400 jobs to scale back and create a better match between revenues and resource utilization in a one-time correction. Jørgen Vig Knudstorp, now Group Chairman, argued that the company would attempt to do a one-time big move, although he could not guarantee this. He argued that the unexpected developments were a consequence of internationalization and growing into a complex—too complex in Knudstorp's judgment—global governance structure. The company was hit by weaker demand in the established markets with an organizational structure too complex to effectively handle the international expansion over the prior years. Incidentally, the slimming of the organization effectively eliminated the strategic risk management function as an excessive administrative function.

Reflections

LEGO provides a very high-profile test of progressive thinking in risk management. In this story, a well-regarded strategic risk management effort at the LEGO Group disappeared as the result of—what turned out to be—a minor crisis. Further irony is found in the fact that the result was due to the challenge of managing success. Additionally, while risk management continues to figure in the official company vocabulary, it no longer features the unique approaches for which it became known. And, in effect, it has reverted to—primarily—a compliance tool. Many aspects of this story warrant discussion. Three that stand out are:

- The strategic risk management approach adopted by LEGO was considered a value-adding feature that contributed to the impressive turnaround after 2006. This approach is outlined in the case study, but the question of why it worked deserves further consideration. What were the ingredients of this approach that allowed it to be embraced by top management, primarily, and by the organization as a whole?
- A part of this story that receives only passing attention is the crisis that led LEGO to embark on a radical overhaul of the company's strategy in 2006. The case references the factors that led to a crisis situation but does not really discuss those factors from a risk leadership perspective. From a risk leadership standpoint, how might the causes of that crisis be diagnosed?
- The, literally, existential episode that ends the LEGO strategic risk management story here, attains a level of philosophical reflection. Does the abrupt relegation of the company's risk management effort tell us anything about the state of risk management itself? Does the way we look at risk management set proper expectations for it? Perhaps even more pointedly, how could a "world-beating" strategic risk management program not foresee the threat and cause of its own demise?

Read more about it

CNBC (n.d.). https://www.cnbc.com/2017/09/05/toymaker-lego-to-cut-8-percent-of-staff-as-sales-decline.html

Frigo, Mark L. and Hans, Læssøe (2012). Strategic risk management at the LEGO Group. *Strategic Finance*, 93(2), 27–35.

Hans, Læssøe (2015). The LEGO group implementation of SRM, Chapter 11. In Andersen, T. J. (Ed.), *The Routledge Companion to Strategic Risk Management*. Routledge, London, UK.

Quartz (n.d.). https://qz.com/1069520/lego-announces-layoffs-after-reporting-an-unexpected-drop-in-sales-and-profit/

The Guardian (n.d.). https://www.theguardian.com/business/2017/sep/05/lego-to-axe-1400-jobs

Notes

1 See, for example, Van Knippenberg, D. and Sitkin, S. (2013). A critical assessment of charismatic-transformational leadership research. *Academy of Management Annals*, 7(1), 1–60.
2 Chemers, M. M. (1997). *An Integrative Theory of Leadership*. Erlbaum, Mahwah, NJ, provides an early overview reflecting research developments over time, including the inclusion of gender factors in leadership.
3 Obviously, a great deal has been written on followership over the past 20 years. A notably helpful overview is provided in Uhl-Bien, M., Riggio, R. E., Lowe, K. B. and Carsten, M. K. (2014). Followership theory: A review and research agenda. *The Leadership Quarterly*, 25, 83–104.
4 See, for example, Mintzberg, H. (2020). An underlying theory for strategy, organization, and management: Bridging the divide between analysis and synthesis. *Strategic Management Review*, forthcoming.
5 Bass, B. M. (2008). *Bass and Stogdill's Handbook of Leadership: A Survey of Theory and Research*. Free Press, New York, pp. 11–20, is particularly notable here for framing classification systems.
6 One of numerous examples is Jacquart, P. and Antonakis, J. (2015). When does charisma matter for top-level leaders? Effect of attributional ambiguity. *Academy of Management Journal*, 58(4), 1051–1074, which focuses on charisma, a trait where interest has particularly re-emerged.
7 See, for example, Hambrick, D. C. and Mason, P. A. (1984). Upper echelons: The organization as a reflection of its top managers. *The Academy of Management Review*, 9(2), 193–206.
8 Stogdill, R. M. (1948). Personal factors associated with leadership: A survey of the literature. *Journal of Psychology*, 25, 35–71 provides an early overview.
9 Stogdill, R. M. (1974). *Handbook of Leadership: A Survey of Theory and Research*. Free Press, New York, offers an updating on his earlier overview of developmental trends in leadership literature.

10 M. Uhl-Bien, R. R. (2014). Followership theory: A review and research agenda. *The Leadership Quarterly*, 25(1), 83-104.

11 Northouse, P. (2019). *Leadership: Theory and Practice.* Sage, Thousand Oaks, CA, is a widely used textbook, but also serves to update previously referenced reviews of the literature by Stogdill, thereby offering something of a sense of the history of research with three distinct time markers (1948, 1974, 2019).

12 Uhl-Bien, M., Marion, R. and McKelvey, B. (2007). *Complexity Leadership Theory: Shifting leadership from the Industrial Age to the Knowledge Era.* Leadership Institute Faculty Publications. 18, set in motion a line of research, inspired by complexity theory and complex adaptable systems research.

13 Simonet, D. V. and Tett, R. T. (2012). Five perspectives on the leadership-management relationship: A competency-based evaluation and integration. *Journal of Leadership & Organizational Studies*, 20(2), 199–213, offers a good overview of the management-leadership discussion.

14 Kotter, J. (1990). *A Force for Change: How Leadership Differs from Management.* Free Press, New York, offers both a sense of academic and professional views on leadership and management.

15 Ibid.

16 Ellis, D. G. and Fisher, B. A. (1994). *Small Group Decision Making: Communication and Group Process (4th ed.).* McGraw-Hill Book Company, New York, offers a good entrée into assigned vs. emergent leadership.

17 Raven, B. H. (1965). Social influence and power. In Steiner, M. F. I. D. and Fishbein, M (Eds.), *Current Studies in Social Psychology* (pp. 371–382). Holt, Rinehart, & Winston, New York, sets out a wider framework for sources of power.

18 Much has been written and tested on the subject of personality factors. A good example is Goldberg, L. R. (1990). "An alternative description of personality": The Big-Five factor structure. *Journal of Personality and Social Psychology*, 59, 1216–1229.

19 Caruso, D. R. and Wolfe C. Jfd. (2004). Emotional intelligence and leadership development. In a Day, D.V., Zaccaro, S. J. and Halpin, S. M. (Eds.), *Leader Development for Transforming Organizations: Growing Leaders for Tomorrow* (pp. 237–266). Erlbaum, Mahwah, NJ, provides an overview of the emotional intelligence concept,

20 Williams, C. A. and Heins, R. H. (1964). *Risk Management and Insurance.* McGraw-Hill, New York, is one of the earliest books to catalog the emergence of risk management as a distinct subject of study and practice.

21 Snider, H. Wayne. Reaching Professional Status: A Program for Risk Management. *Corporate Risk Management: Current Problems and Perspectives.* 112 (1956) 30–35.

22 Williams, C. A., Smith, M. S. and Young, P. C. (1998). *Risk Management & Insurance.* McGraw-Hill Book Company, New York; an update on Williams and Heins 1964 text.

23 Crockford, G. N. (1982). The bibliography and history of risk management: Some preliminary observations. *Geneva Papers on Risk and Insurance*, 7(23), 169–179, provides a good summing up—to that point in time—of developments in the field.

24 Doherty, N. A. (1985). *Corporate Risk Management.* McGraw-Hill Book Company, New York, represents a distinct synthesis of both the emerging finance-based Theory of the Firm view of organizational risk management, with a strong linkage to the early financial risk management research.

25 Stonehill, D. K. (1979). *Multinational Business Finance.* Addison-Wesley Publishing Co., Reading, MA, presents a good overview of the environment that gave rise to developments in financial risk management.

26 Black, F. and Scholes, M. (1973). The pricing of options and corporate liabilities. *The Journal of Political Economy*, 81(3), 637–654, The University of Chicago Press, Chicago, not only presents a discussion of options contracts but has become one of the most influential articles in the field of finance. Note: that the concept of options contracts has been extended in recent decades from focused financial contracts to real options, which appear at various points in this book.

27 Nocco, B. and Stulz, R. (2006). Enterprise risk management: Theory and practice. *Journal of Applied Corporate Finance*, 18, 8–20, is an early and influential paper on ERM.

28 Haimes, Y. Y. (1992). Toward a holistic approach to total risk management. *Geneva Papers on Risk and Insurance*, 314–321, serves as a record of a point in time in the development of risk management when discussion and study began to introduce the idea of integrating various technical risk management practices.

29 Nocco, B. and Stulz, R. (2006). Enterprise risk management: Theory and practice. *Journal of Applied Corporate Finance*, 18, 8–20, laid the foundation for much of what later research explored.

30 Beasley, M. S., Clune, R. and Hermanson, D. R. (2005). Enterprise risk management: An empirical analysis of factors associated with the extent of implementation. *Journal of Accounting and Public Policy*, 24(6), 521–531, pre-dates Nocco and Stulz but features early consideration of the Chief Risk Officer idea.

31 Moeller, R. R. (2007). *C OSO Enterprise Risk Management: Understanding the New Integrated ERM Framework*. John Wiley & Sons, New York, provides an overview of the original COSO statement, which has been updated in 2018.

32 Paape, L. S. R. (2012). The adoption and design of enterprise risk management practices. *European Accounting Review*, 21(3), 533–564, provides evidence of the emergence of a climate of external expectations.

33 Liebenberg, A. P. (2003). The determinants of enterprise risk management: Evidence from the appointment of Chief Risk Officers. *Risk Management and Insurance Review*, 6(1), 37–52, represents early thinking about Chief Risk Officers and the emergence of that idea in organizational settings.

34 Personal profile, Insurance Hall of Fame, International Insurance Society. https://www.insurancehall offame.org/laureateprofile.php?laureate=56.

35 Lam, J. (2003). *Enterprise Risk Management: From Incentives to Controls*. Wiley, Hoboken, NJ.

36 Congress.gov (2002). H.R.3763 - Sarbanes-Oxley Act of 2002, 107th Congress (2001–2002). https://www.congress.gov/bill/107th-congress/house-bill/3763.

37 BIS (2020). *History of the Basel Committee*. Bank for International Settlements (BIS). https://www.bis.org/bcbs/history.htm.

38 BIS (2010). *Principles for Enhancing Corporate Governance*, Basel Committee on Banking Supervision, Bank for International Settlements, Basel, Switzerland, October 2010. https://www.bis.org/publ/bcbs176.pdf.

39 BIS. (2015). *Guidelines: Corporate Governance Principles for Banks*. Bank for International Settlements, Basel, Switzerland.

40 OECD. (2015). *Principles of Corporate Governance*. OECD, Paris, France.

41 Craig, S., Holberton, D. and McAndrew, D. (2019). What makes a successful risk leader? *Risk Management*, 66(3), 44–50.

2 An assessment of ERM leadership performance

Enterprise risk management practice

What does the incorporation of Enterprise Risk Management (ERM) imply for overall organizational management? Is/has the adoption of ERM really been a success? And what does success even mean? Success could simply mean a completed implementation, but it could also refer to the positive effects that may derive from the application of an ERM framework. Presumably, the latter measure of success would vary across sectors and organizational types, but for publicly traded firms, success could be indicated by increasing shareholder value through optimal capital allocation and the deflection of negative loss effects. Outside of a corporate setting, other measures may become more meaningful, and we will consider this in later chapters.

Since most research on ERM adoption has been confined to publicly traded firms, much of the empirical discussion here focuses on financial performance and shareholder value. There are differing views on the merits of those measures as they may represent short-term and fleeting effects where difficulties exist in clearly determining the true causality. For example, can it be confidently concluded that ERM adoption leads to better opportunity identification and profitable growth, or is it that only already profitable companies can afford to implement a comprehensive ERM framework?

If the positive effect on shareholder value is the definition of success, then it seems fair to require or expect that these effects are fairly persistent and reflect what we often refer to as sustainable competitive advantage. Indeed, some scholars conceive ERM adoption as a so-called *dynamic capability* that should have sustainable performance effects if they are valuable, unique, and hard to imitate by other competing organizations.[1] However, in addition to the causality question, short-term firm-specific advantages might not in and of themselves lead to better long-term outcomes, particularly if all firms or society in general are exposed to potential disaster events. So, we may want to also employ other measures of success and contribution.

The concept of time (and time-value) may also play a role here as we often ignore or pay less attention to long-term effects; potential influences of and on climate change in an uncertain future being a very notable illustration. We do not know exactly how, when, and where climatic changes might affect the economic system we currently employ. Things could indeed develop in abrupt and dramatic ways, but it is not possible to predict or delineate the precise circumstances of these future events. These relatively distant effects—that no one hitherto has experienced—tend to be devalued in our minds as well as in common discounted cash flow methodologies that may discard or diminish the economic consequences of events in future decades.

DOI: 10.4324/9781003148579-2

Here we will first summarize what ERM is, with some effort to pinpoint the leadership elements within this view. This is then further illuminated through a discussion of the research findings on the effects of ERM adoption published to date. The chapter concludes with speculations about the Chief Risk Officer (CRO) role as well as the risk leadership implications of ERM adoption more broadly.

The ERM frameworks

The ERM approach is framed by the influential 2004 COSO[2] statement and the ISO 31000 standard introduced in 2009.

COSO updated its 2004 *Enterprise Risk Management—Integrated Framework* in 2017 in view of an increasingly volatile, complex, and ambiguous business environment.[3] The framework is presented as a means to help the board and top management consider risk when setting objectives and formulating strategy, arguing that "integrating enterprise risk management practices throughout an entity helps accelerate growth and enhance performance." It arguably provides an effective way to manage risks and fulfill oversight responsibilities, thereby instilling confidence among external stakeholders. So, it caters to a need for compliance with the general expectations and norms for risk management. It further claims that, since its inception in 2004, the COSO guidance has been successfully applied by all types of organizations by identifying and managing risks within a given risk appetite and supporting the achievement of objectives.

The role of ERM in support of strategy setting and fulfillment of objectives reflects a top management-driven view of strategy formation. In a conventional planning approach, top management first sets strategic objectives where extensive analyses help outline ways to achieve them. These options can be open to input and discussions with decision-makers throughout the organization, although the degree of involvement varies. This presents a rational analytical approach to determine planned courses of action where the strategic direction and action plans are approved by the top management team and board of directors. Further, this implies that strategy is, and can be, formulated and planned by top management and thereafter is, and can be, implemented by people within the organization to achieve the set strategic objectives and goals.[4] It may incorporate periodic feedback loops in diagnostic controls that monitor realized effects against planned outcomes to identify a possible need for adjustments. A typical planning pattern may entail major revisions every three to five years with updated annual and quarterly reviews and shorter-term adjustments to action plans.

The COSO updated ERM statement reiterates the view that ERM involves:

- Aligning risk appetite and strategy. Top management considers the entity's risk appetite by evaluating strategic alternatives, setting objectives, and managing the related risks.
- Enhancing risk response decisions. ERM provides the framework to identify and choose between alternative risk responses avoiding, mitigating, sharing, or accepting risk.
- Reducing operational surprises and losses. Entities identify potential events and establish responses, which reduce being caught off guard or unaware.
- Identifying and managing cross-enterprise risks. ERM facilitates effective responses to interrelated impacts and integrates responses to several risks.
- Seizing opportunities. By considering a full range of potential events, management is able to identify and take advantage of prospective beneficial openings.

- Improving capital allocation. Obtaining robust risk information enables management to assess the riskiness of investment propositions and enhance effective capital allocation.

Direct declarations of the need for a Risk Leader, *per se*, are not part of the COSO language, though responses to COSO's holistic approach certainly influenced the emergence of CROs. And, indeed, it should be said the COSO framework exerts a wide-ranging global influence on how modern risk management—overall—is described, considered, and implemented.

Beyond this, however, what is the direct or indirect evidence of risk leadership-oriented thinking in COSO's statement? An answer may be sought when reading COSO by asking the question: "OK, but *who* is doing this?" COSO says little about who is doing the actual leading and what it entails. Of course, the CEO and the top management team are *de facto* the risk leaders, as may be the board of directors. Nevertheless, there is an implicit assumption that somewhere in an organization's upper echelons leadership is expected to set a risk policy and then assure that compliant risk management practices are implemented and operated accordingly.

ISO[5] updated its 2009 *Risk management—Principles and guidelines* in 2018.[6] It claims to provide "robust, high-level guidelines for the management of risk" in a management standard that emphasizes control and development. The framework outlines risk management policies and processes aimed to formally ensure that tasks are, or can be, accomplished to achieve the stated objectives. It argues that formalized processes are essential for large organizations and "it is increasingly understood that the explicit and structured management of risk brings benefits."[7] And it states that this is achieved by analyzing strategic options and assessing risks and disruptions while complying with legal requirements where senior management and the board are expected to provide robust risk reporting and oversight. Hence, the ISO standard has many commonalities with COSO in its views and approaches, and indeed, in recent years, there has been a recognizable overall convergence between the two.

Beyond the implied evidence, the ERM frameworks have more direct references to leadership-like actions. The most obvious examples include the general emphasis on: 1) exercising board risk oversight; 2) overseeing operating structures; 3) defining desired culture; 4) committing to core values; 5) analyzing the business context; 6) setting risk appetite; 7) evaluating alternative strategies; and 8) assessing substantial environmental change. There are obvious managerial aspects present in these examples, but leadership features prominently as well.[8] A natural follow-up question would be directed to understand how risk leadership actions might be considered and undertaken, and how this contributes to the achievement of organizational goals and objectives. A short review of research on ERM practice provides some useful illumination.

ERM practice and performance: Evidence

The search for evidence

ERM research to date can mainly be described as fitting in three areas of assessment: the characteristics of ERM adopters, the impact of ERM on firm performance, and ERM applications in specific organizational settings. Developing a comprehensive theory of ERM, however, has thus far eluded researchers. And, indeed, the more targeted work that has been done—though important and useful—is somewhat inconclusive.

A fundamental obstacle to a unifying theory is the difficulty of creating a reliable ERM construct. There are various reasons for this. At a most basic level, it has proven difficult to identify organizations where ERM has been adopted. Detailed information on ERM contained in annual reports would appear promising but has proven of limited value.[9] Proxy measures—such as the appointment of a CRO—provide some insight into the presence of ERM programs but beyond flagging the presence of the CRO, they have not produced overly persuasive results.[10] Other areas of research have been more encouraging—though also with important qualifications.

ERM adoption

Why has it proven difficult to identify ERM adopters? As has been observed, ERM exists in a variety of forms "deployed at different levels, for different purposes, by different staff groups in different organizations."[11] The lack of a comprehensive ERM framework, or not having an official CRO, does not necessarily indicate that basic ERM processes are absent. The firms may simply not have an articulated ERM vocabulary or a CRO, yet they could have risk management practices embedded in managerial actions and tactics.[12] It is also possible that other executives (other than a CRO) are responsible for ERM processes.[13]

Empirical research shows that the adoption of ERM is associated with a number of internal factors, such as having a CRO (a slightly circular finding), financial leverage, firm size, profitability and turnover, diversification, institutional ownership, business strategy, and emphasis on shareholder maximization. Other studies looked at links to external factors including globalization, deregulation, and industry consolidation.[14]

The Chief Risk Officer

While COSO essentially identifies the executive as *the* risk leader (the term CRO is not used), an increasing number of firms appoint CROs. A survey by Accenture in 2013 found that 96% of 445 responding large firms had a CRO, an increase of 78% from 2011. The growing emphasis on a CRO is seen as indicative of an interest in having someone represent the "executive perspective" on risk and to fulfill the formal tasks associated with it.[15] These tasks might include:

- Establishing an integrated risk management framework for all aspects of risk across the entire organization
- Developing risk management policies including quantification and allocation of risk appetite establishing specific risk limits/tolerance levels
- Communicating goals and objectives for the group risk policy and framework
- Managing implementation, maintenance, and continuous improvement of the group risk policy and framework
- Managing the information system supporting the risk policy and framework
- Delivering metrics and risk reports to top management, the board, risk/audit committee, and the risk advisory group in support of risk-based decision-making
- Reviewing the risk profiles throughout the organization and propose proper levels of capital to risk exposures.
- Creating a risk-aware culture through communication and training, risk-based performance measures, incentive systems, and change management programs.

Practitioner analysis suggests that CROs should be proactive risk communicators acting as "strategic business advisors" rather than reactive control agents.[16] One author suggests that the CRO role is less about marketing the risk management idea but more to facilitate a common risk language as legitimate business jargon within the organization. By facilitating risk discussions rather than using formal authority, the CRO can heed the principles of risk management in business conduct as opposed to enforcing a control function. The CRO role is about building informal relationships among executives and business managers and balancing the position as compliance warden and business partner—keeping distance yet staying involved.[17] Intriguingly, these observations will be shown to link in interesting ways to many aspects of the general Leadership literature reviewed in Chapter Three.

The appointment of a CRO may be a signal of commitment to ERM by visibly locating the responsibility for risk management processes at an executive level,[18] thereby supporting ERM implementation. In fact, the presence of a CRO is found to have a significant impact on ERM implementation[19] where the CRO encourages engagement in ERM practices.[20] A study[21] found that the presence of a CRO also influences eventual ERM adoption.[22] Other research uses survey data to identify the degree to which firms have implemented ERM and finds a significant affinity with the existence of a CRO. However, findings remain inconclusive as to whether ERM adoption is associated with *effective, successful* risk management. That is, the presence of a CRO could be a proxy for nothing more than an "effort" to introduce ERM—whether well or poorly done.

Other research on adoption

Other lines of inquiry have emerged in the search to better understand the effects of ERM programs. Some studies use changes in stock prices to assess the effects of ERM announcements[23] and others use market-based measures like Tobin's Q.[24] One study develops an index that quantifies the extent to which ERM achieves four objectives established by COSO.[25] Other studies use Standard & Poor's (S&P) risk management rating of insurance companies as a proxy for the level of ERM sophistication.[26] The ERM rating adds to the eight components S&P uses to rate the financial strength of insurers.[27] Although interesting in the context of insurance, there are concerns that the S&P rating is less appropriate in broader ERM studies.[28]

Some studies measure ERM adoption by the risk reporting in annual reports,[29] for example, using a word count of ERM phrases to measure the degree of ERM implementation.[30] Others have attempted to develop measures derived from the COSO framework to indicate the level of ERM implementation.[31] In sum, significant effort has been expended to measure and understand ERM adoption, and yet, convergence toward a more consistent view has not yet transpired.

Performance and other findings

Other factors like financial leverage, firm size, profitability, diversification, institutional ownership, and business strategy related to ERM have been explored as possible antecedents and also producing performance-enhancing effects. The studies of antecedents indicate that adoption of ERM is driven by firm size, performance volatility, management support, and the industry context—all suggesting in some way that ERM implementation is often motivated by external pressures as opposed to a conscious choice. Threatening events or near-death experiences, industry-specific regulation and reporting requirements, signaling of control, and resource richness are common factors that precede ERM implementation. However, there remains little evidence whether (and/or how) these particular antecedents support an ongoing commitment to ERM once it has been initiated.

Some additional relevant findings from the ERM research stream include:

- The empirical evidence on the effects of financial leverage on ERM adoption is inconclusive[32]
- Company size increases the scope and complexity of risks and thereby the likelihood of ERM implementation, although conclusions are tentative[33]
- Institutional ownership provides pressure to introduce control systems that are commensurate with the implementation of an ERM framework. Other factors may be in play, however[34]
- Firms with volatile earnings and poor stock market performance are more likely to initiate an ERM program[35]
- Empirical results, to date, do not find significant relationships between diversification and ERM adoption[36]
- Companies that pursue a "cost leadership" strategy are more inclined to implement ERM compared with companies that pursue a "differentiation" strategy[37]
- Firms in regulated industries like banking, education, and insurance are more inclined to implement ERM[38]

Where research stands

Empirical research, professional studies, and surveys have all contributed to enhancing our understanding of the ERM concept and its implications. Many of these sources provide good theoretical arguments for the potential value to be gained from the implementation of ERM for enterprise-wide risk management assessments—including strategic risks— where ERM can be seen as an input to strategy *formation* as well as strategy *implementation*.[39] However, the empirical evidence on the claimed benefits remains rather inconclusive and provides inconsistent results.

Interestingly, some studies focus on what executives *believe* about ERM, which is not unimportant. There is a belief that ERM can helpfully assist considerations of organizational exposures including strategic risks even though there is an ongoing debate on the tangible and intangible benefits derived from ERM implementation. Executives also see that ERM drives (or may drive) value creation in terms of increased efficiency and downside loss avoidance as well as through more risk-conscious decision-making processes.[40] A survey of 150 audit and risk management executives reveals a belief that the use of ERM enhances management consensus, makes decisions better informed, and improves risk communication and management accountability.[41] Furthermore, ERM is seen as helping identify the upside potential of risk situations and thereby creating a competitive advantage.[42] So, summarizing the prevailing executive beliefs, the purported benefits from effective ERM implementation include:

- Enhancing firm performance
- Reducing the cost of capital
- Improving the efficiency of capital allocation

- Decreasing earnings and stock price volatility
- Increasing firm value

It should be observed here that the use of the term "effective ERM implementation" should lead to some reflection on situations that may arise where these potential benefits are not realized.

Implications for risk leadership

Considering the possible links between risk leadership and general leadership, several interesting observations arise from ERM research.

First, the direct and indirect evidence (professional and academic) makes clear that ERM assumes—by detailing responsibilities and actions to be undertaken by top management and the board—the existence of distinct managerial and leadership dimensions with many component parts. These dimensions would be applied to set objectives and a vision while connecting, promoting, motivating, and encouraging better cooperation. However, while specific tasks, practices, and processes are spelled out in some detail, the actual ways in which they are to be combined and enacted through leadership efforts are much less clear—indeed, they may not be clear at all.

Second, in contrast with the preceding paragraph, the "wider lens" suggested in the guidance could/should be characterized as evidence of a general leadership expectation. The CRO—at least by implication—is a symbol for that leadership expectation where the scope of responsibilities reaches across the entire organization (and even further when addressing shared risks with various external stakeholders).

Third, while many of the reporting and compliance responsibilities outlined by the COSO are part and parcel of general leadership obligations, there are features of the detailed activities that seem to represent and imply the presence of distinct, risk-related knowledge, expertise, and experience. Risk assessment and analysis, risk communication, and risk responses feature prominently, as do broad references to uncertainty and the unknown. For now, call this *risk competence*.

Fourth, a further implication of ERM is the involvement of a wider range of individuals and levels of collaboration (in communication, analyses, and responses); an insight that suggests a very dispersed function, that nevertheless depends on varying levels of coordination.

These observations lead to a view that ERM includes a number of elements that only can be interpreted as, fundamentally, *leadership*. The practical consequence of this is that while the CRO position exists to provide risk leadership, it has to be understood that the CRO represents risk competence within the collective general leadership represented by top management. It is in this express sense that risk leadership is both an aspect of general leadership as well as the principal role of the CRO—the *Risk Leader*.

Risk Leaders/Leadership (intentionally capitalized) is clearly intended to convey a top-level orientation or focus on thinking about concepts and practices. However, previously we have argued that *risk leadership* can be seen at any level within an organization and anywhere in less organization-specific settings. We maintain that the fundamental nature of risk leadership is consistent throughout an organization or in other settings, but it does raise an issue—an issue that will be explored more fully in other chapters but merits an introduction here.

If *Risk Leader* represents a position where a reasonably high degree of *risk competence* is likely necessary, does that *level of competency* hold constant across all types of risk leadership? There is a logical reason why this cannot be true, as all employees will not have the same level of specialized knowledge. So either one of two things must be true. Either risk competence is not an essential feature of risk leadership, or somehow it is. However, perhaps risk competence is not binary but rather exists on a continuum. This issue will need to be explored, but it does suggest an important thing—inculcating some level of risk competence throughout an organization would likely be a key responsibility for Risk Leaders. Indeed, as is later seen, organization-wide risk competence would be a necessity in adaptive and innovative organizations.

A final separate thought. Could it be that some of the organizations that have adopted full-fledged ERM frameworks are actually stifling their ability to respond to the unexpected because they have implemented a standardized set of control-based risk practices? And alternatively, could it be that some other organizations, by the way they structure and support activities and encourage alertness and responsible actions, reveal very effective risk management without, at all, conforming to ERM expectations?

The cases

This chapter probes the evidence of whether, particularly, ERM is a value-adding exercise for firms and provisionally concludes there is no clear support that it does. This gives rise to the possibility that perhaps the ERM concept is improperly conceived, or that conventional measures of its value are measuring the wrong things. These possibilities serve as an entry point for consideration of the three cases presented here—cases that pick up the thread of issues raised in Chapter One's case studies, though coming from a slightly different direction.

Here the cases begin with a famous business disaster that predates this book's modern risk management story. However, it is a story that has gained mythic stature within modern risk management as it reveals fundamental risk-related challenges at the top levels of organizations. There emerges a sense that top management may, itself, be a critical source of risk. The second case fills in spaces in the story constructed in Chapters One and Two by looking at the more technical aspects of modern risk management practices, while the third case introduces a well-functioning approach to risk management that nevertheless misses a critical threat/opportunity.

Case 2.1: An early warning of things to come: Barings Bank

Case overview

The Barings Bank story has been told so frequently it almost seems irrelevant or excessive to resurrect it here. What new can be said? Further, there is very much a feeling of ancient history in the retelling. The world in 1995 seems a very different planet; perhaps especially after the experiences of 2020. Even the idea of Barings Bank as a harbinger of things to come does not hold the same level of foreboding it once did. Could things possibly get worse in the financial services sector? What a silly sounding question to ask after the past 25 years.

Still, it is the distance from today that serves the purpose here. A degree of dispassionate reflection is possible, and this might be helpful in casting a critical eye on the issues we wish to raise. Particularly in the context of risk leadership, new issues are suggested, and this different perspective may cast a new light on seemingly well-trodden matters. To be sure, fraudulent behavior, poor internal controls, governance failures, and a problematic corporate culture must be featured in any Barings story. These are important matters and, among many ways to characterize them, they are risk management matters. Where we may offer a departure is to frame this story from the perspective of what we know about risk management 25 years after the scandal. The preceding chapter's case study on Sarbanes–Oxley provides its own basis for historical reflection, but here we note that SOX takes place seven years after the Barings scandal in response to a gallery of misbehaving executives and managers into which Nick Leeson, Barings' so-called *Rogue Trader* could easily become a member. Did we actually learn anything from the Barings collapse? Apparently not as much as we thought. And then, in the case that follows this case (Société Générale), we see that neither the memories of Barings nor the legal impacts of Sarbanes–Oxley seemed to have gained much purchase.

So here we hope to gain some perspective observing that this case fits into a nearly 30-year story by scanning a historical wave beginning with the Barings scandal, followed by a resolve to do better, followed by a spate of scandals, followed by a regulatory and legal response, followed by another crisis, followed by…what? In 2021 are we in a better position to anticipate and address crises like these? It is hard to be overly confident that we have, but for the sake of this discussion, let us pose the promised possibility that effectively implemented Enterprise Risk Management (ERM) could do the trick. How would ERM be the difference-maker? We will get to this question, but first, the Barings story.

Some background

One of the great fascinations of London's Square Mile is the occasional encounter with a business that has been in operation for hundreds of years. Lloyd's, perhaps the world's best-known insurance market, for example, has been in continuous operation since the mid-1680s. The longevity of such organizations seems to invest them with a sense of solidity and permanence that most modern corporations could only dream of attaining. However, as even Lloyd's demonstrates, that perception can be wrong. Lloyd's near-death experience at the hands of asbestosis liability claims in the 1980s and 1990s (alongside some other challenges) revealed that age and experience offer no iron-clad protection from disaster.

Such was the case of Barings Bank, though in this case with a fatal outcome. Barings was a merchant bank, reckoned to be the second oldest merchant bank in the UK. It had been founded in 1762. In 1995, after 233 years of trading, the bank collapsed as the result of an £827 million loss (£1.6 billion in 2020) due to fraudulent investment practices. As a consequence, two key features in the story of this collapse now live in infamy: misused futures contracts and Rogue Trading.

But first, a brief history. As noted, Barings Bank was founded in 1762 as the John and Francis Baring Company. Through its early years, Barings gradually diversified from wool into many other commodities, providing financial services for the rapid growth of international trade, including the lucrative slave trade, which enriched both family and business. In 1774, Barings started doing business in the American colonies, which included the purchase of 1 million acres of land in what would become the state of Maine. Notably—to US history—in 1802, Barings was enlisted to facilitate the largest land deal in history: the Louisiana Purchase.

For a historical perspective here, a few notable highlights of the Barings story are:

- Barings helped to finance the United States government during the War of 1812 (interestingly, a war with the British).
- In the 1830s, Barings made a bet on future opportunities in North America. By 1843, it became the exclusive agent to the US government. A position it held until 1871.
- Barings was increasingly involved in international securities, especially from the United States, Canada, and Argentina. Barings cautiously and successfully ventured into the North American railroad boom following the Civil War. Barings financed major railways including the Canadian-Pacific Railway, and the Atchison, Topeka, and Santa Fe Railway.
- In 1886, the bank helped broker the listing of the Guinness brewery, but at nearly the same time, got into serious underwriting problems with Argentine and Uruguayan debt. Intervention by the Bank of England was necessary to rescue Barings. This episode permanently reduced Barings' stature. It formed a limited liability company into which the old partnership was transferred.
- The company's struggles to recover, which led to considerable strategic and operational caution further eroded its stature in the world of finance, but saved it from a further disaster when it refused to take a chance on financing Germany's recovery from World War I.
- During the Second World War, the British government used Barings to liquidate assets in the United States and elsewhere to help finance the war effort.

The 1995 collapse

Fraudulent trading in derivatives brought down Barings. The direct cause of the collapse was the bank's head of derivative trading in Singapore, Nick Leeson. Leeson, supposedly, was employing arbitrage tactics to profit from price differences in Nikkei 225 futures contracts (listed on the Osaka Securities Exchange) and in the Singapore International Monetary Exchange (SIMEX). Arbitrage is not illegal nor is it particularly unattractive as a trading tool/strategy. What made this situation different was that Leeson, apparently since 1992, was not buying and automatically selling, and pocketing a small profit. He bought in one market but did not sell in the other market, in effect betting on the future direction of Japanese markets. In trading terminology, his action was completely "unhedged," creating huge exposure for the bank. How was this allowed to happen?

The obvious first response is that Nick Leeson was a criminal. True enough, but the important insights to derive here come from three slightly more technical observations.

First, Leeson was employing a hidden account to trade futures and options on the SIMEX. If Leeson's *motive* was ill-gotten wealth, the futures and options markets presented the *means* to achieve it. Somewhat interestingly, these trades routinely were loss-producing. He was able to cover the losses by meeting margin requirements elsewhere through misuse of subsidiary funds. He covered his tracks by manipulating computer records in such a way that it appeared Leeson was producing substantial profits. An external turn of events was the Kobe earthquake, which sent Asian financial markets into free-fall. Leeson then bet on a quick Nikkei recovery, which did not occur.

Second, a profound failure of internal controls within Barings was found to be hugely significant, which presented Leeson with the *opportunity*. Leeson was the general manager for trading on SIMEX, but Barings committed an egregious internal control mistake by also making Leeson head of settlement operations for SIMEX, which essentially made him his own supervisor (settlement operations concerns the assurance of accurate accounting). Leeson was, in fact, largely unsupervised. Some concerns were raised internally about this situation, but there is no evidence these concerns were heeded.

Third, simple naked corruption must be included in the causes of the collapse. Here the obvious candidate is Leeson himself, but perhaps culpability is not limited to him. Barings' top managers seemed to accept unusual—not to say extraordinary—profits without concern; they were enjoying gains too. Before proceeding, however, a word about the discovery of his wrongdoing.

On February 23, 1995, Barings Bank auditors finally discovered the fraud at nearly the same time that Barings' chairman Peter Baring received a confession note from Leeson. Leeson's activities had generated losses totaling £827 million ($1.3 billion), twice the bank's available trading capital. The Bank of England attempted an unsuccessful bailout and employees around the world did not receive their bonuses. Barings was declared insolvent on 26 February 1995, and appointed administrators began managing the finances of Barings Group and its subsidiaries. The same day, the Board of Banking Supervision of the Bank of England launched an investigation.

What followed?

The short answer to the question, "what followed?" was that Dutch bank ING purchased Barings Bank in 1995 for the nominal sum of £1 and assumed all of Barings' liabilities, forming the subsidiary ING Barings. In 2001, ING sold the US-based operations to ABN Amro for $275 million and folded the rest of ING Barings into its European banking division. Ultimately, the assessment management division was sold to MassMutual. MassMutual retained the Baring name, so though Barings no longer has a legal existence, the name remains alive in MassMutual's division, and as a residual private equity business that was sold to managers with operations in Russia, Brazil, China/Asia, and India.

But what about Leeson and others involved in this story?

Leeson pleaded guilty to two counts of "deceiving the bank's auditors and cheating the Singapore exchange," this included a forgery charge. He was sentenced to six and a half years in Singapore. He was released in July 1999 after serving at least two-thirds of his sentence for good behavior, but partly in response to having been diagnosed with colon cancer, which ultimately he survived. As for colleagues at the bank, hundreds lost their jobs, investors were directly hit, but (surprising or not) the bank directors got their bonuses. More broadly, a government review produced an evaluation of the scandal that led to a number of changes to rules and laws pertaining to internal audit and governance.

Professor Mike Power, who teaches corporate governance and risk management at the London School of Economics, observed that Leeson was an "archetype for all that was wrong in the financial services arena in the 1980s." Interestingly, he argues the story is less about greed than about "hubris," a subject that gets attention later in this book. He also cast a disapproving look at the Barings board, who seemed happy to go along for the ride in the "excessively" good times at the bank without questioning the reasons for those good times.

Leeson's personal defects are one thing, but a general understanding of the purpose of corporate governance and internal audits would encourage the idea that vigilance in these areas is meant to anticipate and address such fraudulent behavior. We must ask, then, what is the bank's culpability in this scandal? A rather weak case could be made in this story that it is possible to hide wrongdoing within an organization, despite the best efforts of any controls. This is very weak, indeed, which can be immediately challenged by the organization's willingness to allow Leeson to be the supervisor/auditor of his own work. This central fact should suggest a couple of things:

1. While abstractly it could be said this was an internal control systems failure, was it really the system or leaders within the bank that was to blame?
2. What goes up must come down, otherwise known as reversion to the mean. Quite apart from wrongdoing, excessive profits should be—yes—good news, but any rudimentary understanding of human behavior and economics should at least raise the suspicion that extremely positive performance should be viewed with curiosity in the same way excessive losses would be considered.

Reflections

Appearing as it does early in this book, this case serves a couple of purposes. First, it is intended to highlight points raised within the chapter and to challenge readers to think about some of the implications of the emergence of ERM, CROs, and the concept of risk leadership. Second, it serves to offer hints of topics yet to come.

However, there is a kind of overarching third purpose, as was referenced in the opening paragraphs of this case. The Barings story recounts events that precede what might be called the modern era of risk management. ERM, COSO, ISO 31000, and even ERM research developments are all effectively post-Barings phenomena. So, possibly in this case alone, modern risk management can escape blame or credit for events that transpired. However, in avoiding that attention, a different question might reasonably be asked. Had ERM existed within Barings in the early 1990s, would the outcome have been different? We can imagine ERM anticipating and addressing this scandal in theory but there is plenty of evidence since 1995 (and some of it will be presented in other case studies here) that even the presence of ERM can fail to prevent really bad things from happening.

The first case in Chapter One recounts one of the foundations of modern risk management: the passage of the Sarbanes–Oxley Act of 2002, which established a number of requirements for internal audit, risk management, governance, regulatory oversight, and legal frameworks. One might reflect on that case and conclude that the Barings scandal exhibited forms of failure in all these requirements. In a future chapter, a different case will demonstrate that Sarbanes–Oxley did not provide the hoped-for remedy. But finally here, in the second case study of this chapter, we will see a return visit from the problems that were central to Barings, to Sarbanes–Oxley, and even to responses to the 2008 financial crisis. Something else is going on here beyond a failure of systems and processes.

It is possible that the other thing "going on here" is more a matter of human behavior as manifested in individual actions AND in collective behavior—what we could characterize as organization culture (its beliefs, its prohibitions, its unspoken rules, its values). Add to this the particular issue of leadership and—we believe—there is a very promising field of investigation for getting to the heart of that "something" that underlies all three cases.

There are many, many points of discussion that might be identified here. We suggest three.

- The case itself raises a seemingly small point—in passing—that actually could be assigned its own chapter. Excessive good or bad news/results should both be a cause for some careful reflection. There may be perfectly legitimate explanations for outstanding performance ("we are just that good!"), but there should always be some critical consideration of outcomes that appear far beyond the range of normal expectations. Typically, such analysis does follow poor performance, but what are the factors that lead critical assessment to NOT be conducted after unexpectedly positive outcomes? It would seem that there is something within basic human psychology that leads us to view exceptionally good performance as a validation of our excellence while looking at exceptionally poor performance is interpreted as someone else's fault. What does this tell us about human psychology generally?
- It is occasionally said that governance is an aspect of risk management that focuses on the risks that impact how the organization is governed. Others might look at the relationship the other way around—governance structures are a source of risk. In any event, this idea manifests itself in the term, *Risk Governance*, which is considered elsewhere in the book. Governance as a risk management tool; governance as a source of risk or even an exposure to risk. Can we think about this in each way: how can we think about Baring's apparent approach to governance as a) a risk management tool, b) a source of risk, and c) and even an exposure to risk?
- A theme that appears in the Sarbanes–Oxley case reemerges here. Can we legislate or regulate morally? One of the central ironies of Sarbanes–Oxley is that the problems it sought to address were largely moral failings, and it did so through the introduction of new regulation and audit procedures. In the Barings case, the issue here is more of a simplified question. In addition to, or in place of, regulatory requirements, is there anything that might be done to anticipate or prevent bad behavior?

Read more about it

Drummond, H. (2002). Living in a fool's paradise: The collapse of Barings' Bank. *Management Decision*, 40(3), 232–238.

Lesson, N. and Whitley, E. (1996). *Rogue Trader: How I Brought Down Barings Bank and Shook the Financial World*. Little Brown & Company, New York, NY.

Rawnsley, J. H. (2011). *Total Risk: Nick Leeson and the Fall of Barings Bank*. HarperCollins, New York, NY.

Stein, M. (2002). The risk taker as shadow: A psychoanalytic view of the collapse of Barings bank. *Journal of Management Studies*, 37(8), 1215–1230.

Case 2.2: The Ghost of Barings Past: Société Générale

Case overview

"Here we go again;" likely uttered countless times in 2008 as the financial crisis swept through the developed world that year. As details of the crisis emerged descriptive terms like "an unimaginable black swan event" began to give way to the question, "how did we not see this coming?" Indeed, as years have passed, the view has emerged that the *unimaginable* is often quite *imaginable*, suggesting that other factors may be in play when catastrophic events occur. There are true black swan events, no doubt, but on closer examination, the 2008 crisis could have been seen in advance—and indeed, many individuals did see it coming.

Buried within the financial blizzard of 2008 were a great number of smaller-scale crises or scandals, many of which featured common elements, and many of which were freighted with a powerful sense of *déjà vu*. One such scandal that brought back memories of past transgressions was the Kerviel scandal at Société Générale.

Société Générale S.A., often nicknamed "SocGen," is a French multinational investment bank and financial services company headquartered in Paris, France. The company is a universal bank and has divisions supporting French networks, global transaction banking, international retail banking, general financial services, corporate and investment banking, private banking, asset management, and securities services. Société Générale is France's third-largest bank by total assets, seventh largest in Europe, or seventeenth by market capitalization. The company is part of the Euro Stoxx 50 stock market index. It is known as one of the *Trois Vieilles* ("Old Three") of French banking, along with BNP Paribas and Crédit Lyonnais.

In 2008, the SocGen was rocked by an event with strong echoes of the Barings Bank fiasco in the mid-1990s. A junior futures trader, Jérôme Kerviel, was found to be the architect of a fraudulent scheme using disguised accounts to mask trades and losses. The ensuing response—including a trial—presented a number of specific questions about legal responsibility, fairness, and governance failures. Interestingly, but peripheral to the case's theme here, the bank experienced a run of further problems between 2008 and 2012, all seemingly unrelated, but collectively raising the specter of *Trouble Comes in Bunches*.

Background

One of France's oldest banks, Société Générale, was formed in 1864. By 1871, its growth and expansion led it to transitioning to public ownership through the French issues market. By the turn of the century, the bank had grown to a sufficient size that it was operating in 148 locations. Although not discussed in detail here, 1870–1900 was a period of great economic instability throughout Europe (and beyond), so the bank's survival was widely interpreted as evidence of sound management. Through the early 20th century, the bank grew functionally into a large modern credit financial institution—managing company and personal deposits, short-term lending, placing shares, and issuing private debenture loans. During this period of time, the bank also expanded operations into Russia. It was in these years that the bank became the largest banking institution in France.

It is worth briefly reflecting on the first half of the 20th century, in which the bank operated through two world wars, the Russian revolution, the Spanish Civil War, the Russo-Japanese War, the Great Depression, and several smaller-scale political and economic crises. The bank's ability to carry on trading is a remarkable part of the SocGen story. In the post-World War II period, however, the bank was nationalized, and it remained so until 1987. During its time as a nationalized bank, it experienced remarkable growth, including a major move into African markets. In large part, growth was the result of the rapid reconstruction of Europe after the war. However, owing to its presence in New York, the bank enjoyed the benefits of serving as a primary vehicle for the distribution of funds under the Marshall Plan. In addition to international expansion, the bank continued broadening its range of financial services.

Key to this case study, beginning in the 1980s and in response to market internationalization, general deregulation trends, and—of course—technological advances, the bank identified two strategic objectives. One objective focused on increased services to private customers, while the other objective involved greater and more diverse activity within global capital markets. The aforementioned re-privatization (1987) was the result of a process undertaken by the French government to choose a bank best suited to succeed as a private entity and Société Générale's post-war track record was seen as a major success story and was—therefore—selected for privatization.

Trouble

Within the full spectrum of dynamics in global financial markets in the first decade of the 21st century, SocGen was an active participant in increasingly complex capital markets, enjoying both the benefits of innovative new products and the roller coaster ride created by the interconnected and lightly regulated world of international finance.

Into that broader story in the late months of 2007 evidence began to emerge suggesting a problem of potentially immense proportions. The circumstances became public in January of 2008 when it was announced that an individual trader had fraudulently generated a €4.9 billion trading loss. It was alleged that this was fully and solely the fault of that trader, Jérôme Kerviel, though an underlying factor was the wider 2007–2008 financial disaster that was engulfing much of the developed world economies. As noted briefly previously, this began an unusual run of difficulties for SocGen, including a missing gold consignment in Turkey and a near disaster (which was averted) that arose from the US government bailout of AIG.

The Kerviel scandal quickly became a sensation in France. In addition to addressing the practical problems of dealing with downgrades by credit rating agencies, SocGen soon realized that the challenge of getting its hands around the full scope of the losses was going to be difficult. At various times, the loss was estimated to be as high as US$73 billion (greater than the bank's market cap), and as low as US$2.8 billion. Subsequently, it can be noted, SocGen listed the cost of closing out the fraudulent contracts at US$7.18 billion. The bank was in the early stages of a recovery in 2010, coincidentally at the same time Kerviel went on trial. The trial lasted the month of June and was the subject of intense focus in the global media, though certainly attention was greatest in France. Among the coverage "themes" that emerged in the media was the fact that this case mirrored the Barings Bank scandal in many ways. How could this happen again?

The court handed down its verdict in October of that year. Kerviel was found guilty of breach of trust, fraudulent behavior, and forgery. He was sentenced to five years (two suspended) and was directed to pay damages of €4.9 billion—over US$7 billion—to SocGen. This verdict was immediately appealed—the immense size of the damages award was judged by the public, and many experts, as being excessive, unreasonable, and unrealistic. In fact, this court decision became something of a *cause célèbre* and there was a public outcry that not only was the award beyond all reason, but it also raised questions about how an individual was able to get away with this fraud in the first place. What was management doing?

Financial institutions have experienced a bumpy ride since 2010, though with generally positive trends. In Europe, a panic around a looming financial crisis in the EU did not help either politicians' or financiers' reputations during this time, and the goodwill lost due to the 2008 financial crisis and the various scandals took a further hit. Though there were improvements in the late 2010s, the COVID-19 crisis in 2020 introduced a new form of challenge and source of instability.

The bigger picture

The SocGen story, standing alone, shines a disproportionately bright light on Jérôme Kerviel, as egregious as his actions were. In linking this story through a reference to the Barings Bank scandal, the scope of the attention widens a bit, so it is worth briefly mentioning that Leeson and Kerviel were far from alone in perpetrating frauds within their firms. For example, consider that since Barings, the following list of trading scandals presents a small but representative example of the scope of trading crimes committed during that time.

- 1995: Toshihide Iguchi of Resona Holdings was sentenced to four years in prison
- 1996: Yasuo Hamanaka of Sumitomo Corp. was sentenced to eight years in prison
- 2002; John Rusnak of Allied Irish Banks was sentenced to seven and a half years in prison
- 2003–2004: David Bullen, Luke Duffy, Vince Ficarra, and Gianni Gray of National Australian Bank were all sentenced to varying terms in prison
- 2005: Chen Jiulin of China Aviation Oil was sentenced to over four years in prison
- 2007: Matthew Taylor of Goldman Sachs was sentenced to nine months in prison
- 2009: Stephen Perkins of PVM Oil Futures was permanently barred from trading
- 2011: Kweku Adoboli of UBS was sentenced to seven years in prison

There are at least two natural reactions to seeing this list, both certainly understandable but both only partly correct. The first is that bad behavior never ceases to emerge—it is always with us. The second is that bad behavior seems to be poorly policed (though, obviously, not in terms of convictions and sentencing cited previously).

There can be no argument that there is plenty of bad/illegal/evil behavior in the world. It is a matter of philosophical deliberation as to whether such behaviors can ever be eradicated. We doubt they can, but the broader question is whether an overall improvement can occur in any meaningful way. It is tempting to argue that in a relatively confined setting like an organization, it should be possible to exert a more powerful effort to shape the overall behavior, values, and expectations within that organization. And, certainly, organizational cultures are more alterable than social/national cultures. Still, all the listed scandals above occurred in organizations, and prominent ones at that. The view that possibly arises from this line of thinking is that nothing can prevent bad behavior *except* somehow enlisting a sincere and realizable individual effort to be good. Regulations and controls do not seem to be effective in imposing good behavior on managers.

Regarding the second reaction to the frequency of bad behavior, it probably is true that the focus on this one type of fraudulent activity should not distract us from the fact that there are lots of other bad acts occurring throughout the organizational world, and we would have to wonder whether regulatory or internal controls and governance systems can keep pace with all of this. Placed alongside this observation, however, is the realization that if things were as bad as we sometimes imagine, organizations would be unable to do their work. There is rare evidence that this is the case. There is reason for hope.

So, what is the answer? The "Reflections" offer some organized way to think about this, but the vital center of this issue is how we balance the desire for virtuous self-regulating managers with the need to enforce standards of behavior. As with most things in life, it is likely that each of the two approaches represents the ends of a spectrum and that the solutions are found somewhere in between.

Reflections

This case begins in France in 2007–2008, bounces back to the mid-1990s and the Barings scandal, and then swings widely into a commentary on illegal trading in general, concluding with an observation on bad/illegal behavior. Can we bring this "Reflections" section into some useful focus?

The three cases appearing in Chapter Two offer a kind of compare-and-contrast challenge. The first two cases (Barings and SocGen) are the obvious "compare" side of the challenge, while the General Mills case offers a kind of "contrast" option…though not precisely in the *either-or* sense of that term. Three observations deserve some attention, especially as they relate to the chapter itself.

- This chapter focuses on the evidence that ERM "works." After having set up the story of ERM in Chapter One and establishing the hopes and aspirations organizations have for risk management and leadership, this chapter challenges proponents to demonstrate that those aspirations are achieved—or perhaps achievable is the better word. What we have found is that the evidence is inconclusive in its totality. There are strong and compelling theoretical ideas that suggest risk management is beneficial to an organization. And there is isolated evidence that risk management practices add value to an organization. Additionally, basic human common sense tells us preventing bad things from happening and optimizing the achievement of good things must be important. And, of course, they are. Still, in holding a more intense focus on risk management/leadership performance as organizational phenomena, we are concerned that analysis shows so many inconsistencies, gaps in the evidence, and—frankly—bigger issues that do not quite seem to fit the current model. Are we looking at risk management the right way?

The SocGen case presents an illustration (along with the Barings story) of an issue that is recognized as a risk management issue—employee fraud—but which sits perhaps just outside the ordinary boundary of risk management thinking in some respects. Conventional risk management responses would tend to gravitate toward the imposition of more formal rules, the imposition of greater oversight, revised governance, and internal control processes—in other words, more command-and-control policing. All important tools, but all demonstrating weakness in incorporating things like self-regulation or virtuous individual behavior. How can we think about the role of risk management in that "human" side of the equation?

- The "contrast" exercise with General Mills, as will be seen, is a relatively dissimilar exercise as the stories represent very different situations—for example, only the SocGen story deals with actual illegal behavior. Still, the General Mills case deals with human perceptions and behaviors—only in a different form. In the case of General Mills, the issue is the seeming failure to identify a major strategic threat, noting (as with SocGen) that this happened while the firm both had an ERM program in place and while the firm had long been lauded as effectively managed and led. This reinforces an idea that gains traction later in the book. Human nature and behavior, including bad or immoral behavior, are probably the most important (certainly the most ubiquitous) sources of risk and uncertainty in organizations. Thinking now about SocGen, how can the human dimension be more firmly "centralized" in the frame of risk management/leadership thinking?

- The SocGen case only lightly touches on the aftermath of the Kerviel case, but it is worth mentioning that post-2010, there was a huge pushback against the bank from the public. It was hard for the public and other observers to imagine that the bank's top managers had no role in or responsibility for the scandal, and yet there was not much official legal attention paid to that side of the story. Additionally, the huge damages award imposed on Kerviel was never paid (nor, it seems, was it expected to be paid). And then, in 2016, Kerviel actually won a wrongful dismissal case against the bank, which reignited media attention on the original scandal. Business leaders uniformly report each year that *reputational risk* sits near the top of their list of strategic concerns. What does the SocGen story tell us about the nature of reputation as an asset exposed to risk as well as a source of risk?

Read more about it

Gilligan, G. (2011). Jérôme Kerviel the "rogue trader" of Société Générale: Bad luck, bad apple, bad tree or bad orchard? *The Company Lawyer*, 32(12), 355–362.

Rafeld, H., Fritz-Morgenthal, S. and Posch, P. N. (2017). Behavioural patterns in rogue trading: Analysing the cases of Nick Leeson, Jérôme Kerviel and Kweku Adoboli: Part 1 and 2. *Journal of Financial Compliance*. 1 and 2, 156–171, and 1 and 3, 276–284.

Reurink, A. (2018). Financial fraud: A literature review. Special Issue: Contemporary Topics in Finance: *A Collection of Literature Surveys*, 32(5), 1292–1325.

Wexler, M. N. (2010). Financial edgework and the persistence of rogue traders. *Business and Society Review*, 114(1), 1–25.

Case 2.3: Strategic risks and risk leadership: General Mills and the yogurt problem

Case overview

Minnesota-based General Mills has been long noted for its commitment to good corporate governance. The Audit Committee oversees internal controls, financial reporting, legal compliance, and ERM. The company has had an ERM process in place since the early 2000s, although according to observers it had become "ripe for a revamp"—needing better risk mitigation follow-ups and alignment with strategic planning. In part, this might be reflected in the past pursuit of a high dividend yield policy that made the stock popular among investors in the low interest-rate environment.

However, this policy also caused an erosion in innovation with falling market shares and declining profits in contrast to its lofty aspirations. It appears the ERM process was mostly applied for financial, economic, and operational risk assessments while strategic risk factors that could affect the long-term viability of the enterprise seemed to be disregarded. A specific challenge involving its yogurt product line produced a vivid example of the pitfalls of not including strategic business risks in the ERM risk assessment process.

The company

General Mills, Inc. is a multinational manufacturer and marketer of branded consumer foods sold through retail stores. It is headquartered in the Twin Cities metropolitan area (Minnesota). It markets many well-known brands including Gold Medal flour, Betty Crocker, Yoplait, Totino's, Pillsbury, Old El Paso, Häagen-Dazs, Cheerios, Cocoa Puffs, and Lucky Charms, among its more than 89 brands.

The company traces its history back to 1856 and specifically to the Minneapolis Milling Company. The name General Mills appears in 1928 when the company merged with two other flour-producing companies. While not relevant to this case study, the story of General Mills for the ensuing 60 years is fascinating as the company at various times owned a radio station, an aeronautics firm, was an early innovator in merchandising and sponsorships via television advertising, an electronics business, a toy company, restaurant chains, and clothing and apparel companies.

It is the late 1980s when General Mills begins a series of moves that led to its current business posture as primarily a food manufacturer and marketer. Notable in this journey is a joint venture with Nestles S.A., which facilitated the marketing of products outside the United States, and the 2001 acquisition of Pillsbury (another historic milling company-cum-food producer based in Minneapolis). Since 2004, General Mills has been producing more products targeted to the growing ranks of health-conscious consumers. Among several product developments, yogurt typified this new focus.

The yogurt crisis

In 2016, General Mills leading Yoplait yogurt brand dramatically and suddenly fell behind its chief competitors, Chobani and Danone, with sales plunging in excess of 20% that year (after having dropped ominously more than 5% the year before). While the company has a number of strong food brands in its portfolio—notably Cheerios, Wheaties, Pillsbury, Old El Paso, and Häagen-Dazs—Yoplait counted for almost a fifth of corporate revenues. Obviously, the deteriorating yogurt sales were a wake-up call. Industry analysts noted that General Mills was late in responding to Chobani's introduction of Greek yogurts and ended up playing catch-up—with mixed results. Putting this situation into a risk management frame, we might say that strategic risks did not seem to figure squarely at the center of the ERM process; though to be fair, managing strategic risks is a very difficult and demanding challenge.

Nevertheless, despite having an ERM process in place, General Mills had missed the high-impact competitive developments in the important yogurt market. Whereas the ERM process appeared to provide detailed reporting on financial and economic exposures with advanced Value-at-Risk monitoring, seemingly it was not able to identify the biggest risks embedded in the competitive market dynamic.

Various initiatives have been taken in the interim to introduce new products across the spectrum, including healthy lifestyle products in its cereal product portfolio, power bars and other energy foods, and a range of new yogurt types with lower levels of sweetener as a means of boosting sales. While evidence of recovering from the shock remains ongoing, observers have noted that these efforts may also increase the cost of more complex product lines that could put pressure on future profit margins and net earnings. That is, the expansion through new product offerings is not without risk either. However, General Mills has promoted new risk management approaches via its Audit Committee, which seem to promise more leadership engagement, use of advanced data analytics, and adoption of a risk appetite statement to foster more risk-taking activities.

The jury remains out on whether the recommended changes will have a positive impact, and it is actually here that this case study finds its focus. This chapter presents an assessment of ERM performance and promise and certainly establishes that research remains equivocal about whether ERM is actually a value-adding endeavor. What is tantalizing is that theory is fairly strong in the argument that managing risk can be a valuable contributor to firm performance—the problem seems to be that empirical evidence stands on a far less firm footing. So, here we encounter a real-world situation that once again poses the following question:

> General Mills has introduced a number of measures that align firmly with ERM concepts, principles, and practices. This is to be applauded in the wake of the yogurt challenge, but will it work? Or to be slightly more precise, if it works will it matter?

This chapter offers critiques of ERM in general as well as in the context of specific actions and applications. Overall, the general line of critique focuses on whether ERM is positioned to meaningfully deal with things that really matter. Risks seem well-covered, but what about uncertainties and unknown or emergent threats and opportunities. This is worth contemplating in the General Mills case because strategic challenges are specific responsibilities for top managers and a strong case can be made that strategic challenges are not *risks*, they are *uncertainties*. And, as such, they are hard to see, hard to assess, and hard to address. Further, the fact that they tend to be interpreted as risks is actually an additional problem. Organizational leaders seek (and demand) data, but data on strategic issues is limited, which can tempt decision-makers to over-interpret or over-value the limited information they have.

Beyond this, however, the chapter and future chapters provide evidence that the problem is not so much the efficacy of the measures taken—though there is even some concern there. Rather, the issues pertain more to what might be called the *executive milieu*. How do executives interpret and use these measures?

While not specifically referring to the General Mills leadership team, it is worth remembering that individuals rising to the top of organizations bring with them not just the ordinary experiences humans all have but have particular pressures unique to working at high levels, and so have some susceptibilities in thinking about risk, uncertainty, and the unknown. Furthermore, as has already been established, ERM carries the burden of being perceived as a "must do" rather than a "want to do" exercise. Therefore, the reasons for concern about a firm adopting ERM measures might be summarized as:

1. Strategic uncertainties are hard to assess and address
2. They tend to not be seen for what they are—uncertainties and emergent challenges
3. Executive decision-making is challenging and highly pressurized
4. Human factors intrude (behavioral psychology, cultural sociology, moral and ethical factors), meaning even the most talented and intelligent leaders are imperfect observers of the world they encounter
5. And yet … leaders are charged with handling the most important challenges that organizations face

In sum, human perception and behavior—not systems and processes—tend to lie under most risk management issues.

A final note. As things stand today, US companies with assets in excess of $10 million and shares held by more than 2,000 owners must file annual reports with the Securities and Exchange Commission (SEC) disclosing, on a Form 10-K, new emergent risks that may affect the business. In other words, when General Mills and other larger companies have to identify and define major strategic risks, we may be witnessing the consequence of a legal reporting requirement rather than the outcomes of conscious strategic risk management processes and thinking.

Reflections

We await the *and … therefore* moment with this short case study. Current events, such as the pandemic, the economy, and civil unrest in Minneapolis–St. Paul have swept away more conventional commentary on corporate performance everywhere. And it most certainly is also true for General Mills. It is difficult if not impossible to say that the introduction of modifications to its ERM has "worked." But as with all "Reflections," the point of the case is to prompt consideration and discussion about issues raised in the chapter.

Here, the focus is on the workability of ERM and particular issues that arise when we consider strategic threats and opportunities. In that light, three questions or discussion topics seem particularly important.

- From a risk management perspective, one of two things likely explains why General Mills experienced the challenges that threatened its Yoplait business. Either the emerging threat was a complete surprise or it was known but was devalued in importance. Of course, a possible third reason—an almost existential reason in the case of its impact on Yoplait—would be that General Mills knew about the threat but could do nothing about it (or could not quickly do anything about it). None of these explanations would be well-received by investors. This observation must be leavened by the sheer reality of uncertainties, which is that sometimes things happen that we cannot foresee, plan for, and respond to, no matter our level of managerial excellence. But most post-mortems reveal that most surprises can be seen in advance. So, the question for discussion here is:
  - What would a reasonably effective Strategic Uncertainty Assessment process look like? In thinking about this, acceptability among executives would also be an important dimension, given the specific demands on the leadership team's time.
- One of the frequently cited issues CROs face is gaining appropriate access to the executive team, which is somewhat paradoxical because CROs are intended to signify a top-level engagement with risk management. Alongside access, the matter of credibility presents another challenge. Partly this is due to the newness of the CRO function and—indeed—the newness of some aspects of ERM. How would executives know that someone was credible or was doing a good job when the position is new and comparisons with past practices are limited? Perhaps more important is the question of how a CRO seeks to gain standing and credibility. How would a new CRO look at the process of establishing the necessary support and recognition to be able to effectively do his/her job? What does a game plan look like for a CRO's first six months on the job?

- A somewhat hidden aspect of modern risk management is to get all managers to see the value-adding relevance of risk management to their jobs. For the executive team, value is seen in strategic and organization-wide terms. For other managers there has to be evidence that 1) the risk manager/leader is helping them do their job better and 2) where possible or relevant the risk manager/leader needs to be able to show direct value enhancement from risk management to the company's output—that is, its products or services. What would be the evidence that the practice of risk management is directly leading to customers more highly valuing the company's products or services?

Read more about it

David, Kolpak (2016). General Mills: The risks run deeper than its sky-high valuation, August 24. https://seekingalpha.com/article/4001886-general-mills-risks-run-deeper-sky-high-valuation.

General, Mills (n.d.). *Annual Report.* https://investors.generalmills.com/financial-information/annual-reports/default.aspx

John, Kell. (2017). General Mills loses the culture wars, May 22 (in the June 1, 2017, issue of *Fortune*). http://fortune.com/2017/05/22/general-mills-yoplait-greek-yogurt/

Michelle, Lodge (2018). General Mills' plans to emphasize sales growth carry risks: Packaged goods giant counting on new cereals, energy bars and yogurt to boost sales, July 11, *TheStreet.* www.thestreet.com/investing/general-mills-plans-to-emphasize-sales-carry-risks-14648218

Notes

1 See, for example, Nair, A., Rustambekov, E., McShane, M., Fainshmidt, S. 2013. Enterprise risk management as a dynamic capability: A test of its effectiveness during a crisis. *Managerial and Decision Economics*, 35(8), 555–566.

2 The Committee of Sponsoring Organizations (COSO) was established in 1985 by five major US-based accounting and auditing associations (American Accounting Association [AAA]; the American Institute of Certified Public Accountants [AICPA]; Financial Executives International [FEI]; Institute of Internal Auditors [IIA]; the National Association of Accountants—now Institute of Management Accountants [IMA]) to advance internal controls and enterprise risk management. COSO commissioned PricewaterhouseCoopers (PwC) to develop the integrated ERM framework in 2001, which is used in the PwC risk management practice. The detailed ERM framework can be purchased from COSO against up-front payment.

3 COSO (2017). *Enterprise Risk Management—Integrating with Strategy and Performance* (Executive Summary), Committee of Sponsoring Organizations of the Treadway Commission (COSO). https://www.coso.org/Documents/2017-COSO-ERM-Integrating-with-Strategy-and-Performance-Executive-Summary.pdf.

4 See, for example, Andersen, T. J. (2013). *Short Introduction to Strategic Management.* Cambridge University Press, Cambridge, UK. http://libsearch.cbs.dk/primo_library/libweb/action/dlDisplay.do.

5 ISO (International Organization for Standardization) is an independent non-governmental international organization headquartered in Geneva, Switzerland, with 165 national standards bodies as members. It develops, maintains, and promotes the ISO standards and guidelines globally and the detailed frameworks and guidelines can be purchased against up-front payment.

6 IRM (2018). *Standard Deviations—A Risk Practitioners Guide to ISO 31000*, The Institute of Risk Management, London, UK. https://www.theirm.org/media/6884/irm-report-iso-31000-2018-v2.pdf.

7 ISO (2018). *Risk Management—ISO 31000*, International Organization for Standardization (ISO), Geneva, Switzerland. https://www.iso.org/files/live/sites/isoorg/files/store/en/PUB100426.pdf.

8 ibid.

9 Two papers that shine a light on the challenges of looking for ERM evidence in annual reports. Quon, T. K., Zeghal, D. and, Maingot, M. (2012). Enterprise risk management and firm perfor-

mance, *Procedia—Social and Behavioral Sciences*, 62, 263–267. Lundqvist, S. and Vilhelmsson, A. (2016). Enterprise risk management and default risk: Evidence from the banking industry, school of economics and management, department of business Administration, Lund University and Knut Wicksell Centre for Financial, pp. 45–99.

10 Three journal articles representing different approaches to assessing ERM and CRO adoptions. Liebenberg, A. P. and Hoyt, R. E. (2003). The determinants of enterprise risk management: Evidence from the appointment of Chief Risk Officers. *Risk Management and Insurance Review*, 6, 37–52. Pagach, D. and Warr, R. (2011). The characteristics of firms that hire Chief Risk Officers. *Journal of Risk and Insurance*, 78, 185–211. Beasley, M. S., Clune, R. and Hermanson, D. R. (2005). Enterprise risk management: An empirical analysis of factors associated with the extent of implementation, *Journal of Accounting and Public Policy*, 24, 521–531.

11 Mikes, A. and Kaplan, R. S. (2014), Towards a contingency theory of enterprise risk management. Harvard Business School. Working Paper 13-063. Illustrates an effort to look for theoretical framing for ERM.

12 Corvellec, H. (2009). The practice of risk management: Silence is not absence. *Risk Management*, 11, 285–304. Among other things, a paper that reinforces the idea that just because you cannot see ERM, it does not mean it is not there.

13 Liebenberg, A. P. and Hoyt, R. E. (2003). The determinants of enterprise risk management: Evidence from the appointment of Chief Risk Officers. *Risk Management and Insurance Review*, 6, 37–52; an early effort to identify factors that influence the adoption of ERM.

14 Liebenberg, A. P. and Hoyt, R. E. (2003). The determinants of enterprise risk management: Evidence from the appointment of Chief Risk Officers. *Risk Management and Insurance Review*, 6, 37–52. Lamm, J. C. and Kawamoto, B. M. (1997). Emergence of the chief risk officer. *Risk Management*, 44(9), 30–35. Miccolis, J. and Shah, S. (2000). Enterprise risk management: An analytic approach, Tillinghast-Towers Perrin, TTP Monograph; collectively, three representatives of the earliest serious writing on ERM and CROs—with the Lamm paper perhaps one of the very first.

15 Lam, J. (2003). Ten predictions for risk management. *The RMA Journal*, 85, 84–87.

16 Razali, A. R., and Tahir, I, M, (2011), Review of the literature on enterprise risk management. *Business Management Dynamics*, 1(5), 8–16. A good summary of ERM research to that point in time.

17 Mikes, A. and Kaplan, R. S. (2014). *Towards a Contingency Theory of Enterprise Risk Management*. Working Paper, Harvard Business School, Cambridge, MA.

18 Paape, L. and Speklé, R. F. (2012). The adoption and design of enterprise risk management practices: An empirical study. *European Accounting Review*, 21(3), 533–564. Few papers include ERM design considerations.

19 Beasley, M. S., Clune, R. and Hermanson, D. R. (2005). Enterprise risk management: An empirical analysis of factors associated with the extent of implementation. *Journal of Accounting and Public Policy*, 24, 521–531. An early assessment of implementation.

20 Lamm, J. C. and Kawamoto, B. M. (1997). Emergence of the chief risk officer. *Risk Management*, 44(9), 30–35. Referenced previously.

21 Kleffner, A. E., Lee, R. B. and McGannon, B. (2003). The effect of corporate governance on the use of Enterprise risk management: Evidence from Canada. *Risk Management and Insurance Review*, 6(1), 53–73.

22 Beasley, M. S., Clune, R. and Hermanson, D. R. (2005). Enterprise risk management: An empirical analysis of factors associated with the extent of implementation. *Journal of Accounting and Public Policy*, 24, 521–531. Previously referenced.

23 Beasley, M. S., Pagach, D. and Warr, R. (2008). Information conveyed in hiring announcements of senior executives overseeing enterprise-wide risk management processes. *Journal of Accounting, Auditing and Finance*, 23, 311–332. Does the presence of a CRO actually signal a changing or progressive view to risk management in organizations? This paper provides a view.

24 Hoyt, R. E. and Liebenberg, A. P. (2011). The value of enterprise risk management. *The Journal of Risk and Insurance*, 78(4), 5–69. An updating of the authors' previous work.

25 Gordon, L. A., Loeb, M. P. and Tseng, C. (2009). Enterprise risk management and firm performance: A contingency perspective. *Journal of Accounting and Public Policy*, 28, 301–327. Notable for the coverage of contingency in assessing performance.

26 McShane, M., Nair, A. and Rustambekov, E. (2011). Does enterprise risk management increase firm value? *Journal of Accounting, Auditing, and Finance*, 26, 641–658. Baxter, R., Bedard, J., Hoitash, R., and Yezegel, A. (2012). Enterprise risk management program quality: Determinants, value relevance, and

the financial crisis. *Contemporary Accounting Research*, 30(4), 1264–1295. These two papers present different approaches to assessing ERM performance.

27 Standard & Poors (2019). *Enterprise Risk Management Evaluation Framework*. S&P Global Ratings, New York, NY.

28 Lundqvist, S. A. (2014). An exploratory study of enterprise risk management: Pillars of ERM. *Journal of Accounting, Auditing and Finance*, 29(3), 393–429; provides a good overarching look at ERM.

29 Quon, T. K., Zeghal, D. and Maingot, M. (2012). Enterprise risk management and firm performance. *Procedia—Social and Behavioral Sciences*, 62, 263–267; provides yet another approach to performance assessment.

30 Lundqvist, S. and Vilhelmsson, A. (2016). Enterprise risk management and default risk: Evidence from the Banking Industry, *Journal of Risk and Insurance*, 85(1), 127–157.

31 Beasley, M. S., Clune, R. and Hermanson, D. R. (2005). Enterprise risk management: An empirical analysis of factors associated with the extent of implementation. *Journal of Accounting and Public Policy*, 24, 521–531. Referenced previously.

32 Liebenberg, A. P. and Hoyt, R. E. (2003). The determinants of enterprise risk management: Evidence from the appointment of Chief Risk Officers. *Risk Management and Insurance Review*, 6, 37–52. Pagach, D. and Warr, R. (2011). The characteristics of firms that hire Chief Risk Officers. *Journal of Risk and Insurance*, 78, 185–211. Golshan, N. M., Zaleha, S. and Rasid, A. (2012). Determinants of enterprise risk management adoption: An empirical analysis of Malaysian public listed firms. *A World Academy of Science, Engineering and Technology;* the first two cited papers are previously referenced, the third presents an assessment in Southeast Asia.

33 Paape, L. and Speklé, R. F. (2012). The adoption and design of enterprise risk management practices: An empirical study. *European Accounting Review*, 21(3), 533–564; which examines adoption and design from a different perspective.

34 Liebenberg, A. P. and Hoyt, R. E. (2003). The determinants of enterprise risk management: Evidence from the appointment of Chief Risk Officers. *Risk Management and Insurance Review*, 6, 37–52. (Liebenberg and Hoyt, 2003, 2011), Referenced previously.

35 Pagach, D. and Warr, R. (2011). The characteristics of firms that hire Chief Risk Officers. *Journal of Risk and Insurance*, 78, 185–211. Referenced previously.

36 Hoyt, R. E. and Liebenberg, A. P. (2011). The value of enterprise risk management. *The Journal of Risk and Insurance*, 78(4), 5–69. Pagach, D. and Warr, R. (2011). The characteristics of firms that hire Chief Risk Officers, *Journal of Risk and Insurance*, 78, 185–211. Golshan, N. M., Zaleha, S. and Rasid, A. (2012). Determinants of enterprise risk management adoption: An empirical analysis of Malaysian public listed firms. *A World Academy of Science, Engineering and Technology*. All three papers are referenced again in regard to a different issue.

37 Soltanizadeh, S., Abdul Rasid, S. Z., Mottaghi Golshan, N. and Wan Ismail, W. K. (2016). Business strategy, enterprise risk management and organizational performance. *Management Research Review*, 39(9), 1016–1033; reflecting emerging interest in the strategy/risk management relationship.

38 Beasley, M. S., Clune, R. and Hermanson, D. R. (2005). Enterprise risk management: An empirical analysis of factors associated with the extent of implementation. *Journal of Accounting and Public Policy*, 24, 521–531. Referenced previously.

39 Andersen, T. J. and Sax, J. (2018). Making risk management strategic: Integrating enterprise risk management with strategic planning. *European Management Review*, 16(3), 719–740; n paper that examines the directionality of the ERM-Strategic Management relationship.

40 Bromiley, P. and Harris, J. D. (2014). A comparison of alternative measures of organizational aspirations. *Strategic Management Journal*, 33, 338–357. A wide-ranging paper with relevance for ERM and CROs.

41 Gates, S., Nicolas, J. L. and Walker, P. L. (2012). Enterprise risk management: A process for enhanced management and improved performance. *Management Accounting Quarterly*, 13(3), 28–38; provides an argument for ERM's contribution to overall organizational performance.

42 Beasley, M., Branson, B. and Pagach, D. (2015). An analysis of the maturity and strategic impact of investments in ERM. Journal of Accounting and Public Policy, 34(3), 219–243: a paper looking at the specific issue of investing in the development of ERM programs.

3 Risk leadership in a complex and uncertain environment

Leading in a complex environment

This chapter continues to examine risk leadership in organizations and seeks to investigate links to the broader Leadership research. It further attempts to isolate and explain the associated, or implied, core component of risk leadership—what will be termed *risk competence*. While Chapter Two focused on the recently updated ERM frameworks in the context of turbulent environments, we extend this discussion and consider the implications of increasingly complex risk landscapes for risk management practice.

An evolving risk landscape

According to the World Economic Forum, the most significant risks to affect business and society refer to climate change, extreme weather, cybercrime, and socio-economic instability—all incidents beyond the immediate control of individual companies or communities.[1] In other words, there may be a need for collective solutions—a theme we will return to later. The global links between individuals, organizations, and societies are accentuated by pervasive cross-border flows of people, goods, capital, and information—all enabled by an open economic system and digital technologies. This has created a vast intertwined network of interacting global players, which has increased the complexity and interconnectedness between agents. It constitutes a complex system comprised of many interacting entities with a structure that defeats simple comprehension where outcomes are often unpredictable because the actions of each entity are linked to, and depend on, all the others. These relationships follow irreversible paths where current actions influence—and partially determine—the options available for future actions. Hence, it is important to make prudent responses, while it is difficult—even impossible—to forecast events accurately as the many interacting elements can have unexpected consequences. In short, the complex settings force us to a foursquare encounter with uncertainty—and the unknown.

Complexity: A portal of entry

Many organizational theorists have been drawn to Complexity Theory inspired by multiple streams of scholarship across the natural sciences (and including more recently the fields of Big Data and Artificial Intelligence).[2] A view on complexity here can be useful while recognizing that the translation from natural sciences to management produces some wrinkles that require further scrutiny. Nevertheless, a usable working definition might be:

DOI: 10.4324/9781003148579-3

> Complexity is a characterization or condition of the behavior of a system, model, or other context—as a whole or within its constituent parts—all behaviors (interactions) guided by localized rules with no higher instruction evident.[3]

A very critical implication of this is that complexity can be studied and described, although the outcomes—as far as can be known—are not predictable, which makes the ability to quantify and assess potential exposures a demanding—possibly futile—exercise.[4] *Systems theory* frames the study of complex behavioral patterns among interdependent agents in a social system with purpose, structure, and functions influenced by environmental changes where change in one part of the system can affect other parts or the entire system. These patterns may appear chaotic and counterintuitive. And they are often *nonlinear* as the observed effects of the component parts cannot simply be aggregated to form a cohesive whole—events may rather lead to unexpected, and possibly, extreme outcomes. *Chaos theory* studies dynamic systems that seem to reach disorderly states at random over time, identifying patterns between linked effects and feedback loops where a small change in one state of the system can cause large effects in a later state.[5] Climate change is illustrative of such a system dynamic.

These systems can create spontaneous order—often referred to as *self-organization*—formed by interactions between local parts, or agents, in the otherwise disorderly context. This is not controlled but is driven by sufficient energy among individual agents that respond to various stimuli. A *multi-agent system* is a form of self-organized system composed of autonomous interacting intelligent agents that can resolve emergent problems through negotiated solutions based on updated local information—possibly supported by a facilitating digital technology.[6]

As a further extension, a *complex adaptive system* may appear in the form of a dynamic network of interactive agents where the agglomerated, or collective, effect of their combined behaviors can be adaptive. That is, together the individual responses mold and reshape the system so it becomes more compatible with the environment.

So, research on complexity has advanced some important perspectives into the management sciences, including the idea of organizations as Complex Adaptive Systems (CAS).[7] As with complexity itself, there are numerous variants of the CAS concept, where the essential attraction for management scholars is the belief that CAS may suggest remedies to the limitations of the traditional linear and deterministic strategy model.[8]

For management scholars, CAS has focused attention on the ways in which social systems, and by implication organizations, innovate and adapt in response to internal and external tensions, pressures, forces, and disruptive events.[9] From a *leadership* perspective, the challenge has been, and remains, to find ways to think about leading in an organization where—owing to the nature of complexity—supporting, but not interfering with, independent network interactions is preferred to command-and-control leadership in achieving successful adaptations.[10]

This idea, obviously, sits uncomfortably alongside a traditional top-down management/leadership perspective and is not aligned with the systems/processes/controls approaches that permeate management—and risk management for that matter. In addition, there are accompanying assumptions of trust and common purpose as needed leadership skills that heretofore may not have been prominently in view. A recent paper attempts to reorganize earlier thinking around the idea of Complexity Leadership and identifying the most probable of necessary leadership abilities as:

(Facilitating)…(b)oundary spanning, organizing and implementing aligned actions, promoting cross-functional training, joint planning and decision-making, deploying resources across units to foster interconnectivity.[11]

In other words, leadership is here largely about lubricating and maintaining the system as a whole and enabling social networks within so the individuals can better interact with one another guided by a network *schema*—to be thought of as the mental/localized rules-of-the-road. Empowering and motivating the individual agents to interact and decide for a common purpose would seem a necessary feature as well.[12]

Emergent (evolutionary) management/leadership

Adaptation as a topic has been studied in the management field from its very inception as a necessary condition for organizational survival and sustained growth in a competitive environment.[13] Strategic adaptation has, in more recent times, become subsumed by the concept of *dynamic capabilities* that supposedly reflect the ability to reconfigure the organization to deal, and cope, with rapidly changing environments.[14] A condensed version of these ideas is that adaptive processes require basic abilities to *sense* environmental changes, *seize* resources around adaptive responses, and *restructure* the organization to enact the adaptive moves. The basic logic is not fundamentally different from a conventional risk management view, although it has a greater focus on opportunities and attempts to add sophistication by delving into extensive analyses of underpinning capabilities. Yet even this approach says little about which actors in the organization do what, and it hardly considers the implied leadership styles—if at all.

The conventional strategy view—as largely adopted in the ERM frameworks—sees the CEO (and executives at the upper echelons of the organization) as the instigator that sets the strategic path from prior analyses and then makes the organization act accordingly to achieve the stated objectives. It typically distinguishes between the *formulation* of the strategic plan followed by the *implementation* as organizational members carry out the planned actions. This is commensurate with the risk management logic to identify, assess, mitigate, and monitor major exposures and, therefore, fits well with command-and-control leadership.[15]

However, it is generally recognized that uncertain environments, which are more likely to feature unexpected events, make it difficult to foresee and consider all possible scenarios when setting objectives and planning the strategy. This inspired the astute observation that realized strategic actions may derive from *intended* (formulated and planned) activities as well as from *emergent* (unformulated and improvised) activities that respond to opportunities that arise along the way in rapidly changing environments.[16]

Various studies show how the emergent elements of strategy execution can be shaped from autonomous initiatives inside the organization that eventually become very important strategic options.[17] As emergent activities respond to changing environmental conditions, they provide an adaptive element to the formation of strategy. An implication of this is that initial objectives formed on the basis of expected future conditions may change and, therefore, cannot/should not be permanent or fixed target points. This reflects an *evolutionary* perspective on strategy-making, where a primary top-management role is to impose enabling structures and policies on the organization, while lower-level managers are the instigators of new adaptive business initiatives. An emphasis on decentralized initiatives can advance responsive actions to environmental changes retaining a certain balance between CEO-induced direction and an ability to foster autonomous adaptive initiatives.[18] The autonomous initiatives are a source of opportunities with the potential to adapt current activities guided by strategic *intent*, or purpose, and objectives set by top management.[19] So, corporate strategy-making is generally conceived in a more nuanced way than captured in the conventional model and it affects the way we—and/or managerial decision-makers in general—can think about risk management and its relationship to strategy and objective setting.

Leadership for organizational adaptability

Leadership for Organizational Adaptability (for brevity's sake only, LOA), envisions that three interlocking leadership components—Entrepreneurial Leadership, Enabling Leadership, and Operational Leadership—align with the necessary dynamic capabilities.

Entrepreneurial Leadership emphasizes the generation and development of new ideas—including adaptive and innovative responses to threats or opportunities observed in or outside the system/organization.[20] Enabling Leadership focuses on the conversion of ideas into functional adaptations and innovations. [21] Operational Leadership illuminates an effort to transpose the organization into an adaptive mode. In say, an environmental ecosystem, basic laws of nature provide system structure and coherence. Organizations, as social systems are different by being constructed systems susceptible to human interference with few naturally occurring constraints. So, Operational Leadership also serves a "regulatory" function—maintaining overall organization structure, integrity, and functionality in compliance with laws and social norms.[22]

These LOA perspectives uncover some obvious connections to Risk Leadership:[23]

- The notion of networks and interactions between independent agents presents an opportunity to test how ERM can deliver on the intention to distribute risk responsibilities throughout the organization.
- ERM facilitates the use of basic tools, such as risk registers, reflecting the idea of creating a comprehensive list of critical organizational risks and uncertainties to develop a useful view of the corporate risk profile. The basic methods of identification, analysis, and assessment are helpful, but also have limitations as they assume an ability to foresee major events, as well as free and unimpeded flows of information. A better understanding of interactive agent networks may help diagnose how ongoing agent interactions might serve to identify emergent risks and unexpected events.
- The tensions that catalyze innovation and adaptive responses seem to require further analysis, perhaps utilizing new analytical methodologies. How leaders might actively seek or promote tensions, or stressors, could shine a new light on emergent risk assessment and consciousness about uncertain conditions.
- The idea that engaging networks of independent individuals around the organization may be, in some way, a "better" approach to sensing emergent changes in order to make needed innovative and adaptive decisions. However, this may also conjure difficult emotional conversations with top management where only the bravest may engage. Exploring this further has resonance with a CRO's wider efforts to achieve support and commitment from executives.
- There is a particular tension between exploring new opportunities and exploiting existing business activities. Control-based management approaches seek to optimize

the economies of the existing activity and to eliminate "wasteful digressions." However, firm value is a combination of business-in-use and the potential of new opportunities, where the latter consequently need attention as well.[24] Achieving the right balance between exploiting the present and exploring for the future is a key strategic concern that also seems to fit squarely within the risk management debate. Thinking about how to mediate this echoes the risk management issue of prioritizing and aligning the past, present, and future as evolving states of being.

- Alongside these implied leadership capabilities in the face of complexity, there are more distinctly risk-related competencies, skills, abilities, and attributes. They would probably include an understanding of complexity and networks, an understanding of entrepreneurial contexts, awareness of innovation and adaptive processes, and a more nuanced view on how strategies actually come about and take form in real organizations.

Risk competence in context

Here it is appropriate to first reflect on three contextual issues regarding the application of *risk competence* to overall leadership, and then discuss risk competence itself.

First, COSO, ISO, and other frameworks provide guidance on ERM-building—often in significant detail. What ERM should do, what tools may be deployed, what risk communication might look like, and how risk governance should be structured including the role of internal controls and audits. What is less evident are the details on how all this gets properly introduced and managed/led.[25]

Second, considerable work has been undertaken to describe the things done in ERM and in particular the *maturing* of an ERM program—to use common parlance.[26] ERM maturity indices show evidence of specific accomplishments that characterize progress toward certain levels of maturation, but they are less clear on the mechanisms that can facilitate progress.[27]

The third issue is the emergence of Risk Leaders (mainly CROs) where the idea of risk leadership seems to suggest that a risk leader is representative of *assigned leadership*. That is, they are given official authority to lead on all organizational risk issues. They also hold formal responsibilities to assure that proper processes are in place, which in turn may challenge the ability to impose risk leadership on others in the organization. In reality, the standing that this title conveys—authority, sanction, responsibility, and legitimacy—is frequently only tenuously given and held. This often means that establishing standing is the first—and perhaps the only—task a risk leader can or must address (building *emergent leadership*) before moving on to specific risk objectives.[28]

Risk competence

In light of these factors, how do we then define the differentiating features of risk leaders? What constitutes the knowledge/skill base possessed by risk leaders and risk leadership?[29] The term *Risk Competence* is used here to capture what seems to be the core knowledge around which risk leadership could be built:

An aggregation of knowledge, experience, and capability that includes 1) an understanding of complexity, risk, and uncertainty, 2) insights about human behavior under conditions of uncertainty, 3) comprehension of risk management thinking and practice, and 4) sufficient comfort in these areas to think creatively about addressing complexity, risk, and uncertainty while acting ethically.

The reference to "comprehension of risk management practice" suggests a working knowledge of ERM and other guidelines, but not necessarily devotion to any of them. In other words, comprehension should be interpreted as an awareness of the strengths and weaknesses of each. Additionally, the definition presumes some data-analytic insight referring to systematic methodologies for assessing risk and uncertainty. The degree of data-analytical knowledge necessary would seem to depend on the context. For example, in banks where regulation requires a CRO, the "CRO should have the ability to interpret and articulate risk in a clear and understandable manner and effectively engage the board and management."[30] Furthermore, "The risk management function should have a sufficient number of employees who possess the requisite experience and qualifications, including…command of risk disciplines." This seems to indicate a risk leader that has general leadership skills but who may or may not necessarily possess high-level data analytical capabilities her or himself. Leadership competence appears to take precedence over risk competence, but presumably, the Risk Leader's ability to ask the right questions would imply a reasonable level of—can it be called—risk *conversance*. So, risk leadership must also entail an ability to apply critical thinking assessing the potential riskiness of the broader context in which the organization operates, but again, the degree of technical mastery necessary might be higher in some situations.

When might greater mastery than conversance be necessary? Summarization is difficult, but one way to think about this is to consider organizations where the management of risk is core to its organizational function or purpose. High Reliability Organizations (HRO) would be a good example; in other settings, scientific research centers, medical device laboratories, and various engineering specializations might be examples. It would seem that such organizations would be more likely to have a CRO with a background in an underlying technical risk function defined, or heavily influenced, by data analytics.[31] Here, we would be remiss if we did not mention the insurance industry where technical/traditional risk management functions remain highly data-analytic and offer recognized pathways toward various operational risk management roles and the CRO position.[32] Many insurance company CROs began their careers as actuaries.[33]

So, certain industries may require a high data-analytic competence, although it remains the case most other industries/sectors call for might be referred to as the aforementioned *risk-conversant* understanding of risk analytics.[34] Indirect evidence of this is found in the observation that outside the examples mentioned previously, there is not yet a definable or obvious pathway from traditional risk manager to Risk Leader.[35]

While not wishing to descend into minute detail, this issue of risk competence levels and career advancement does have very practical implications. This is because a significant proportion of people entering the many specialty fields of risk management are initially drawn by the appeal of *data analytic* components and it is only over time that their experience leads to opportunities to consider the wider-ranging contextual and non-quantitative dimensions affecting risk management practice. This is hardly a controversial observation since most entry-level risk positions focus on data analysis for various practical purposes. *Risk Analyst*, in fact, is probably the most common entry-level job title.[36]

Here is where things get interesting in the risk management field. Gaining experience in the risk management field does—in most cases—allow practitioners to arrive at a level of comfort, knowledge, and capability that enables them to think beyond the technical functions. Broadly speaking, however, very few technical risk managers to date have made the jump to CRO-level positions (except in the few industries mentioned earlier). What is the missing ingredient? Of course, it depends on the situation and the person, but one way to think about that "next step" is having the opportunity to develop what might be called *outside-in* thinking and *inside-out* thinking,

An *outside-in* analytical perspective means the person is deeply cognizant of the context in which the surrounding world has evolved and influenced the organization and shaped its history. In doing so, that person attempts to interpret the context through a wide lens recognizing oneself as an imperfect observer practicing critical thinking and considering cognitive, behavioral, and ethical angles to explain past and recent decisions and actions in the organization. Risk management guidance emphasizes the importance of understanding *context* but it is much less clear on how to think contextually. An *inside-out* perspective may be equally important to understand the influence of self-awareness and the human aspects in risk management and leadership, but it only infrequently figures into the ERM literature. Where do these perspectives get developed?

To be fair, in recent years, risk management professional organizations have taken some steps to fill in the professional development gap. And many of these efforts are innovative and helpful. However, a question that can only be asked, but which may not be answerable at present is this: Is it possible that technical/operational risk management and CRO positions simply require a fundamentally different type of person? This is not judgmental, nor does it suggest one is better than the other. In the same way that some people are extremely unlikely to succeed at sales, physically demanding jobs, or jobs requiring a high level of numeracy, it is possible that—taken as a whole—the two jobs may require a person with different skills, interests, capabilities, career aspirations, personality, and so on.[37] To date, we have seen no examination of this issue.

Fitting complexity into risk competence

Risk competence, then, refers to a conceptual set of knowledge, insights, experience, skills, and capabilities that constitute some differentiating features risk leaders possess. As noted, yet to be determined is whether risk competency means different things for risk leaders, with broader organizational responsibilities, than in more general applications of risk leadership, as it applies to all engaged organizational members. It seems probable that there is a difference, although it likely is a difference in complexity, intensity, degree, breadth, and depth. The broader the risk responsibility, the higher the degree of complexity the risk leader has to oversee and comprehend, and the higher the degree of complexity, the more the risk leader must be able to deal with uncertainty and the unknown. As noted previously, developing varying levels of risk competence throughout the organization would seem to be a primary role for risk leaders.

Risk, uncertainty, and the *unknowable* appear throughout this book and—indeed—describe what we might call the "stuff" of risk management and the justification for its presence in practice.

Begin with *Risk*. Risk is a descriptive term informed by a capacity to measure objective phenomena. Measurement need not be quantitative, but the application of the term does imply that the risk phenomena can be described in terms of an expected effect and a likelihood of occurrence from a triggering state. In most fields of risk analysis—there is the idea that such assessment will lead to some ability to predict future outcomes and thereby ascribe a "price" to a related economic exposure. This can be based on statistical actuarial calculations reflecting a distinctly financial/mathematical nature of risk management—but it need not, at least not directly.[38] For example, in reinsurance where disaster losses can vary considerably over time, the contracting between reinsurers has been characterized by a certain collegiality and fairness to retain long-term relationships.

Uncertainty requires a bit more attention for reasons already given. Uncertainty is simply the absence of certainty. It is distinct from risk—defined as measurable uncertainty— by the fact that the underlying events, or phenomena, are beyond quantification (or present limited quantifiable evidence) since when they happen, they are unique, and fail to provide reliable data for calculative analyses.[39] In addition, uncertainty may also be a function of how humans perceive, or misperceive, the surrounding world as well as pure ignorance. For the ignorant, everything may be uncertain, though there is such a thing as being too ignorant to realize one's own ignorance. The risk management literature has advanced the idea that humans, as observers, are a source of *subjective risk*, in contrast to *objective risk* as observed and independently verifiable phenomena.[40]

The *unknowable* reflects something that is objectively unknown or cannot be known because it represents a thing that never before has happened, or in some sense is unimaginable. There are, essentially, three forms of the unknowable—unknowable/unknowns, knowable/unknowns, and one supposes, unknowable/knowns—sometimes referred to as *predictable surprises*,[41] which is often the case, with hindsight at least. Recognizing our limitations in dealing with the unknown, or the *emergent*, is important in the pursuit of effective risk management. As future risk events are difficult to identify, and quantify in advance, control-based risk management is challenged, and we need other approaches to deal with uncertainty and the unknown.

Where does *complexity* fit into this outline of risk, uncertainty, and the unknown? As a reminder, a seemingly useful fit is that complexity describes and defines the structure and behaviors—dynamics, some might say—of the environment as a system of interacting elements that shape the conditions for decisions in the face of uncertainty.[42] The observable dynamic system (an organization) is affected, or disrupted, by environmental jolts and is also influenced by the human responses to them.

Many resources are available to develop critical thinking/analytical skills for dealing with uncertainty including games/simulations, game theory, and scenario planning, but all require some *ex ante* identification of "things that could happen." These tools and techniques can be useful to stretch the imagination, identify weaknesses, stress test the organization, and prepare for whatever might come. However, they cannot deal with unexpected and truly unknown events that—sooner or later—will occur in the form of chaotic markets, dramatic political events, or environmental disruptions. A focus on the LOA approach may suggest and inspire a way forward here.

The cases

In conditions of true complexity—as far as we know—outcomes cannot be predicted. In complex organizational settings, we may fare a bit better in terms of prediction, but in many respects, day-to-day management operates in *effectively complex* conditions, meaning our forecasts are frequently only slightly better than guessing. However, there are also conditions that seem unpredictable, but which—upon reflection—could have been anticipated. The challenge in such situations is not complexity, it is faulty thinking and perceiving. The term *faulty* encompasses numerous sins—large and small. Limited knowledge of a highly technical process may lead to incorrect predictions; lack of resources to fully examine a situation may lead to decisions based on incomplete information; laziness or complacency might be the problems in other settings. It turns out there are many examples of events that seemed unpredictable, but which—on closer examination—could have been predicted. It is in this context that three different cases offer consideration of this point—but in doing so highlight numerous other ideas appearing in this chapter.

The first case presents a problem that comes close on the heels of another significant problem, leading to a brief consideration of the old adage "trouble comes in bunches." However, other issues are in play as well, including a fixation on an objective, perhaps at the expense of understanding the means to achieve that objective. Faulty judgment appears as do heuristics (mental rules of thumb). The second case offers an even starker example of what might be called a strategic blind spot. It appears that this particular blind spot was unique to the firm in question, but not to competitors. The third case offers a novel story that, while true to life, serves as a kind of metaphor for risk leaders functioning at an everyday level and the bewildering array of risks and uncertainties that leader encounters. Everything is connected, and this is never more evident than when a group of individuals are isolated on a small sailing ship bobbing in an immense ocean.

Case 3.1: Trouble comes in bunches: Seeing and not seeing at Target Corporation

Case overview

Data security has become one of the top reported risk concerns for organizations around the world. Contemporaneously with the Target breach, other highlights, if that is the right word, included:

- Adobe in 2013
- eBay in 2014
- LinkedIn in 2012 and 2016
- US election breaches in 2016
- Equifax in 2017

and…of course…many more incidents could be named.

Electronic data have been vulnerable for decades, but three key risk management issues have been driving factors in more recent years: increasing complexity, broadening interconnectivity, and increasing global accessibility. All three have increased vulnerabilities and added new dimensions that heretofore have not been fully appreciated. Into this general picture, Target Corporation's major data breach in 2013 stands as one of the more vivid recent reminders of the risks associated with increasing reliance on digital technology. The data breach had a huge financial and reputational impact on the firm, and even though an argument might be made that it could not have been anticipated and prevented, a compelling argument could also be made that a different outcome was possible. In any event, an entire case study could be written about this incident by itself.

Equally, the contemporaneous failure of Target's entry into the Canadian market might also stand-alone as a separate case study. In this case, the evidence is very strong that this is not just a story of globalization gone wrong, though it certainly is that. Rather, this case seems to offer a more general consideration of strategy-making, including an opportunity to reflect on blind spots, mental models, and strategic leadership.

What seems of particular interest here is the fact that these two crises occurred at—essentially—the same time. They present themselves as distinct and separate issues; certainly, the details of each story are quite different. However, from a risk analytic perspective, the possibility cannot be ignored that they are connected in some way. Of course, at a very basic level, they are connected because they both occurred at roughly the same time to the same firm. However, more clinically the question may be asked whether they are the result of a specific, common *root cause*. Publicly available information does not exist in sufficiency to find compelling direct evidence of a root cause, but since all case studies here are written to prompt more general discussion of key arguments in the book, evidence that does exist permits discussion and debate.

The Target Corporation

Minneapolis-based Target Corporation has been a successful retailer for many decades. It has positioned itself near the top of the discount retailer segment, meaning it has been financially successful when compared with competitors, but also that it has conceived itself as providing affordable, but high(er) quality products. Target's product range includes apparel and accessories, health and beauty products, toys, furniture, sporting goods, groceries, pharmacy services and products, and more. This includes own-brand products and periodic creative design partnerships with international suppliers. Target operates in all 50 US states with nearly 1,800 retail stores, and at the time of this story reported annual revenues in excess of US$70 billion.

The earliest incarnation of Target began in the early 1900s as part of Dayton's department store business—which has had a long and distinguished history in Minnesota and the US Upper Midwest. Alongside leading organizations in Minnesota (3M, General Mills, Pillsbury, Cargill, and others), Dayton's for a long time was lauded for promoting fair business practices, exercising admirable corporate social responsibility, and active community citizenship. Target initially worked within Dayton's structure, but slowly developed its own identity and regional following. In 1967, an IPO launched Target as an identifiable and distinct national corporate entity—positioning itself as a high-quality mass-market discount retailer.

Since that time, Target has experienced relatively steady growth and increasing complexity in the services and products it offers. Technological developments that today seem rather ordinary were pioneered early—automated checkout lines, inventory management systems, and so on. A grocery section was included, and has been extended in recent years, to provide more products that accommodate changing consumer lifestyles. Pharmacy services were also added and expanded. The company made notable advances in mobile and online retailing; steps that included the introduction of the Target REDcard; a company-specific debit card that offered customers additional discounts when used.

By 2010, Target had begun to emerge from the effects of the 2008 financial crisis and was looking forward to pursuing promising future strategic opportunities. The challenge of remaining a discount store while pushing the boundaries of quality and unique offerings—all within a highly competitive discount store sector—was a specific matter of concern, as was the intention to move internationally. Target's supply chains had already been internationalized with special initiatives to reach international designers, quality products, and producers existed, but Target's direct retail identity had remained US focused.

The data breach

It would be highly misleading to convey a picture of smooth sailing for Target prior to the two crises discussed here. The discount retail market in the United States is extremely competitive, so on top of the 2008 financial crisis, the company faced fierce competition from Walmart (primarily, but also from other traditional discount retailers). Owing to its size and market share, Walmart had considerable ability to dictate prices, which put significant downward pressure on retail prices and margins. Alongside this specific competitive dynamic, Amazon emerged during this period to represent a completely different set of competitive challenges in terms of inventory management, online services, customer responsiveness, and—of course—pricing. In combination, Walmart and Amazon represented an existential challenge for discount retailers and, indeed, several have subsequently shut their doors (Kmart being one of the more notable disappearances).

In this environment, Target discovered it had fallen prey to a huge data breach, which occurred during the 2013 holiday season. As the story unfolded, it was discovered that criminal data hackers had stolen credit/debit card information from nearly 40 million customers; 2014 brought additional bad news when it was further found that additional personal information (emails, mailing addresses) had been stolen from up to 110 million people, most of whom were not in the original 40 million identified in 2013. The breach specifically impacted the Target REDcard, and customer worries led to a significant and rapid weakening of sales and loss of confidence in—particularly—the REDcard product as well as general IT security at Target. The Target response included a significant effort at upgrading and expanding IT security measures, providing free credit monitoring and identity theft services to customers, and additionally, the company agreed to a US$10 million settlement with victims of the breach.

Target's leadership displayed some disagreement over the short- and long-term effects. The prevailing view, however, was that the impact on the firm's financial performance and reputation would be felt over an extended period. It was nevertheless true that from 2014 forward, the breach echoed throughout the business world as a dramatic example of IT insecurities and vulnerabilities in the business world. In subsequent years, the company rebounded financially, but future events warrant a very brief mention here as the COVID-19 pandemic and the associated economic challenges in 2020 (and social unrest, particularly in Minneapolis) have not afforded Target much strategic breathing space.

Target Canada

Alongside, but beginning prior to the data breach, Target had committed to a major international initiative; an expansion into the Canadian market. In 2011, Target purchased 133 sites across Canada. These sites were all former locations of a failed Canadian retailer—Zellers. The stores were reopened under the Target brand in 2013. Public information is limited on the strategic reasoning process behind the swiftness of the move into Canada, but evidence hints at a number of issues that, by implication, were not adequately addressed—possibly because the marketplace north of the border looks so similar to the United States market.

- It seems that store locations were fundamentally problematic, and there was specula-tion that the locations were a contributing factor in Zellers' own failure.
- Within the acquired sites, the physical layout was incompatible with design and man-agement requirements Target sets for all its sites.
- The management of logistics proved to be dramatically problematic.
- Specific problems occurred in inventory management (notably, software problems).
- Target's rapid scaling-up of operations introduced new difficulties in terms of embed-ding flexibilities that would have allowed the company to respond to fluctuating demand throughout the year. This was, first and foremost, an inventory management problem, but vivid examples of customers encountering empty shelves had a major impact on reputation and customer loyalty (such as it was).
- Staffing issues emerged and existed throughout Target's time in Canada.
- Questions arose about the degree to which cultural and linguistic differences had been properly identified and appreciated.

Other evidence could be cited, but the general impression of a wide-ranging lack of detailed planning and preparation seems to capture the general sense of the Canada initia-tive. And, indeed, efforts to rectify these problems between 2013 and 2015 were almost entirely unsuccessful. Ultimately, Target made the decision to close its Canadian opera-tions in January 2015. The decision underlined the huge scope of the losses arising from the initiative: 17,000 employees put out of work with Target declaring a quarterly loss of $5.4 billion. It is worth noting here that Target's CEO since 2008, Gregg Steinhafel, had been asked to step down in May 2014, with the data breach (and its handling) cited as the primary motivation, although the failing Canadian initiative was also seen as part of the rationale. Thus, it was that the actual closure of Target Canada occurred under the direction of a new CEO, Brian Cornell.

Aftermath and looking ahead

The after-effects of the twin crises are still being felt in 2020, though the change in leader-ship is presently seen as positively responding to (and learning from) the past events, while not allowing those events to unduly influence strategic thinking and implementation. The current CEO, Brian Cornell, was publicly quoted as offering a vision and strategy to transform Target's competitive advantages; a vision and strategy that included significant investment in omni-channel capabilities, a search for greater product differentiation, and moves toward alternative and flexible store formats. Beyond online security concerns, Target's online presence was broadly considered to have been, and continues to be, in need of upgrading.

Especially in light of the Canada experience, a significant restructuring of supply chain and inventory management systems was undertaken; interestingly proving itself to be a particular competitive advantage in weathering the COVID-19 pandemic. Its inventory management system, even in the United States, was judged to be inefficient and expen-sive, indirectly leading to higher labor costs. Logistics management was a contributing factor as well and has been the focus of particular attention. Adjunct to inventory man-agement, forecasting consumer demand was identified as a significant issue—an insight that was, ironically, brought fully to light by an otherwise successful partnership with a clothing designer, where Target was unable to keep up with the huge demand for the partner's products.

In one sense, it could be said that the twin crises had the salutary effect of identifying a number of weaknesses already existing within Target, prompting—in turn—positive strategic investment responses. However, this itself raises the relevant issue of why it took full-blown crises to make these issues visible and motivate the necessary changes.

Reflections

In this chapter, perception of risk and uncertainty, the challenges of detecting emergent challenges, and the overarching difficulties in managing in the face of complexity are key subjects of interest. Central to all this is how managers think, see, and interpret their uncertain world. Among the insights that are worthy of revisiting or highlighting in these reflections are the particular challenges executives have in understanding and dealing with *uncertainty*, underscored by our belief that top-level managers mainly deal with uncertainties, where adequate data are rarely available. There are two sides of this challenge that might be considered within the Target story. First, how do executives in general need to approach and handle uncertainty? And second, what does the leader bring to the table (personality, experience, skills) to manage the encounter with uncertainty? Beyond this, a particular meditation on the "trouble comes in bunches" *leitmotif* presents an opportunity to reflect on connectivity, complexity, and the effort to think critically about the root causes. And then, the very difficult challenge of learning from the past and applying those lessons to strategic thinking emerges as a key risk leadership issue.

It is difficult to say that the data breach and Canada venture are now fully in Target's past. The echoes continue to reverberate, exacerbated by the COVID-19 pandemic and the associated economic difficulties in 2020. However, several directed observations are possible regarding the two crises occurring between 2011 and 2015.

- *Memory* (remembering) is perhaps the most underappreciated facet of risk management. Among the array of human contributions to our perception of risk and uncertainty is a cluster of mental properties that contribute to remembering, forgetting, and imagining. The Target story features this matter in several forms. In a present-day context, the question that captures a very practical observation is this: "Why does it take a disaster to motivate humans to do something about disaster preparations?"
    - Looking back on the effects of the two crises, it now seems evident that many weaknesses in Target predated the crisis events. These weaknesses are now being (or recently have been) addressed, but there seems to be a sense that the motivation to do so required the bracing impact of two crises. Updating or modernizing inventory management, technology improvements including IT security, supply chain modifications, and improved monitoring of customer trends, all were accelerated in the context of the crises. Why not before?
    - Furthermore, as the two crises drift further into the past, will we observe a slackening of attention or energy in the efforts to address endemic business issues. If history is any indicator (and we think it is), there is ample evidence that humans tend to forget and that eternal vigilance or the ability to easily recollect is simply beyond our capacity…that is, absent memory aids. What can be done about this? How do we support institutional memory, acknowledging that there also can be a role for "forgetting" and moving on?
- *Does trouble come in bunches?* Here the question is simply whether the data breach and the Canadian initiative were in some sense products of an underlying root cause.

However, the broader question of "trouble in bunches" deserves attention here. The concept of *complexity* features prominently in this chapter and drawing on the associated literature it could be said that the interconnectivity within complex systems presents an environment in which one variant action or input could create a domino effect that results in a cluster of connected outcomes. However, we should also acknowledge that complex systems produce unpredictable outcomes, and so variant outcomes might simply *seem* to be related.

- In the Target case, the quest for root causes seems particularly challenging as they are quite different situations—indeed, superficially they do not seem to be linked in any obvious way (except that they both occurred at Target). However, systems being what they are, there is most assuredly connective tissue. What might that be? It could be suggested that the corporation, by dismissing the CEO, implied that he was the essential root cause. But CEOs are dismissed for many reasons that are not related to direct causation—including symbolic sacrifice.

- *Leadership vision.* In later chapters, investigation tightens its focus on leadership styles, behaviors, beliefs, and even the idea of "bad" leaders. Here the question of leadership vision orients toward the specific strategic choice of entering Canada. There is a public consensus that the initiative failed, and there are visible pieces of evidence as to the elements of that failure. And, in fact, the elements of the failure were rather wide-ranging and comprehensive, from the obvious multi-faceted misalignment (and inappropriateness) of the physical properties acquired, to the inventory, supply chain, marketing, cultural, and financial problems. How does a leadership team so egregiously misjudge a major initiative like this?

Read more about it

Dahlhoff, D. (2015). Why Target's Canadian expansion failed. *Harvard Business Review*, January 20. https://hbr.org/2015/01/why-targets-canadian-expansion-failed

Hoffman, A. and Gold, N. (2015). *Target Corp's Tarnished Reputation: Failure in Canada and a Massive Data Breach*. Sage Business Cases. Rotterdam School of Management/Erasmus University.

Olavsrud, T. (2014). 11 steps attackers took to crack target. CIO Magazine, September 2. https://www.cio.com/article/2600345/11-steps-attackers-took-to-crack-target.html

Target Corporation Annual Reports. https://investors.target.com/annual-reports

Case 3.2: Nokia Corporation: The world's premier mobile phone producer—over and out!

Case overview

Nokia was considered one of the most successful first movers in the mobile phone industry and became the world's dominant producer within a decade. By 2007, almost half of all mobile phones sold were Nokia phones, whereas iPhones from Apple only made up 5% of the market. Nokia's profits peaked around US$4 billion in 2007 as new smartphones emerged and disrupted the existing market order. However, Nokia seemed unable to respond to these market changes imposed by new competitors like Apple and Google. Hence, the company's market dominance gradually deteriorated, and the decay was so complete that Nokia's entire mobile phone business was sold to Microsoft in 2014 for US$7.2 billion at a fraction of the company's market value of around US$250 billion at its peak in 2000.

A brief history

Nokia was founded in 1865 by the Finnish engineer Fredrik Idestam. The company started as a wood pulp and paper manufacturer but evolved to become a conglomerate, operating in a variety of businesses including forestry, rubber, cables, power generation, and electronics. Nokia has been engaged in the production of large-scale telecommunications infrastructures since the 1990s and contributed to the mobile telephony industry engaged in the development of GSM, 3G, LTE, and now 5G standards. For a period of time, the company was the world's largest vendor of mobile phones making Nokia a worldwide brand at the peak of the telecom bubble in 2000. The company headquarters is located in Espoo, Finland (the outskirts of Helsinki).

From a banking career with Citibank/Citicorp, Jorma Ollila became head of finance in Nokia in 1986, then chief of mobile phones in 1990, and appointed CEO in 1992. He pointed the company toward an exclusive focus on telecommunication and mobile phones. In many ways, Nokia was a pioneer in mobile telephony, introducing Europe's first fully digitalized telephone exchange in 1982 and the first provider of GSM calls in 1991.

After the sale of the mobile phone business to Microsoft in 2014, Nokia has focused on telecommunications technologies and the Internet of Things and was the third-largest network equipment manufacturer in the world by 2018. The company employs some 100,000 people in more than 100 countries with annual revenues of around US$28 billion. Nokia is listed on the Helsinki and New York Stock Exchanges.

Background

Nokia's engagement in mobile telephones is referred to as a classical example of an otherwise successful company that sticks with its winning formula too long, leading to difficulties adapting to changing market conditions. The following case offers insights to analyze Nokia's eventual failure to deal with emergent competitive risks as Apple and Google disrupted the industry and walked away as the winners.

According to the risk management policy outlined in the annual reports, Nokia used highly sophisticated risk management tools, which listed a variety of relevant risk factors included in the corporate exposure considered in the risk governance process.

Enterprise risk management

Nokia used many state-of-the-art risk management tools and practices, signaling strong managerial capabilities and, according to Nokia's annual reporting, the company was in good control of its major exposures. Nokia used derivative instruments to hedge its financial exposures calculating Value-at-Risk (VaR) to assess overall corporate exposures. The substantial overseas business activities engaged Nokia in the international financial markets to manage exposures to foreign exchange and interest rate volatilities. Nokia distinguished between market, credit, and liquidity risks measured and monitored in a central risk management function. The market risks comprise exposures to foreign exchange rates, interest rate rates, security prices, and commodity prices. Credit exposures relate to accounts receivables, customer loans, and other counterparty obligations. Liquidity relates to the ability to honor payments at all times managed in an efficient cash management system.

The board of directors received reporting on major risks and aggregated exposures in accordance with risk policies imposed by the Audit Committee. The risk management function looked at financial, operational, and strategic risks to identify key factors that could prevent Nokia from achieving its business objectives. The risk factors comprised threats as well as opportunities and the risk analysis was not preoccupied with the elimination of downside risk. It also specifically noted that everyone in the organization had a responsibility to identify risks that could influence firm performance.

Strategic risk management

Strategic risks typically relate to exogenous factors beyond the control of senior management including things like competitor moves, technological innovations, socio-political developments, regulatory changes, and so on. These types of risks are often difficult to foresee and quantify using conventional risk management techniques. They present what is referred to as "true uncertainty" as influences caused by unique events that often unfold in unpredictable ways and may constitute the most significant exposures that can make or break a firm.

Nokia identified an extensive list of potential risks in the annual report at the time when some of its most pronounced exposures related to changes in the industry including new complex technologies and intensified competition. There was also a focus on the need to grow, create a more competitive product portfolio, attain skilled employees, and implement an effective organizational structure. While the key strategic exposures appeared to have been identified, the company found it difficult to generate effective responses to those risks as they emerged, which judging from the outlined risk management practices should have been a pure formality.

Managing the exposures

The mobile phone industry changed dramatically in the decades up to 2007 where Nokia became the clear market leader. Some of the major competitive differentiators included product quality, stable functionalities, and supportive technologies. From the mid-2000s, changes emerged, particularly with respect to the use of software, which gave some advantages to companies like Apple and Google, and others.

Apple introduced the iPod in 2001 and Steve Jobs, then the CEO, feared that mobile phones would include music download capabilities, so by cannibalizing an existing successful Apple product, the iPhone was developed to be a winning entry into the mobile phone market. The iPhone was introduced in 2007, and initially did not have 3G functions, although that capability was promised for later versions. The phone used a proprietary operating system, iOS, for Apple computers. The phone introduced an app store with a cohesive but broad set of offerings with the phone tied together by iOS allowing cross-selling that generated incremental revenues for Apple. Google bought Android Inc. in 2005 to become their new OS in smartphones, introducing their product to the market in 2008.

Both Google and Apple created open software platforms allowing uploads of different application software from the app stores for use on smartphones. This created a paradigm shift in the industry, basing competition on software rather than hardware quality. The iPhone was appealing due to its design and effective handling across an integrated platform ecosystem.

While Nokia had an enormous reservoir of technological patents and high-quality mobile phones that were extremely robust, with good battery capacity, and cost-competitive, they were unable to comprehend or appreciate the shift toward an integrated software platform. This appears rather paradoxical since the competitive threat was identified as a strategic risk in the company's 2007 Annual Report.

Nokia created the Symbian OS as an open source to compete, which was widely used by around two-thirds of the global mobile market by 2007. However, Symbian had difficulties working with the complexity of the system, which only increased when integrating various internet connections. It was designed for mobile phones with modest use of touchscreen technologies, so Nokia phones gradually became uncompetitive in the developed markets. The company developed a new OS, MeeGo, at the beginning of 2007 on a Linux-based open platform, but it only supported the N9 model released in 2011 and was hailed as Nokia's best design of all times. Nokia launched its own app store, Ovi, in 2009 but it was abandoned in 2011 due to insufficient interest. Stephen Elop, the CEO of Nokia at the time claimed that MeeGo was disorganized and lacked support as a rationale for replacing it with Microsoft OS.

Analysis and discussion

A key reason for Nokia's failure was the inability to adapt to the changing industry with new competitors, technology developments, and market demands. Apple and Android took advantage of their capabilities and strengths to create valuable software offered on open platform ecosystems, accessed by smartphones. Nokia was still the largest telecommunication equipment producer at the time, so it may seem strange why they were unable to take advantage of their strong technology and market position.

Nokia had the opportunity to join the Android network but declined and stuck to the Symbian OS. If Nokia had joined Android, it might arguably have become a successful ecosystem, but the company seemed more inclined to exploit what they already were good at, rather than explore new opportunities. Nokia did see the emerging threat from Apple and Android but failed to see the significance of the evolving platform economics. While Nokia was one of the first mobile phone providers to introduce touchscreen, wi-fi connectivity, cameras, and so on, it proved to be very slow in adapting these technologies to the mobile ecosystem.

Internal organization

If someone, or something, was to be blamed for Nokia's failure to understand the changing competitive environment, should the candidates for blame be the top management team, the many employees, or the organizational culture? Around 2000, Nokia's organizational culture focused on internal competition and flexibility, which created agility as a source of competitive advantage. However, by 2007, the culture was better characterized as governed by hysteria. Nokia tried to introduce multiple products to counter their rivals rather than trying to deal with the underlying issues. Jorma Ollila had linked Nokia's prior success to an experienced and tight executive team that welcomed open employee thinking and initiatives taking chances with new developments. So, earlier success was attributed to management agility and employee engagement.

This culture of agility seemed to change as a new management team took over during 2006, shortly after the company formed the Nokia-Siemens network. The former CFO, Olli-Pekka Kallasvuo, replaced Olilla to become the new CEO. He had a background in business control and finance with a reputation for a somewhat conservative outlook. The senior management team did not represent deep technological experience, and either because of that, or for other reasons were more concerned about meeting investor expectations than developing new market offerings. Hence, one of the first executive changes imposed by Kallasvuo was to dissolve the company's Future Technologies team.

This move was also motivated by a need to restructure and accommodate the Nokia-Siemens network joint venture announced in June 2006, which was aimed at consolidating the network equipment businesses with expected annual savings of more than €1 billion by 2010. Notably, this move would result in cutting about 60,000 staff in the process. In short, Nokia became less agile and flexible while also enflaming other problems of cannibalistic rivalry between business units and introducing complex decision processes with ambiguous chains of command. As a consequence, Nokia was poorly prepared and positioned to respond to competitive challenges.

Jorma Ollila, who had become Chairman of the Board, announced in early September 2010 that Stephen Elop, the head of Microsoft's Business Division, would take over as the new CEO for Nokia, replacing Kallasvuo and becoming the first non-Finn to run the company. Elop had a strong background from prior senior positions with Juniper Networks and Adobe Systems before joining Microsoft and was considered a technology-savvy executive. It was later announced that he received a signing bonus of US$6 million to compensate for lost income from his prior employer.

Elop assessed Nokia as a firm sitting atop a "burning platform" and he asserted that it needed to undergo fundamental changes. These needed changes turned out to be a broad strategic partnership with Microsoft introducing a new Windows Phone, investing in "next-generation disruptive technologies," and setting a new leadership team in place.

Jorma Ollila resigned as Chairman in May 2012, a position he had—according to his own assessment—retained with some reluctance. In early September 2013, Nokia announced that Elop would step down as CEO as Microsoft acquired Nokia's handset mobile business. Elop reportedly received a bonus of €18.8 million triggered by his resignation. Elop would subsequently assume the role of EVP of Microsoft's devices and services business and Risto Siilasmaa would take over as interim CEO and continue to serve as Chairman of Nokia.

In short, the prior successful organization attributed to entrepreneurial risk-taking eventually came to resemble more of a machine bureaucracy with a structure and culture that seemed to waste talent (and money) rather than use it to create responsive agility.

Emotions and cognitive biases

It is argued that fear among managers can partially explain why Nokia lost the smartphone battle.[1] There appeared to be a hostile environment around the new top management team and this hostility transmitted fear across people throughout the entire organization. The top managers experienced fear themselves through the intensified competitive pressures and increasing investor demands. They sensed the need for a better OS, which would take years to develop. The middle managers in turn faced increasing demands from top management to react.

The inability to innovate in the situation may also be attributed to over-optimism among top management and a blind reliance on organizational capabilities. There was a strong belief in the strength of prior glory. They had time, resources, and technological capabilities to handle the situation, but seemed embedded in a comfortable complacency rather than creating a risk-conscious culture with everybody looking for emergent risks and attractive solutions.

Top managers' cognitive biases seemed destined to serve as obstacles to the development of a risk-aware culture as those biases reduced the firm's ability to understand threats and opportunities in the risk landscape. Top management engaged in formal ERM-based analyses of emergent risks and competitive threats and listed them all. Yet, they were unable to respond to them, with a middle management increasingly focused on implementing the directives from top management in fulfillment of the long-term performance goals and strategic objectives, but without addressing the emergent strategic risks. However, many middle managers stated their awareness of the iPhone project at Apple well in advance of its introduction, but these competitive issues were just not discussed openly with top management. So, Nokia's top management (and board) formally noted the pending threats and listed them in the official annual reports, but failed to act, possibly blinded by prior success, cognitive biases, and structural deficiencies in the organization.

The Nokia management probably exhibited severe confirmation bias with a mindset of "what has worked in the past will also work well in the future." This reduced their ability to identify and exploit opportunities that surfaced from within the firm. They noted key trends but failed to understand the extent to which the trends would affect them. There were also signs of internal disputes and emotional distress, which had a negative effect on the organizational culture.

In the end, Nokia suffered from a risk-averse consensus-based culture short on entrepreneurial spirits and collaborative efforts. The lack of risk awareness was partially a direct result of cognitive biases at top management. Essential market knowledge among lower-level managers remained unsolicited and emotional pressures refrained employees from involvement that would have identified the weak signals of emergent competitive threats calling for swift responses.

Reflections

The case provides a reasonably detailed description of events at Nokia and even sets out some ideas as to causal factors and responsibilities for the outcome. However, the "why" is only lightly touched upon and thus three points for discussion are raised.

- This chapter focuses on complexity and perceptions of complex situations. What is interesting about the Nokia case, in this light, is that—retrospectively—the competitive challenge of Apple and Google was not complex. Indeed, many within Nokia were aware of and understood this challenge. Perhaps the complexity of this case is not in the challenge but within Nokia itself. Considering Nokia to be a Complex Adaptive System, how should we look at the causes or reasons for a failure to adapt?
- Perception of uncertainty and risk is also featured in the chapter. Cognitive biases are mentioned as probable contributory factors, but here it might be beneficial to step back and think about leadership attributes in general. Can we think about the kind of leadership most likely to handle the competitive challenge? In suggesting this as a point of discussion, the question is not asking for reflection on the actions leaders

might take, but rather on the attributes of a leader who might have effectively been able to respond to the challenges described.

- A more methodical and forensic evaluation of this case would likely include the insights contained in the case itself. However, more broadly, such an evaluation would attempt to be structured to organize the various factors in relation to one another. How could this story be presented to specifically demonstrate how the factors are related to one another and which are most important? In doing this, the risk analysis question might be "What is the *one thing* that Nokia might have done that would likely have produced the *largest positive effect* in addressing the challenge from Apple and Google?"

Read more about it

Cuthbertson, R., Furseth, P. I. and Ezell, S. J. (2015). Apple and Nokia: The transformation from products to services. In *Innovating in a Service-Driven Economy*. Palgrave Macmillan, London, UK. https://doi.org/10.1057/9781137409034_9

Doz, Y. L. and Kosonen, M. (2008). *Fast Strategy: How Strategic Agility Will Help You Stay Ahead of the Game*. Pearson Education, New York, NY.

Fox, J. (2010). Nokia's secret code. http://archive.fortune.com/magazines/fortune/fortune_archive/2000/05/01/278948/index.htm (accessed on 10-12-2016).

GeekWire (2011). Nokia pays big bucks for Elop: Former Microsoft executive receives $6M signing bonus. *GeekWire*, March 11, 2011.

Guardian (2006). Nokia and Siemens announce joint venture. *Guardian*, June 19, 2006.

Hayes, J. (2014). The Theory and Practice of Change Management (4th ed.). Palgrave Macmillan, London, UK.

Nokia (2008). *Nokia Annual Report 2007*. http://company.nokia.com/sites/default/files/download/investors/request-nokia-in-2007 (accessed on 07-12-2016).

Nokia (2016). *Our Story*. http://company.nokia.com/en/about-us/our-company/our-story (accessed 07-12-2016).

Shaughnessy, H. (2013). Apple's rise and Nokia's fall highlight platform strategy essentials. http://www.forbes.com/sites/haydnshaughnessy/2013/03/08/apples-rise-and-nokias-fall-highlight-platform-strategy-essentials (accessed on 05-12-2016).

Slywotzky, A. J. and Drzik, J. (2005). Countering the biggest risk of all. *Harvard Business Review*, 82, 78–88.

TechCrunch (2011). Nokia confirms Microsoft partnership, new leadership, and organizational changes. *TechCrunch*, February 11, 2011.

Vuori, T. O. and Huy, Q. N. (2016). Distributed attention and shared emotions in the innovation process: How Nokia lost the smartphone battle. *Administrative Science Quarterly*, 61(1), 9–51.

YLE News (2013). Nokia boss Elop to make €18.8m from Microsoft deal, *YLE News*. September 19, 2013.

Case 3.3: Small boats in the great big sea: The Volvo Ocean Race

Case overview

The original idea for an around-the-world race was conceived by The British Royal Naval Sailing Association as a retracing of the global trade routes followed by square-rigger ships in the 19th century. Initially run in 1973, and reflecting its original commercial sponsorship support, the race was known as the Whitbread Round the World Race. It continued under that name until 2001 when Volvo took over principal sponsorship. The title, Volvo Ocean Race, remained until 2019 when it was changed to The Ocean Race, though Volvo remains involved. The race is conducted every two to three years. It has not been run since 2018 owing to the ordinary sequencing of the race cycle, but also due to the global COVID-19 pandemic.

The route of the race varies for reasons related to scheduling, promotional considerations, and sponsorships. Consequently, the ports of call will differ from race to race. However, there are typically eight to ten legs—and there may be several in-port races along the way. Each leg will keep the boats at sea for around 20 days, meaning that the crews are effectively on duty day and night during each leg. Breaks of varying lengths occur between the legs, but a two-week break is representative. The race is expected to begin and end in Europe and normally commences in September–October, ending nine months later. The overarching timing of the race reflects an attempt to avoid the most worrying of ocean conditions. Typically, the most concerning of the legs will occur in the oceans of the Southern Hemisphere where waves have been measured at 150 ft and winds have exceeded 70 knots.

The distances traveled will vary from race to race. The longest version of the race covered over 45,000 nautical miles. As already noted, the routes are variable. However, to provide an illustration, a recent version of the race commenced in Alicante, Spain and ended in Galway, Ireland. Along the way stops included Cape Town: South Africa, Abu Dhabi: United Arab Emirates, Sanya: China, Auckland: New Zealand, Itajai: Brazil, Newport: United States, Lorient: France, and the Hague: the Netherlands.

Notably, there is no cash prize. Certainly, however, public recognition of the victor is likely to lead to pecuniary rewards from future sponsorships as well as potentially lucrative relationships with shipbuilders and other specialists in ocean boating technology.

The boats and crews

Onboard crews range from seven to ten individuals both male and female, but competitive teams will include onshore specialists as well. Also, since 2008, a dedicated media crew representative has been a requirement. That individual (called the On Board Reporter) does not participate in the crew's work. Responsibilities include sending images/video to the race headquarters via satellite. It is fair to assume that the demands of the race require extensive technical preparation from crew members, and, indeed, maintaining physical and mental fitness, adhering to a regulated diet, and maintaining the capacity to meet and endure varying environmental rigors are essential to success—the term *success* could mean just completing the race.

For many years, the race included a range of boat types. Over time, however, there was an evolution toward requirements leading to a greater commonality of boat types. This was partially due to an emulation of types that performed best—not surprisingly—but issues of race equity and fairness were contributing factors as well. For example, the 2021–2022 race is scheduled to have two classes of boats. In both classes, the boats are expected to be broadly similar, though one of the classes will feature technologically advanced designs.

Preparations

For purposes of case structure and focus, a hypothetical boat—the Columbia—is identified here. It has a distinctly (but not unusually) international team and crew consisting of:

Onshore team:
- Project manager:(German)
- Boat designer representatives (Australian)
- Boat builder representatives (Japanese)
- Shore support/transportation/emergency response (United States)
- Meteorologist (Norway)
- Communications, public relations, sponsor relations (Spanish)

Boat crew:
- Captain: (French)
- Watchkeeper: (British)
- Foredeck and general crew members: (Swedish, six members)
- Navigator and tactician: (Philippines)

Figure 3.1 sets out the general framework for Columbia's preparation process. It should
be noted that the boat design process begins much earlier but is included in the first stage
for simplicity.

The timeline labels summarize a range of preparatory activities that will engage
some or all of the crew. The middle column represents social and strategic elements
that occur over the entirety of the preparations (as well as before and after). The individual behavior and the cohesiveness and collaborative sensibilities of the crew are
critical issues—sources of risk, in fact—and so it is very likely that crew selection would
include the involvement of psychological profiling, assessment of cultural considerations, and identification of issues pertaining to team dynamics. For purposes here, the
assumption is that each of the crew members has been determined to be suited for the

General Timeline – 2xx1 Race

Early Planning	Yacht & Team Building	Practice Runs	Team Planning, Strategy, Risk Mgmt	Final Race Preparation	Race	Race Completes
Race Sponsor Committed	Team Selected	Boar Delivered	Individual Perspectives	Race Yacht Inspected	Competitive Objectives	Final Strategy
First Team Members Recruited	Yacht Build Starts	Qualifying Race	Cultural Perspectives	Boat Stocked w/ Supplies	Sponsor Objectives	Team Outlook
Boat Design Started	Training Boat Purchased	Practice Race	Group Perspective	Team Training Completed	Individual Objectives	Sponsor Goals
June 2xx0	Nov-Dec 2xx0	Summer 2xx1	Ongoing	August 2xx1	Sept 2xx1	Sept 2xx1

Figure 3.1 General framework for Columbia's preparation process.

race, but in addition to each having specialized roles, they are individuals who will be exposed to extreme pressures and conditions so personalities and team cohesiveness remain as ongoing issues. Regarding specific risk management/leadership elements, the captain obviously maintains absolute leadership responsibilities, but the practice of risk management is very much the case that *every crew member is a risk manager within the scope of his/her responsibilities.*

From the standpoint of strategy, the obvious objective is to complete the voyage with boat and crew intact and healthy. Beyond that, specific goals related to time and finishing order will be raised and discussed by the team. Alongside this discussion will be a consideration of the strategic and tactical measures that will most likely achieve the goals. Here, discussion will take place about the view of risk that will prevail throughout the voyage. The crew's past experiences have shown that pressurized situations (a storm, damage to the boat) can affect decision-making and can lead to an elevation of risk-taking in pursuit of the goal of a respectable finish. What is the threshold of unacceptable risk? How do we decide to stop or to carry on? What are the Columbia's sponsors' goals and views on risk? Perhaps this last question is not paramount for crew members, but the sponsors' perspectives cannot be ignored.

The race

A nine-month race is impossible to summarize in short form. However, to capture a sense of the dynamics of such a trip, a very abbreviated and selective summary of the captain's log follows:

Leg 1: October
- Weather conditions difficult with heavy headwinds during much of this leg. Progress was also slowed by equipment failure and a torn spinnaker.
- Slow race the first few days for all competitors. Early crew frustrations and tension mount.
- Winds of 50 knots (over 100 kph) blowing in a storm off the proximate coastlines: "We went up this huge wave and just kept going up. There was nothing behind it except air—the back was as vertical as the face. It was like driving a car over a cliff. I've no doubt that the only thing still in the water was the tip of the rudder. I'm sure even the keel and bulb (depth 13 feet) were completely out of the water and in mid-air. The crash was unbelievable when we landed. It was like landing 30,000 pounds on concrete. I couldn't believe that nothing broke" was a notable comment by one crew member.
- "A big wave washed across the deck and nearly took our navigator with it. He smashed his head on a deck fitting and came to a rapid halt. This knocked him out for a few seconds then he came down below with blood pouring everywhere" commented a crew member, reflecting the personal risk dimension of the race.

Leg 2: November
- Air and sea temperature just above freezing for the greater part of this leg.
- We have 30–40 knots (wind about 100 kph from behind the boat), huge rolling seas and we're surfing up to 28 knots. All we have to do is to keep it together and not crash and burn.

- "It was pitch black (night) and blowing up to 35 knots—we needed to get weed off the keel. So we dropped the headsail (and started sailing the boat backward) while we all looked over the side to see if the weed was coming off. 'Look out, there's another boat!' Our closest competitor went screaming right past us like a runaway train in the middle of the night" was the watchkeeper's observation.
- Concordia team's crewman was diagnosed with serious illness. Australian rescue plane dropped medical supplies. Crewman remained on board. Recovery was relatively swift; three to four days.
- The navigator commented, "One crew member and I are recovering from back injuries we suffered two days ago when we were thrown from the wheel of the boat by a huge wave. I have cracked ribs and heavy bruising to my back (because of the pressure of safety harness keeping him in the boat), and the crew member has suspected bruised kidneys." This occurred near the end of the second leg.

Leg 3: December

- As Leg 3 commences, weather problems challenge progress. Tornadic conditions experienced. The wind screeched through the rig at more than 60 knots and the yacht began to lie over on its side. Suddenly the twister changed course ever so slightly and roared down the port side of the yacht like an out-of-control locomotive, the outer edge being less than 100 meters away.
- Halfway through this leg, the rudder split when a shark swam under the boat and became wrapped around the blade.
- One yacht team was the only one to come up with an analysis of developing weather patterns which led them to steer well north of the other yachts and find advantageous winds—in 24 hours they were 85 miles ahead of us. We are currently in the fourth position.

Leg 4: January

- When crews set out on this leg no one knew that the ice would be 800 miles north of the usual limit for the year.
- I am seriously worried now with the night approaching. We have the radar on full-time and are praying like hell we miss.
- At one stage, while watching the radar and seeing nothing, we sailed just 100 feet away from a growler that was ten feet out of the water.
- When you're driving a yacht in those conditions the average guy on the street has no idea of the stress involved when you have someone's life in your hands. It destroys you emotionally.
- We hit a small iceberg while doing 21 knots. I was steering and all I felt was a loud crash on the hull and then the rudder.
- Another team reported icebergs everywhere. It was pitch black, the middle of the night, and a snowstorm howled around them. The wind leaped from 32 to 48 knots—equivalent to 65 knots (130 kph) in normal conditions. This team had already been submerged several times, jumping from one wave straight into the back of the wave ahead, then going straight through it.
- We were scanning for squalls on the radar. We saw this big squall coming and knew there was no way out of it. Tone, the steersman yelled "guys, it's gone"—describing his loss of control over the boat in a relatively calm manner. We rolled to windward, and the cockpit filled with water. I was the only one clipped on at the time. With the hatch now one meter underwater all the guys down below were woken with a ton or so of icy water flooding the cabin. Bang! The

unmistakable sound of carbon blowing up. We rolled upright; the mast had twisted off about two meters above the boom from the force of hitting the water at 28 knots. We were lucky it broke otherwise the boat would have filled with water and sunk. ... We would have lasted only half an hour in survival suits.

- On day 19, the rudder broke off, likely because of being weakened after hitting ice. Commenting on the leg The navigator: "On a scale of 1 to 10 for danger, it was 10. I openly admit I was seriously worried and on occasions, however really scared." We limped into port, remaining in fourth place, largely because every other boat had problems of their own.

Leg 5: February

- During shore leave, a mob approached four of the crew. The first guy pulled a knife and held it at one of the crew's throats. Police intervened, but the experience proved hugely distracting during the run-up to Leg 5.
- To add to the distractions, Dengue fever struck members of several crews that had spent time on shore.
- We briefly took the lead after two days of nifty racing. Then we looked for greater gains instead of staying with the fleet and covering their moves. A soul-destroying tactical blunder sent us from first back to fifth.
- Obstacles have included unlit fishing boats at night, oil rigs, cargo ships, and pirates.
- A day 7 crisis looming. Do we have enough fuel? With water ballast pumping, battery charging, making drinking water we have underestimated our fuel supplies.
- Everybody else in the fleet seems to understand this, and it now been beaten into us…the first four boats stayed together, raced all the way around, and finished one, two, three, and four. They hardly deviated more than four to five miles from each other. We, on the other hand, were 100 miles out to one side hoping for a miracle and it didn't come.
- By virtue of some luck—and luck alone—we remained in fifth place at the end of this leg.

Leg 6: March

- The racing was so tight that margins were measured in boat lengths.
- We analyzed the wind and decided it was dying on the right side of the bay. Thunderstorms were starting to develop over the land to the left. We changed course after drifting along for only a short while we found our breeze. We soon found ourselves four miles ahead, back in first place for only the second time thus far.
- In a 200-meter-wide shipping channel into the destination harbor, the Columbia was caught between a large ship and a tug towing a large barge coming from opposite ends of the channel.
- As they closed in on us it became apparent that our only option was to position ourselves right in the center of the channel so we would be between the ship and the barge. There would be only boat lengths to spare on either side and we knew that if we didn't get the move right either the barge would plow right over the top of us or we'd crash into the side of the ship. It worked—we missed the stern of the ship by meters.
- We came to port effectively in the first place, but second through fourth places were within hailing distance.

Leg 7: April

- On a test run eight days before Leg 7 began, our boat hit a shark or sunfish. The tip of the rudder was knocked off, resulting in a dramatically slower boat.
- The boat was dismasted when rigging failed. Had to sail to port and hope to find a cargo ship to transport the boat in time for the start of the next leg.
- The dismasted boat was shipped in a cargo ship to Liverpool, where it was transshipped on to Southampton, then shipped by road to Portsmouth for a new mast. Then the crew that accompanied the boat sailed it across to Leg 7 starting location. This was all completed in the eight days before the Leg 7 start. "A miracle, someone is looking down on us," was the project manager's comment.
- Navigator's nightmare. Crew was challenged by massive tides and currents; shipping congestion, North Atlantic, North Sea oil rigs, sandbanks, shoals, and rocks and reefs off the coastline.
- Heavy winds and steep 20-foot waves experienced during the first half of the leg. Most crew seriously seasick. Having half the crew down is a disaster. And the other half are exhausted covering for them.
- The top five yachts were sometimes racing fully abreast. It is a remarkable sight, though we hardly have had time to take it all in.
- The five yachts cross the finish line within seven minutes of the leader, and the finish was the closest of the race thus far. We ended in third place at that point.

Leg 8: June (Owing to day-to-day weather issues, May eventually ended up being scratched)

- Scratching May was a blessing in disguise. It led to a reconfiguration of the balance of the race, but the crew was really worn down and the rest was helpful. Of course, it was helpful for our competition too!
- Leg 8 begins in very good conditions. Columbia remains in third place, though five boats remain easily in contention to win.
- Halfway through the leg. It was night and we were sailing just meters off the seawall on the coastline, so close in fact we couldn't see over the top of the wall and into the harbor. We'd spent 24 hours getting past the, at that time, leader boat and at that stage had expanded to a lead of ten boat lengths.
- As we came to the (final) harbor entrance, a ferry appeared from behind the wall two boat lengths in front of us and charged across our bow. It just filled the sky. We had no clue it was coming. All we could do was alter course toward the seawall and hope we'd get behind it. We missed the back of the thing by less than a boat length, but with all the turbulence it created, we just stopped. Suddenly almost everything we'd gained in the past day was lost.
- We held to our lead, but it was very close to the very end. The five contending boats cross the finish line all within the span of 15 minutes. It would have been an even closer finish, but the second and third place boats actually encountered a backwash from a nearby ferry which led to a few harrowing minutes where they both might be swamped.
- Our victory was the happiest of conclusions, but the entire race will take some time to process. A race report will follow in the next two months once debriefings have occurred.

Reflections

Each leg of the competition posed any number of risk management and leadership issues. This chapter's focus on leading in a complex, risky, and uncertain environment suggests at least three particular questions or discussion topics.

- The crew and the Columbia itself could be construed as part of a Complex Adaptive System. Whether we confine our attention to the shipboard crew or extend our vision to include the shore-based crew, there is a very vivid image of needing to empower and authorize each member to make adaptive decisions in response to situations they encountered. This decision-making would be presumed to be based on a generally developed view of what the team's collective risk tolerance would be, but in many senses that decisions would have to be situational, and it would assume that each crew member knew which other members needed to be involved and what other considerations needed to be included. How should we envision this idea working in practice? Leg 7 was particularly event-filled, so this may be a portion of the voyage on which to think about CAS agents, networks, and schema to develop some substance on how this dispersed approach to risk management would work.
- The captain's role is interesting to contemplate in a book on leadership. On the one hand, CAS-based thinking might suggest a light touch—a "facilitative" approach to leading. On the other hand, the captain's role is not dissimilar from military settings where big picture decisions can be required on the spur of the moment. Elsewhere in this book can be found the idea of command as a form of leadership. How would we demarcate the captain's responsibilities in light of an otherwise dispersed, loose-jointed approach to risk management?
- It is clear from the captain's log that no one could have predicted many of the issues that arose during the trip. Or could they? Time, location, level of intensity certainly cannot be accurately forecasted, but the potential *perils of the sea* are well understood by maritime insurers and, of course, by seasoned crew members (including the captain) who will have a deep understanding as well. Consider here, then, the process by which the team/crew might have set out developing an understanding of what might happen during the trip and how they would decide to rank or prioritize their preparations. Note that some time would need to be spent thinking about the unknown, interconnectivity, and the idea that trouble comes in bunches.

Read more about it

Guthrie, C. (2008). Life at the extreme: An investigation into the experiences of professional sailors competing in a fully crewed around the world ocean race. ProQuest Dissertations Publishing. https://search.proquest.com
The Ocean Race website. https://www.theoceanrace.com/
Videos from the Ocean Race. https://www.youtube.com/watch?v=h04_4Msuw2k
Volberda, H. W. (2009). ABN AMRO in the Volvo ocean race: A bank learning to sail as one team. RSM Case Development Centre. Retrieved from http://hdl.handle.net/1765/38683

Notes

1 World Economic Forum (2020). *The Global Risk Report 2020.* http://www3.weforum.org/docs/WEF_Global_Risk_Report_2020.pdf.

2 Dooley, K. J. (1997). Complex adaptive systems model of organization change. *Nonlinear Dynamics, Psychology, and Life Sciences,* 1, 69–97, offers one of many descriptions of the transition of CAS to organizational settings.

3 Johnson, S. (2001). *Emergence: The Connected Lives of Ants, Brains, Cities.* Scribner, New York. [Page 19 provides this particular definition that has general application across all complexity studies.]

4 Plsek, P., Lindberg, C. and Zimmerman, B. (2005). Some emerging principles for managing complex adaptive systems (unpublished). Cited in Grobman, G. M. (2005). Complexity theory: A new way to look at organizational change. *Public Administration Quarterly,* 29(3), 350–382. [The article is oriented toward public sector organizations but offers an accessible entry to understanding CAS.]

5 See, for example, Gleick, J. (1998). *Chaos: Making a New Science.* Vintage—/Random House, London, UK.

6 See, for example, Mařík, V., et al. (2002). Organization of social knowledge in multi-agent systems. *Integrated Computer-Aided Engineering,* 1(9), 195–206; Mařík, V. and McFarlane, D. (2005). Industrial adoption of agent-based technologies. *IEEE Intelligent Systems,* 20(1), 27–35; Vrba, P. and Mařík, V. (2010). Capabilities of dynamic reconfiguration of multiagent-based industrial control systems. *IEEE Transactions on Systems, Man, and Cybernetics—Part A: Systems and Humans,* 40(2), 213–223.

7 Weaver, W. (1948). Science and complexity. *American Scientist,* 36(4), 536–544. [This is an influential and early paper that introduced the idea of disorganized vs. organized systems, which is considered a discussion on which complexity's application to organizations emerges.]

8 Dooley, K. J. (1997). Complex adaptive systems model of organization change. *Nonlinear Dynamics, Psychology, and Life Sciences,* 1, 69–97; illustrate applications of CAS to organizations.

9 O'Reilly, C. A. and Tushman, M. L. (2008). Ambidexterity as a dynamic capability: Resolving the innovator's dilemma. *Research in Organizational Behavior,* 28, 185–206. [This article offers a good representation of many papers that suggest and reference the very large amount of research that has been focused on managing and leading for adaptability and innovation in organizations.]

10 Ibid.

11 Uhl-Bien, M. and Arena, M. (2018). Leadership for organizational adaptability: A theoretical synthesis and integrative framework. *The Leadership Quarterly,* 29, 89–104. [This is the foundational paper on the Leadership for Organizational Adaptability concept.]

12 Grobman, G. M. (2005). Complexity theory: A new way to look at organizational change. *Public Administration Quarterly,* 29(3), 350–382. [This article provides an accessible introduction.]

13 See, for example, Andersen, T. J. (2015). Strategic adaptation. In J. D. Wright (Ed.), *International Encyclopedia of the Social & Behavioral Sciences* (2nd ed.), Elsevier, London, UK, 12, 501–507.

14 Teece, D. J. (2007). Explicating dynamic capabilities: The nature and microfoundations of (sustainable) enterprise performance. *Strategic Management Journal,* 28(13), 1319–1350; Teece, D. J. (2009). *Dynamic Capabilities and Strategic Management: Organizing for Innovation and Growth.* Oxford University Press, New York.

15 As an example, consider the following state-of-the-art recipe for risk handling (the risk management cycle). https://assets.publishing.service.gov.uk/government/uploads/system/uploads/attachment_data/file/550688/Tool_1.pdf.

16 Mintzberg, H. and Waters, J. A. (1985). Of strategies, deliberate and emergent. *Strategic Management Journal,* 6(3), 257–272.

17 Burgelman, A. and Grove, A. S. (1996). Strategic dissonance. *California Management Review,* 38(2), 8–28. [This article is a classical illustrative case.]

18 Burgelman, A. and Grove, A. S. (2007). Let chaos reign, then rein in chaos-repeatedly: Managing strategic dynamics for corporate longevity. *Strategic Management Journal,* 28(10), 965–980.

19 Lovas, B. and Ghoshal, S. (2000). Strategy as guided evolution. *Strategic Management Journal,* 21, 875–896.

20 Uhl-Bien and Arena (2018) offer the central development of the Leadership for Organizational Adaptability. Two complementary papers are Augier, M. and Teece, D. J. (2009). Dynamic capabilities

and the role of managers in business strategy and economic performance. *Organization Science*, 20(2), 410–421 and Newey, L. R. and Zahra, S. A. (2009). The evolving firm: How dynamic and operating capabilities interact to enable entrepreneurship. *British Journal of Management*, 20, 81–100.

21 Uhl-Bien, M. and Arena, M. (2017). Complexity leadership: Enabling people and organizations for adaptability. *Organizational Dynamics*, 46(1), 9–20. [This article is particularly interesting in revealing the progression of thinking first proposed in the 2007 paper and leading to the 2018 Leadership for Organizational Adaptability paper.]

22 Uhl-Bien, M. and Arena, M. (2018). Leadership for organizational adaptability: A theoretical synthesis and integrative framework. *The Leadership Quarterly*, 29, 89–104.

23 Beasley, M. S., Branson, B. C. and Hancock, B. V. (2019). *State of Risk Oversight: An Overview of Enterprise Risk Management Practices*. 10th ed. NC State, Enterprise Risk Management Initiative. [North Carolina State University serves as a reference point for the bulleted statements.]

24 See, for example, the classical article on the topic: Myers, S. C. (1977). Determinants of corporate borrowing. *Journal of Financial Economics*, 5(2), 147–175.

25 COSO (2017). *Enterprise Risk Management Integrating with Strategy and Performance,* Committee of Sponsoring Organizations of the Treadway Commission. ISO 31000: 2018. Risk Management— Guidance, International Organization for Standardization. [COSO is the most widely referenced guidance in the United States. ISO 31000 is more commonly followed outside of the United States.]

26 Underlying this is an assumption that it takes time to make things right, but when the maturity stage arises, after time and effort, the prescribed benefits will accrue. If no visible results have arisen, it is because things are in progress, slowly, but will eventually come about if the effort continues.

27 Monda, B. and Giorgino, M. (2013). An ERM maturity model (unpublished paper). Presented at the Society of Actuaries 2013 Enterprise Risk Management Symposium (Chicago). [This paper offers a discussion of a particular version of a maturity model representative of the many versions that exist.]

28 Ellis, D. G. and Fisher, B. A. (1994). *Small Group Decision Making: Communication and Group Process*. 4th ed. McGraw-Hill, New York. [This book offers a good entrée into assigned vs. emergent leadership.]

29 De La Rosa, S. (2007). Moving forward with ERM: By working together, chief risk officers and internal auditors can guide their organization around enterprise risk management pitfalls. *Internal Auditor*, 64(3), 50+. [This article is useful for its indirect references to what CROs are expected to know—or don't know.]

30 BIS (2015). Guidelines—Corporate governance principles for banks. The Basel Committee on Banking Supervision, July 2015—See, Principle 6: Risk management function, pp. 25–26.

31 ibid.

32 ibid.

33 O'Brien, C. (2012). Risk management: Actuaries as CROs? *The Actuary*. Institute and Faculty of Actuaries. [This article emphasizes the specific career path from actuary to CRO.]

34 Entire books could be written on the data-analytic components of risk management (and many are readily available)——for example, Bedford, T. and Cooke, R. (2001). *Probabilistic Risk Analysis: Foundations and Methods*. Cambridge University Press, Cambridge, UK. [This book provides just a single illustrative example of the wide range of informative literature on risk analysis. The book has additional relevance in that it has a focus on the analysis of infrequently occurring events.]

35 University of St. Thomas (2013). *The Risk Leadership Challenge: Final Report*. UST Press. [This is a survey of nearly 100 Minnesota firms with top-level risk managers ("Risk Leaders") that sought information on issues pertaining to career paths and challenges in establishing ERM programs.]

36 McDonald, C. (2013). The path to risk management. *Risk Management*, September. RIMS.

37 Seivold, A., Leifer, S. and Ulman S. (2006). *Operational Risk Management: An Evolving Discipline*. Supervisory Insights. Based on BASL guidance. [This paper defines operational risk for financial institutions as "the risk of loss resulting from inadequate or failed internal processes, people, and systems or from external events. This definition includes legal risk but excludes strategic and reputational risk."]

38 Bedford, T. and Cooke, R. (2001). *Probabilistic Risk Analysis: Foundations and Methods*. Cambridge University Press, Cambridge, UK.

39 This largely corresponds to Frank Knight's distinction between risk and uncertainty. See, Knight, F. H. (1921). *Risk, Uncertainty and Profit*. Houghton Mifflin, Boston, MA.

40 Williams, C. A. and Heins, R. H. (1964). *Risk Management and Insurance.* McGraw-Hill, New York. [This is probably the most widely used textbook on risk management from its initial publication date until the early 21sth century.]

41 See, for example, Bazerman, M. H. and Watkins, M. D. (2008). *Predictable Surprises: The Disasters You Should Have Seen Coming, and How to Prevent Them.* Harvard Business Press, Boston, MA.

42 Padalkar, M. and Gopinath, S. (2016). Are complexity and uncertainty distinct concepts in project management? A taxonomical examination from literature. *International Journal of Project Management,* 34(4), 688–700. [This article presents a recent effort to square the concepts of complexity and uncertainty.]

4 Risk leadership as a moral endeavor

The ethical organizational culture

Let us start with a simple question. How would we describe an "admirable" ethical organizational culture? Presumably, it would be one that embodies specific traits or qualities with a commitment to act and behave in accordance with certain concrete values. Some fundamental traits would likely include things like reflectiveness, humility, anticipation, and community involvement. Those traits, or values, would signify its formally stated values and would be reflected in the way activities are being executed by individuals scattered throughout the organization. Thus, one might say that an ethical organizational culture could be described both by its *substance* and as a *process*.[1]

The concept of an ethical organizational culture has emerged over time as the product of a moral inquiry that defines an institution as its essential unit of measure. One feature of this approach is that a corporate conscience—the collective sense of right and wrong among the people that make up an organization—can be viewed as not dissimilar to the conscience of individuals. It should be noted that the idea of a corporate (or collective) conscience is not a new construction. Indeed, in Book II of *The Republic*, Plato notes that there are respects in which an organization is similar to an individual human, thereby suggesting that an organization possesses a faculty analogous to the moral conscience of an individual; that is, a *corporate conscience*.[2]

This faculty shapes how an organization—through its decisions, enacted by many organizational members—pursues certain objectives and goals (profitability, market share, competitiveness, efficiency, innovation, etc.) by accounting for its moral obligations to various groups and individuals. Furthermore, it falls to an organization's leaders to create and cultivate the corporate conscience. This can come about as a subconscious, or unconscious, effort or it can be a very consciously intended leadership effort. The leaders are described as pursuing this by *orienting* the firm toward particular moral values; *institutionalizing* those values in its operations; and *sustaining* the values over time, making them an enduring part of the organization's identity.[3]

A model for an ethical organizational culture has been proposed as possessing five characteristics:

- *Values Driven*: Values and mission as integral components of an organization's strategic focus—its strategy and objective setting.
- *Stakeholder Balance*: The organization recognizes the presence and importance of multiple stakeholders and seeks to hold those interests in balance.

DOI: 10.4324/9781003148579-4

- *Leadership Effectiveness*: Leadership, most notably senior management, must embody the organization's values in their own behavior and must articulate those values in a way that is compelling for employees and all other stakeholders.
- *Process Integrity*: The organizational values are institutionalized throughout all functions in key operational units, e.g., recruiting, hiring, firing, evaluating, compensating, promoting, and communicating.
- *Long-term Perspective*: The organization seeks to gain a proper balance between short-term gains and a long-term sustainable orientation.[4]

This model presents a particular point of view, and we do realize that both competing and complementary views exist. Indeed, it might be important to note that some would argue that the above framework is predicated on a Western cultural orientation. We also recognize that operating in a multinational context may require a more nuanced perspective as organizational members confront different institutional and national contexts when they operate in different parts of the world.[5] However, a counter-argument is that the definition of the characteristics may change across different cultural settings; an acknowledgement that national cultures are in flux as well and may affect different individuals in different ways. Nevertheless, as this model rests upon substantial inquiry and discussion within the ethics field, we believe it offers a useful structure for thinking about the relationship of values/ethics and risk leadership, even in complex organizations.

Responsible leadership and culture

Ethical decisions in organizations rely on the traits of the individual decision-makers—their moral development and personal qualities—as they are applied to deal with the specific circumstances of emergent work situations and changing environmental conditions. Responsible organizational behavior can be seen as a function of the moral principles, or core values, demonstrated by the senior decision-makers—as representative of the general leadership—and most visibly exemplified by the CEO.[6] The core values that permeate an organization are enforced by concrete executive decisions that show the way as commitments to act in particular ways. These actions—in turn—can create a corporate reputation as trustworthy and reliable in building good stakeholder relationships.

The implicit standards for responsible behavior might be described as *utilitarian*; meaning actions could be conceived as "good" or "bad" according to the degree of wellbeing, or hardship, they inflict on or impart to those affected by the decision outcomes. Or the standards might also be based on the extent to which actions generate benefits for the *common good* and generate outcomes that are perceived to be the best for people as a whole showing compassion for more vulnerable beings.

The associated human virtues of *good character* ascribed to the involved leaders, or decision-makers, are linked to their individual personalities as they become important behavioral role models. This leadership will be eventually defined by the moral impact it has as it gains trust, respect, and admiration among organizational followers and provides inspiration to engage in just proactive behaviors.[7] Hence, the predominant leadership values derive from the morality of senior management, and the CEO, who as a role model will imprint those values among organizational members as the ethically correct behavior.[8] As such, the core values reflected in the executive behaviors become the foundation of a corporate culture that will guide all actors and actions throughout the organization. [9]

The imprinted culturally embedded core values can help (and will influence) decision-makers as they deal with unexpected situations that may arise from highly uncertain environmental conditions. In those situations, the core values can become a compass that gives direction, where analytics will fail to comprehend the complexity of an uncertain emergent risk situation. Hence, the core values embedded in a corporate culture can be conceived as informal priorities that specify duties and proper procedures where formal contractual arrangements fall short because the *unexpected* cannot be specified and accounted for in advance. The implied generally accepted social norms are a form of "unwritten contracts" that can guide optimal actions when events and contingencies arise that could not be foreseen.[10]

Edgar Schein argues that a corporate culture forms from the beliefs, values, and assumptions of a company founder and, as the organization evolves, by the joint experiences of organizational members, and eventually the beliefs, values, and assumptions brought in by new leaders that join along the way.[11] In other words, *organizational culture* is a dynamic phenomenon that can change over time, although it often retains the key characteristics manifested in informal rituals, priorities, and beliefs. These artifacts may be unseen by the naked eye but can nonetheless be identified by an astute observer. So, traditional core values can become challenged as new leaders enter an organization, which can be an opportunity for needed adjustments, but also a potential source of eroding values.

All the while, various *subcultures* can take form as a consequence of organizational expansion where subunits may become more segregated entities due to operational and geographical diversification. Hence, it will become more difficult for the leadership to oversee a larger more complex and extensive international presence where the organization is increasingly seen as a coalition of specialized business units. Local management practices and national customs across distant geographical locations can form pockets of diverse values and behaviors. It may become difficult for the leadership to impose a common organizational culture across diverse business activities—often incorporated through acquisitions—and national institutional norms in the local environments.[12]

Corporate responsibility

What does corporate social responsibility (CSR), or corporate responsible behavior, actually mean? Formally, CSR can be conceived as a self-regulating corporate behavior where the organization is accountable to a broader constituency of stakeholders including society in general. However, the way CSR is practiced is not uniform, and it can take distinctly different forms across business sectors and international contexts.[13] Some argue that responsible corporate behavior must ensure that business expansion and economic growth are achieved without causing damage to the natural environment and social conditions in the countries where they operate.[14] But, this claim hinges on an interpretation of the word "damage," which can mean somewhat different things to different constituents. That aside, responsible corporate behavior can be likened to genuine attempts to avoid exerting adversity on the natural and social environments that are represented by major stakeholders to the organization.[15] This can be further modified to—at least—not knowingly causing harm to the stakeholders, and if such should occur, then rectifying discrepancies when they are discovered.[16] In other words, acting in good faith and with good and honest intentions.

This is the hallmark for *values-based leadership*, which is supposed to balance all stakeholder interests and thereby avoid the prospect that negative economic externalities can, or will, arise. Hence, one of the primary leadership tasks is to consider important stake-holder concerns when making major resource-committing decisions.[17] The stakeholder perspective argues that leadership is about how to make customers, suppliers, employees, financiers (shareholders, creditors, banks), and communities collaborate with the organization to create value.[18] In principle, a *stakeholder* means anyone who can affect, or who can be affected by, the organization. A key justification for a stakeholder approach is that it may generate economic benefits from improved corporate relationships including knowledge-sharing, innovation, and increased goodwill. Maintaining good stakeholder relations may further facilitate collaborative solutions in situations where unexpected risk events might occur.[19]

Leadership in ethical organizational cultures

The term *Ethical Leadership* does appear in some professional and academic writing, but there is not a consistent usage of the term. As is the case with Risk Leadership, the possible reason for its limited appearances is that it is not a specific category of leadership but rather an aspect of leadership. So, perhaps the more useful term to apply here is *Leadership Ethics*.[20] Given this affinity, ethicists and risk leaders might benefit from a meaningful exchange of ideas and experiences. Fortunately, some language has begun to develop around the idea of *ethical risks*, and this may provide a foundation for clarifying the connections between ethics and risk management—and might even serve to propel that exchange of ideas.

A rather subtle but very important issue deserves attention in this discussion—the relationship between *espoused values* and *values in action*.[21] Even with high standards and aspirations to live a moral life, we all can fall short—as can organizations. This presents something of a paradox for leaders as setting lofty standards of behavior may itself increase the chances of failing to live up to those goals. Ethicists would observe that morality involves a profound personal commitment and therefore an intentional setting of lower expectations to reduce risk would be to miss the point of ethics entirely. And yet, from a risk management perspective, it is worth recognizing that committing to ethical standards of behavior is a serious business because a failure to adhere to the standards an organization has *chosen of its own volition* comes at a very high cost—loss of reputation and trust being perhaps the most obvious and consequential results.

Moral and virtuous behaviors have been subjects of intense consideration for well over 2,000 years, and it would be foolish here to aspire to anything more than a brief overview. Four basic questions will be relevant to pose here:

• What can be said about morality in the specific context of risk leadership?
• Is it possible to give some structure to the idea of *ethical risks*?
• Is there a way to fit a thorough-going effort to assess and address ethical risks within more conventional risk management efforts?
• Can we, at least speculatively, describe the placement of ethics within risk leadership?

Let us start with a short commentary on ethics and risk leadership.

Perhaps the first thing is to state the obvious; leadership can be moral or immoral, and therefore leadership itself is a critical source of risk or uncertainty. Indeed bad, or even evil, leadership may—as a general proposition—be one of the biggest strategic concerns facing an organization. Furthermore, it should be stipulated that a discussion about morality, risk, and leadership must remind us that many attributes we ascribe to good leadership (charisma, ambition, and persuasive communication skills) are two-sided coins.[22]

Leadership ethics may be measured by the values a leader possesses (known as a deontological perspective) or by the ethical value of the outcomes of the leader's actions (the teleological perspective).[23] By what measure should such leaders be judged?

This question deserves some further consideration. The definition of a virtuous leader has changed dramatically over the centuries.[24] In the current era, there are many different frameworks for virtuous leadership but a summation, if possible, would be: a person who 1) *respects and serves other human beings*; 2) *seeks justice*; 3) *is open, honest, and transparent*; and 4) *has a wider sense of responsibility for/service to community, society, and planet*.[25] In different contexts, these characteristics may be more or less important or relevant in relation to one another.

It would seem that there are two potential ethical challenges facing the virtuous risk leader. First, how are virtues translated into objectives and goals, or strategic intentions; and second, how are virtuous intentions translated into virtuous short-term effects and sustainable long-term outcomes? Virtuous leaders, it may be assumed, will set virtuous objectives and establish virtuous goals. However, is a virtuous leader, with admirable goals actually virtuous, if the consequences of pursuing those goals result in great harm? Alternatively, is an amoral leader with self-serving goals actually virtuous, if the consequences of some action unintentionally produce a positive outcome for others? Such controversies are not resolvable here, but it is worth observing that the goals and expected outcomes—as well as unintended and adverse unexpected side-effects—are inextricably linked. As a simple example, if the goal of a particular action is to maximize shareholder wealth and that goal is not achieved—but the organization's reputation is enhanced among stakeholders due to, say, the nobility or sincerity of its efforts, should this then be considered a moral failure?[26]

The concept of *teleopathy* ("goal sickness") is relevant to introduce here.[27] Teleopathy proposes that most ethical breaches are found in the interplay between Goals, Means, and Values. With a well-functioning alignment between goals, means, and values, ethical consistency would be the evidence—goals are achieved by means that are consistent with the corporate values. When breaches or misalignments occur, we find evidence of "ends that justify the means," or "objectives and goals that are inconsistent with the values." Note here that organizational goals and means not only need to be internally consistent with one another, but they also have to be consistent with the prevailing societal values. Misalignments or breaches between goals, means, and values, according to teleopathy, constitute potential *sources of ethical risks*.

In other words, it seems to be good, or prudent, risk management practice to try to assess whether discrepancies in this triangular relationship introduce potential organizational risk events. All the while, it is important to recognize the role of probability, fortune, and luck.[28] It is possible that a bad or immoral leader could be the beneficiary of a lucky turn of events, while a virtuous leader could be simply unlucky. The notion of luck tends to be somewhat undervalued in the leadership literature, but in a complex world, luck is an active agent. It might reveal itself in various guises; nonlinearity leading to unanticipated outcomes, good fortune being ascribed to personal characteristics, and then there is the unknown—which can certainly produce outcomes that appear to be purely random. Here the word *luck* is employed as shorthand for a recognition that there is much we do not understand or are unable to predict.

One characteristic of leadership ethics arises from changes in societal values and the fact that research has followed those changes. Broadly speaking, this might be referred to as "the leader among the followers" phenomenon.[29] In other words, the leader does not sit on an elevated throne but leads through more direct engagement with followers. Various current theories adopt this orientation: followership research, transformative and adaptive leadership, authentic and servant leadership—all see a more engaged and lateral leader-follower relationship. These theories could be said to capture a spirit of the modern age, which places a higher value on justice, fairness, equality, and respect. Even in the less studied area of collaborative leadership, an effective leader's worldview would extend beyond narrow self-interest into what might be called *communitarian* sensibility.[30]

Ethical risks and risk leadership ethics

Within the risk management literature, the relationship between ethics and risk management is not a well-developed subject of study. It is hard to pinpoint why this is so, though it might—might—have something to do with C. P. Snow's well-known "two cultures" thesis, which is to say that the history of risk management has meant that scholarship has been focused on a particular way—and as a result, what might be called *humanities-based* perspectives are less prominently featured.[31]

Ethical risks

Conventional risk management has developed a variety of ways to categorize risks as a practical value for risk managers who are charged with wide-ranging responsibilities. In the following discussion, a relatively new category of *ethical risks* is offered.[32] The term *ethical risks* might be interpreted in at least three different ways. The term could refer to threats to an organization's values. Or, it could mean consequences (good or bad) arising from the organization's values—for example, values in action not being consistent with espoused values. Or, it might even be a reference to the personal ethics of risk managers/ leaders. Consider each of these meanings one at a time.

If ethical risks refer to threats to values, the challenge is to consider the things that might present that threat, and here the concept of teleopathy provides a perspective. What are the threats to the Goals-Means-Values construction, and how would those threats actually disturb the balance between them? If this is the meaning of ethical risks, maintaining alignment would be a critical risk management objective.[33]

If ethical risks refer to the consequences of values held, alignment is still a likely objective. In this case, however, it would be alignment between *values espoused* and *values in action*, and it probably also means that an organization's values should align with generally accepted societal norms and values.[34] Consideration of stakeholder values would be expected to have a particularly important place in aligning organizational and societal values.

The idea that ethical risks might refer to the personal ethics or virtues of the risk manager/leader—well, of everyone really—suggests a deeply personal challenge to our own character. This may be the hardest interpretation to formally address, as it relates to issues that call for something beyond institutional responses. Yes, training programs can be offered to employees and other developmental or remediating opportunities may be made available. But, there are important cultural (organizational and social) influences, and personal traits, attributes, and predispositions—some nearly immutable—that influence the presence of personal ethical risks.[35] This is muddied ground suggesting matters related to character-formation, personal experiences, innate attributes, and even a crossover into the realm of psychiatry, behavioral psychology, and personal counseling, all of which introduce their own distinct moral and legal considerations for individuals and organizations.

Risk leadership and ethics

It is true that *all* decisions and actions carry implicit or explicit moral considerations and the chapter has argued that risk management decisions and actions are particularly freighted with moral considerations. In part, this is because a significant part of the work of risk management is dealing with critical, high-impact challenges and their consequences. Risk management could be defined as expressly toiling in an ethical hothouse.

Of course, though dealing with fraught moral issues is a constant condition, it is also true that risk managers and leaders often do, or do not, have the luxury of time to carefully assess future challenges and develop deliberate plans, which means many challenges do not afford risk leaders with time for reflection or critical consideration. We could say here that this adds weight to the notion that values must be so fully embraced as to be instinctive at moments like this. Relatedly, there are two particular issues here. First, while planning—we might even say that planning would include rehearsing the application of moral considerations to future challenges—is commendable, frequently those plans and rehearsals prove useless or irrelevant to actual events. Put differently, focused and detailed plans tend to fall apart when the metaphorical first shot is fired. So, planning is important, but it turns out that it is a particular type of planning that seems to be necessary. Sometimes that type of planning appears in the guise of *scenario planning*, sometimes as *real options reasoning*, sometimes as *game theory* (and other similar methods). All different, but all with a common feature—consideration and planning for multiple possible outcome alternatives. Certainly, these methods could be applied to moral planning as well.

The second issue is that *risk competent* and morally engaged thinking is less often seen than one might care to admit—whether there has been planning or not. Almost invariably in such cases unanticipated challenges arise and must be handled in a confusing, highly-charged, emotional environment—not the best circumstances in which even an "instinctive" grasp of goals and values can guide decisions.[36]

The preceding discussion sets the stage for the case studies in this chapter. Risk managers/leaders are particularly tasked to address high stress/high impact future possibilities. Such events evoke strong emotions, whether considered at a remove or close up. And, critically, these possible futures almost invariably carry serious moral implications and consequences. Therefore, risk leadership has to be a Values Driven undertaking—or to reference this chapter's title, a Moral Endeavor.

Two final thoughts. First, following on from the Ethical Organizational Culture model, the five characteristics (if an organization subscribes to them) are both exposures to risk and sources of risk—but as importantly, they also are critical assets that serve as the basis for an organization's integrity and reputation. Therefore, they represent the field of play for perhaps the most important concerns in risk management.

Second, in Chapter Three, the Leadership for Organizational Adaptability construct views leaders serving more of a facilitating role, though with responsibilities for the system's—and individual network's—functioning.[37] The leader's role relative to the roles of agents reflects an emerging theme in this book, which is recognition of what might be called the dynamic tension between centralization and decentralization. Though not yet expressed in those terms, the Leadership for Organizational Adaptability idea rests upon that dynamic tension, as does Enterprise Risk Management thinking. Further, general leadership research promotes a more direct leader-follower approach, emphasizing dispersal of responsibility and authority, heightened support for human interactions as responses to the needs for organizational adaptation and innovation.

In this more—let us call it—organic environment questions arise. What are the rules? How do agents in networks make decisions and act? How do all the agents working within a system know what to do? Their guidance, it would seem, must come from the organization's values. At the center of this, and within all interactions, it would seem that values shape the schema (local rules). Having noted this, the previous sentence begs another important question. How do organizational values come to be known and understood—how do they come to shape the schema? Plaques on walls, ethics testing and training, and exhortations from top management have a place, but the essence of what we are seeking to answer may be illustrated in the following image and question:

> Imagine an individual manager/employee, alone and considering a threat, an opportunity, or simply a decision that needs to be taken. What is necessary for everyone within that organization (along with relevant stakeholders) to have utter and complete confidence that the shared values of that organization reside centrally within the mind of that manager/employee?

This is not an easy question to answer but touches upon an issue worthy of further consideration.

The cases

This chapter explores the relationship of ethics and risk leadership, arguing as it does for a recognition that risk management and leadership fundamentally are moral exercises. The concept of *teleopathy* hovers in the background of each case study that follows. While all addressing the issue of ethical behavior, these three case studies offer distinctly different views of the role of ethical standards and behaviors as matters of concern for risk managers and leaders. Risk Leadership does not just possess a relationship with virtuous behavior, it is a moral endeavor.

Case 4.1: A. P. Moeller–Maersk: Values-based risk management

Case overview

The company founder, A. P. Møller, set the initial standards for ethical conduct in the company enforced by imposing encouragement, securing career advancements, and displaying the moral principles as carried out in various decisions and actions. These core values in the corporation were passed on by the son, Mærsk Mc-Kinney Møller, and they were made visible in written instructions and concrete decisions, such as, investing in double-hull tankers and quickly correcting mistakes, should they arise. However, the company grew in size to operate across more than 90 countries, including more than 100,000 employees. In expanding the reach of the organization across diverse national cultures and acquired companies, it became increasingly challenging to enforce the original core values, as that expanded reach made local managers less attached to the core values assumed by top management. So, while the organizational culture remained strong at headquarters, it could no longer be taken for granted among the many employees around the world.

As this issue became more visible, a new top management team attempted to introduce corporate guidelines and policies in order to express more declaratively the traditional "Mærsk Values" and thereby increase awareness among all organizational members.

The Mærsk values:

- Constant care—Take care of today, actively prepare for tomorrow.
- Humbleness—Listen, learn, share, and give space to others.
- Uprightness—Our word is our bond.
- Our employees—The right environment for the right people.
- Our name—The sum of our Values: Passionately striving higher.

Notably, socio-economic conditions had been changing over time, introducing external interests into the equation, the standards of good social behavior set out in the UN Global Compact were emblematic of this changing business climate. Beyond the UN Compact, other formal guidelines regarding responsible behavior, working conditions, environmental conditions, social engagement, and human rights were getting Maersk's attention.

The company established a corporate social responsibility (CSR) department and signed the UN Global Compact in February 2009. The Director of CSR, Annette Stubbe, noted that responsible behavior entails transparency and accountability, being open about both good—and not so good—performance, and being clear about how to do better. The group CEO, Nils Smedegaard Andersen, argued that good behavior simply made good business sense.

The corporate context

A. P. Møller–Mærsk can trace its roots to 1904 when Arnold Peter Møller at age 27 incorporated *Dampskibsselskabet Svendborg* together with his father Captain Peter Mærsk-Møller and eight years later established the sister company *Dampskibsselskabet* in 1912. A. P. Møller was influenced by his father's Christian values and his employees were recognized for hard work and commitment with expectations of high performance without slacking. Competence, wholehearted effort, and loyalty earned respect and were rewarded with promotions to higher ranks and responsibilities within the company. A. P. Møller practiced a patriarchal leadership style with strong core values many of which have prevailed at corporate headquarters to the present day.

Arnold Mærsk Mc-Kinney Møller was A. P. Møller's second child and oldest son. He was born in 1913 by A. P. Møller's American wife Chastine Estelle Roberta Mc-Kinney. Mærsk Mc-Kinney Møller became co-owner of the shipping company in 1939 and moved to New York. When troops from Nazi-Germany invaded Denmark on April 9, 1940, Mærsk Mc-Kinney Møller received legal authority to manage the entire company fleet from New York throughout the Second World War for as long as Denmark was occupied. The concern for 'Constant Care' so frequently referred to in the company dates to this time as A. P. Møller sent a letter to Mærsk Mc-Kinney Møller advising him: "that no loss should strike us that can be avoided through constant care."

The company business grew steadily during the post-war period and corporate activities expanded during the ensuing decades of European reconstruction and international industrial growth. When A. P. Møller died in 1965, Mærsk Mc-Kinney Møller became the CEO of A. P. Møller–Mærsk (APPM). The gradual abolishment of import restrictions and tariff barriers increased global trade and provided ample opportunities to grow the international shipping business. Container technology revolutionized sea-borne line traffic. APMM was recognized as leading the way by establishing effective terminals in key locations around the world. The company's own shipyard made advanced container ships and modern oil tankers. The group also expanded into other business activities including retail distribution, oil exploration, and air transportation.

Mærsk Mc-Kinney Møller resigned to assume Chairmanship of the company in 1993, and Jess Søderberg became CEO. APMM continued to expand the container-line traffic as globalization required extensive movement of goods between continents. The APMM group acquired two friendly competitors *Safmarine* and *Sea-Land* in 1999, thereby enhancing the global network in Europe, Africa, and North and Central America. Mærsk Mc-Kinney Møller retired as Chairman in 2003 and was replaced by Michael Prahm Rasmussen. APMM subsequently acquired the Anglo-Dutch worldwide container shipping line *P&O Nedlloyd* in 2005 to forge a leading market position although post-merger integration produced big challenges. Jess Søderberg was replaced as CEO in late 2007 by Nils Smedegaard Andersen, until then CEO of Carlsberg A/S and non-executive member of the board.

The maritime industry was severely hit by the global economic crisis 2007–2008 with contracting trade volumes and low freight rates. In response, the company focused on cost-consciousness and resourcefulness divesting marginal activities to trim the business portfolio. The company placed orders for the largest container ships (triple-E) ever made in 2011 with a capacity of at least 18,000 containers to forge efficiency in the industry while engaging in different capacity-sharing arrangements. However, the strategy also entailed an increasingly flexible fleet of ships in varied sizes to enhance door-to-door delivery services. In 2016, Søren Søren Skou became CEO of APPM having been employed in various positions within the group since 1983. Jim Hagemann Snabe was appointed as Chairman in 2017 to replace Michael Prahm Rasmussen in the post.

Leadership values

In the early 1990s, the company was seen to have maintained strong cultural traits dating to the founder A. P. Møller, with particular emphasis on decent behavior, honesty, and respect. These values had never been written down but permeated communications from Mærsk Mc-Kinney Møller to business associates as the pillars of management thinking across the organization. These corporate values were further reflected in executive decisions as well as in written instructions. They became an engrained way of thinking, acting, and behaving and were seen to constitute the spine of corporate managers that advanced through the ranks. Additionally, evidence shows the core values were enforced through concrete actions.

For example, Mærsk Mc-Kinney Møller committed to building double-hull tankers right after the Exxon Valdez oil spill in Prince William Sound, Alaska, on March 24, 1989, as a first step in replacing the entire company's fleet of oil tankers. This impressive and demanding overhaul was completed by 1993. However, the more costly ships did not earn a return for many years as most charterers continued to opt for the cheaper single-hull transport option. Indeed, things did not change until the international maritime conventions were changed in favor of double-hull oil cargos after another major environmental catastrophe took place. On December 12, 2000, the Erika, a tanker chartered by Total Fina, spilled around 11 million liters of oil off the French Atlantic coast. Although the spill was only a fourth the size of the Valdez incident, a heavy winter storm turned it into an ecological disaster affecting a 350-km vulnerable coastline killing around 100,000 seabirds.

As a consequence, new international maritime conventions scheduled a gradual phasing out of single-hull tankers from 2002 and created a two-tier freight rate system with special rates for double-hull tankers. By that time, the APMM group only had double-hulled ships and, therefore, faced no immediate requirements to renew the fleet. A combination of foresight, luck, and responsible behavior eventually seemed to pay off after a decade. In the meantime, charterers would continue to choose the cheapest single-hull rates to save costs in stark contrast to the official statements they made about environmental concerns expressed in glossy corporate brochures. This observation made the APMM leadership pledge not to make public announcements, but rather instill in employees to do the right thing and be "fair and square" in corporate relations. The mantra was that there are limits to what you can deliver, but if you make a commitment, you must honor your promise.

International conventions

After the Exxon Valdez ran aground in Alaska in 1989, the US authorities introduced the Oil Pollution Act of 1990 (OPA 90) requiring new oil tankers to be double-hulled while phasing out the old single-hull tankers between 1995 and 2015. Outside the United States, the International Maritime Organization (IMO) imposed other requirements in 1993, which are described in Annex I of the international convention for the prevention of pollution from ships (MARPOL). These rules attempted to phase out all the large, single-hull tankers from use by 2026. However, subsequent to the sinking of the Erika off the French coast in 1999, the MARPOL rules were amended effective from September 2002 to accelerate the phasing out of single-hull tankers by 2015. The European Union (EU) instated similar regulations during 2002 to accelerate the in-phasing of double-hull designs within the EU.

Executive decisions

The global shipping industry has always been governed by national restrictions and complicated international treaties making good relationships with public authorities essential. Having the most modern fleet does not guarantee access to national harbors, but good relations with governments, regulators, trade associations, business partners, and local customers can. By the late 1990s, the global shipping volume continued to grow as did the corporate activities in retail distribution, oil exploration, and air transportation. But the increasing complexity of the expanding group created new exposures. Hence, the company was taken by surprise in 2000 when its airline business was charged with infringements of European competition laws.

The APMM subsidiary Mærsk Air and Scandinavian Airlines System (SAS) had filed a cooperative agreement with the European Commission in late 1998, informing them that they engaged in code-sharing and exchanged frequent flyer benefits among customers. However, inspections conducted by the Commission in June 2000 revealed a more restrictive agreement with non-compete clauses on certain inter-European flights. Mario Monti, the Competition Commissioner at the time, stated that it was a clear case of two airlines illegally sharing the markets at the expense of the customers. The incident showed a lack of regulatory compliance with significant fines that could hurt economically and damage their reputation. In this situation, the corporate leadership accepted the wrongdoing and worked closely with commission officials to get things right.

Maritime regulation and competition

International maritime regulation seeks to impose common standards on shipping transportation to ensure efficiency in international trade. The shipping industry is primarily regulated by the UN agency—the IMO—established to protect the marine environment, safety, and labor standards at sea. These regulations are governed by diplomatic conventions and agreed upon by member countries. The rules are imposed and enforced by the flag states where ships are registered and by the port state controls of the harbors that host the ships. The IMO was instituted at an international conference in Geneva and put into force in 1958.

The ILO, another UN agency, bridges the views of governments, employers, and workers to safeguard working conditions at sea. Historically, the global shipping industry was characterized by collusive arrangements where the shipping firms met at conferences to set freight rates and coordinate schedules and exclusive regional coverage. These conferences came under increased scrutiny and were challenged, e.g., in US courts, as well as by UN guidelines for liner conferences with effect from 1983 to ensure broader representation. The adverse effects of restrictive price and market conferences now succumb to national anti-collusive legislation and enforcement efforts.

Competition laws within the EU aim to counter abuse of market power by major corporations to the detriment of economic welfare. Hence, the EU treaties have provisions to ensure that competition prevails, and cartel agreements and monopolistic price fixing are avoided comparable to the US antitrust laws. Articles 101 and 102 of the Treaty on the Functioning of the European Union (TFEU) deal with collusion, anti-competitive practices, and abuse of dominant market positions giving the Commission authority to enforce the competition laws within the EU. The Directorate-General (DG) for Competition was responsible for implementing the competition policies within the EU while enforcing the antitrust regulations. Mario Monti was Commissioner in charge of the DG from 1999 to 2004.

Reflections

The management literature often presents executives with a potential conundrum between adopting rational economic reasoning to their investment decisions and using ethical motivations to guide corporate responsible behaviors. Some scholars distinguish between opposing rationales to consider the stakeholder concerns in social responsibility presented as pure "economic reasons" in contrast to "intrinsic merit" in the sense of good behavior. Other scholars voice similar tensions between corporate responsible investments based on "profit-maximizing" cost-benefit analysis and assessing corporate actions based on "moral values."

However, the APMM case suggests that these alternating views are not contradictions but actually may reflect shrewd considerations by executives that assume a long-term sustainability perspective. Hence, Mærsk Mc-Kinney Møller's decision to convert the entire tanker fleet into double-hulled ships was arguably the right ethical decision to make because it reduced the potential for adverse environmental effects from disasters. Conversely, it was also a rational decision to make for the long-term—to implement technological capabilities ahead of the competition—envisioning an inevitable trend toward tougher environmental regulations. The implied cost-benefit analysis is obviously challenged by high uncertainty about future regulatory regimes, their timing, and the implications for the investment value. Yet, the act also creates positive spillover effects in the form of an improved corporate reputation. What is more, the goodwill derived from a strengthened corporate reputation as a trusted, accountable, and reliable counterpart may help the company deal more effectively with complex emergent risks that require collaborative solutions.

The decision to invest in double-hull tankers was not driven by regulatory requirements but by a combination of moral values and rational reasoning. One may even argue that public regulation primarily motivates the laggards in the industry to behave properly and not the proactive companies that lead developments. From this reasoning, we can (probably) deduce that the value-enhancing rationales for corporate responsible behavior can relate to rational investment analysis that takes account of effects from positive economic externalities that create goodwill and concerns about subsequent penalties and fines caused by negative economic externalities.

Three particular issues may warrant further discussion:

- How are (can) important core values (be) executed to enhance corporate reputation and facilitate collaborative solutions?
- How do functional specialization, multinational diversity, and business acquisitions affect the core values in an organization?
- How may (can) leadership influence corporate responsible behaviors in a large and complex multinational organization?

Read more about it

Andersen, T. J. (2017). Corporate responsible behavior in multinational enterprise. *International Journal of Organizational Analysis*, 25(3), 485–505.

From the A. P. Moeller: Maersk website, "Maersk Core Values." https://www.maersk.com/about (downloaded 27-12-2020).

Harrison, J. S. and Freeman, R. E. (1999). Stakeholders, social responsibility, and performance: empirical evidence and theoretical perspectives. *Academy of Management Journal*, 42(5), 479–485.

Hornby, O. (1988). *"With Constant Care …" A.P. Møller. Shipowner 1876–1965*. Schultz. Copenhagen, Denmark.

The Ten Principles of the UN Global Compact. https://www.unglobalcompact.org/what-is-gc/mission/principles

Waldman, D. A. and Siegel, D. (2008). Defining the socially responsible leader. *Leadership Quarterly*, 19, 117–131.

Case 4.2: Connecting virtue with value: South African breweries in Sub-Saharan Africa

Case overview

The South African Breweries Ltd. (SAB) story contains numerous complex social and commercial imperatives—all interesting, and instructive in their own way. Indeed, some attention will need to be paid to the socio-commercial history preceding international expansion because it was arguably these unique factors that placed SAB in the position to pursue its very ambitious international strategy. However, this case study ultimately focuses on SAB in the early process of expanding into regional markets throughout Sub-Saharan Africa. Developments that followed this initial expansion will receive a mention, but the setting for this case remains confined to the period between, roughly, 1995 and 2005.

SAB did have some early history of operating outside South Africa, but before the end of apartheid in 1994, the company was largely confined to its domestic market. Its first international expansion relevant to this case was a joint venture with the government of Tanzania, which was quickly followed by entry into Zambia, Mozambique, and, later, Angola. While this case focuses on the African continent, SAB was moving farther afield at the same time; the Canary Islands, Hungary, China, Romania, Poland, Slovakia, Russia, the Czech Republic, India, and Central America—all occurring before 2001. These markets warrant a mention here because they reflect a central feature of the story. Beer consumption had been flattening or declining in most developed markets, while beer consumption was level or growing in developing parts of the world (not just in Africa), where social-economic-political unrest was common and business underinvestment common. This fact illuminates a central challenge for SAB. Its strategy required moving into higher-risk markets where the most promising opportunities were found. Can risk management be positioned to support a conscious, aggressive risk-taking strategy?

Focusing on its African neighbors, the high levels of risk come into an even sharper focus. Political instability, environmental degradation, social inequities, economic impoverishment, food and water shortages, underinvestment in infrastructure, and corruption all featured to varying degrees in these markets. And, as was the case throughout most of the world, a full-blown health crisis (HIV/AIDS) had swept across the region.

Apartheid ends/early developments

Although SAB was primarily identified as a beer brewer, the company's history since the mid-1900s reveals a wide-ranging diversification of its business holdings. Earlier diversification into soft drinks, associated retail, and other affiliated businesses were intrinsic strategic moves, but regulation—both at the national and international level—as well as anti-apartheid policies around the world placed SAB in a position where an already highly profitable brewing firm was restricted to investing almost exclusively within South Africa and into numerous sectors with little or no connection to its core business. Acquisitions included plate glass, hotels, hospitality and entertainment, manufacturing, and a range of different retail businesses.

This is critical history because when apartheid ended officially, SAB chose to divest itself of holdings across sectors, leading to a strong cash-rich position in which to support a strategic decision to return to a focus on beer and soft drinks. This strategy implied—indeed, required—internationalization since SAB already dominated its local market. However, moving to international markets presented business challenges. Notably, throughout the world, the industry is dominated by local brands and powerful consumer loyalty to those local brands. Indeed, despite public perception of beer production at that time, it was not cost-effective to internationally ship a product that is 90% water. Parenthetically, SAB later proved to be an early innovator in this regard with its decision to designate products from its acquisition of Miller (USA), Peroni (Italy), and Pilsner Urquell (Czech Republic) alongside its own Castle products as global brands; that is, products were produced in their home countries but shipped and sold worldwide. By overcoming technical constraints, SAB created a unique selling point. Consumption of Pilsner Urquell, for example, became a common experience worldwide. It was brewed to the same recipe, using the exact same ingredients and copper tanks that had been used for hundreds of years.

Global brands would come later. SAB's early growth primarily occurred through acquisitions of local breweries or through partnership/joint venture strategies. Thus, a picture emerged of a rapidly growing global firm that was constituted of many regionally or locally oriented breweries focused exclusively on their local and historic markets. Winning in the various local markets required attentiveness to local market demands as well as conditions. The strategy set by the CEO Graham Mackay was "think globally, but execute locally," the challenge being to translate this exhortation into implementable actions.

Given this business structure, however, it might be reasonably wondered what the value-adding motive would be if SAB were merely accumulating largely independent brewers who continued to (indeed, had to) operate locally. Certainly, SAB might be able to direct significant financial resources to revitalizing and modernizing individual brewers. This would offer some competitive advantage, though perhaps less so than might be thought since most of the acquisitions were already likely to be market leaders. Seemingly, significant value-adding would have to come from technical and managerial advantages that only SAB might provide. In fact, this appears to be the firm's line of reasoning because almost all acquisitions during the relevant time period included the installation of a SAB leadership team from South Africa—suggesting that SAB believed there was a distinct "SAB way" to manage breweries and the transfer of this know-how would be a key driver of success. Interconnectivity in overall corporate management and investment was seen as a critical adjunct, but the SAB country leaders were, in effect, the sharp end of the spear.

The regional risk profile

The story of Sub-Saharan Africa is one offering great promise, but also presenting significant challenges. Indeed, cataloging and discussing these challenges would overwhelm the scale and scope of this case study. Political instability, revolutionary turmoil, economic instabilities, poor infrastructure, crime and terrorism, extreme poverty alongside extreme wealth, food and water shortages, environmental concerns (natural and human-caused), poor-to-nonexistent educational opportunities—and more. The great potential of the region—human and natural resources, varied and unique flora and fauna, and significant business potential—should not be discounted here. However, this case pivots to a particular challenge; the struggle to cope with a significant HIV/AIDS crisis.

HIV/AIDS

The HIV/AIDS story is one of the most profound public health tragedies in the past 100 years. At the time of SAB's early international expansion, it was estimated that about 20% of the entire regional population in Africa was HIV positive, and in some specific locations, it was much higher. There were numerous reasons for this including the general view that Central and Southern Africa were likely among the origination points for HIV/AIDS, that limited capacity to respond in the health care systems was a common feature, and that public sanitation and food/water insecurity were factors—as were educational levels, knowledge of the disease, and—some have theorized—the rather more liberal cultural views on pre-and-extra-marital sex.

In combination, these factors posed a particular problem for SAB, which was that the home countries of its newly acquired breweries were exposed to a very serious health risk. Put in purely transactional terms, HIV/AIDS were massive threats to SAB's workforce and its customers—*ergo*, to its profitability. If this were the extent of SAB's worldview (that is, the HIV/AIDS risk was solely measured by its threat to profitability), it would seem that the company faced a dilemma. On the one hand, high profitability was seemingly achievable in these new markets, meaning a singular focus on "making money" would be a logical approach; but on the other hand, the inherent social, economic, and political instabilities would highly likely degrade the company's performance over time if issues beyond pure profitability were not considered and addressed. The higher probability of unforeseeable "surprises" was also not far from the minds of company leaders.

Close observers of the SAB story at this time noted that while South Africa had been branded with a reputation for a racist past, the company's own culture represented a slightly subtler mix of that country's history and national culture. This is to say, while the broader social and cultural overlays were present even in SAB, the company's history was distinctly working-class oriented, and the working-class population—demographically speaking—was disproportionately black but included other ethnic backgrounds as well. As a consequence, central features of race relations were, perhaps, more acutely felt in this multi-cultural setting—at least it could be argued that equality was very much a cutting-edge business issue for the company. Relevant here, there seems to have been a sensibility shaped by the social, cultural, economic dynamics—which meant the company had encountered the presence and impact of HIV/AIDS well before its international expansion. Perhaps here the best summarization would be this: SAB was very aware of cultural sensitivities when entering into neighboring markets.

SAB responds

Motives can be difficult to verify; actions are visible. However, first consider the possible motives for responding to the challenges of SAB's new markets.

Leaders within SAB have stated that its culture has always been shaped by the values it has espoused throughout its history. Central to this assertion is the notion that SAB's circumstances, its products, and its specific local focus did not permit it to develop a purely exploitative view of its business and its customers. In the eyes of key leaders at SAB, profitability only came by understanding the context in which it operated. A local focus (by necessity during apartheid) made customer and employee relations, in many respects, highly *personal*. Exploitative behavior would be noticed and remembered. This approach, coupled with the religious and ethical values of SAB's leadership, led to what might be called a rather distinctive white South African commitment to its values. Those ethical values were not to be tampered with.

Regarding actions taken, the leadership's particular values in action were built around the notion that it needed loyal and able employees who—importantly—took accountability, had access to sufficient support (in whatever forms) to enable them to show up for work, and to perform in alignment with company expectations. Given these goals in combination with company values, an exploitative approach simply would not work.

The company implemented a strategy that aligned with company values—and particularly was shaped by the view that SAB, itself, had an obligation to address the sources of insecurity—beginning with HIV/AIDS but ultimately progressing along a path that considered other security needs. In the early stages this included free HIV testing and medical advising for employees, but then expanding to include family members, then eventually to the communities where employees lived, and involving a wider range of HIV/AIDS support services.

Interesting questions arose from this growing willingness to extend HIV/AIDS service and support. How far should a company be willing to go to address insecurities or support needs that threaten the workforce and the customer base? Does SAB have an obligation for food and water insecurity? Certainly, water quality/security is a business issue as it is a fundamental input in beer production, but should SAB's interest extend to the wider community's water-related issues? What about the worker's children and their security? Should SAB be interested in supporting schooling? The welfare of workers' children is a source of insecurity, but the children are also future employees. What about the risks of just getting to work? Roads may be unsafe, personal safety from crime/terrorism may be at risk, even matters pertaining to clothing and general sanitation might translate themselves into both moral and business effects.

Early on, leaders noted that increasing loyalty to SAB proved to be a salutary side-benefit of its work against HIV/AIDS—loyalty from employees, but also increased brand loyalty from customers. Recognizing that most of its future market opportunities around the world would feature high-risk environments—and HIV/AIDS might not feature as prominently in many regions—consideration of its willingness to go far down the road of social engagement became a matter of top management concern.

Alongside these vexing questions, the moral dimensions of responsibly producing and selling alcoholic beverages were never far from the surface. Put in its most simple terms, the success of SAB was based on customers responsibly consuming more beer to enhance social occasions, but which could lower inhibitions, leading to increases in irresponsible behavior—all of this occurring while also focusing on addressing the spread of a communicable disease. SAB engaged in ambitious marketing and communications efforts to promote responsible consumption, but it must be plainly stated that this remains a core risk management challenge for SAB and, indeed, for all organizations in the alcoholic beverage sector.

Reflections

The case directly or indirectly suggests at least three important risk leadership questions that are relevant to this chapter:

• Business schools are fond of framing a debate about the central purpose of a firm. Is the purpose firm value maximization measured by increasing the wealth of shareholders or is it measured by balancing stakeholder satisfaction? It seems possible that the premise is wrong—it need not be one or the other. And, in alignment with this book, one aspect of risk leadership certainly suggests that responsibility for the impacts of organizational decisions would have to consider a wide-ranging field of vision. This is a matter of values and morality, but even a purely financial view would seem to have to reflect on the costs that might be imposed by regulators, the law, community activists, and governing bodies when an organization's actions result in harm to individuals, communities, the environment, and so on. Using the SAB story as the basis for consideration, is there a limit or boundary to how far a company can/should go in defining what is in-bounds and out-of-bounds when making business decisions?

- Is doing good, in this case, measured by *motives* or by *results*? What is the argument for each measure, and which aligns with your views? Here the particular issue of promoting beer consumption seems to serve as a starting point for discussion. If it is presumed that excessive beer consumption has a direct effect on less responsible behavior (and here, sexual promiscuity should be stated as a central concern), how do we consider the moral dilemma of investing considerable resources in improving community safety with the promotion of beer consumption? Can an acceptable compromise be found while recalling that teleopathy would argue that compromising on values is a prime illustration of ethical risk?
- Corruption is a feature of many environments in which SAB operates. A SAB leader stated that the company would never pay bribes as this is inconsistent with its values. Without challenging the sincerity of that statement, the example of paying bribes frequently appears in business ethics courses to contextualize a discussion about morality "in action." Here the question can be extended to note that SAB seems to be *doing well* financially and *doing good* in addressing critical community needs. Does it change the equation in any way if a local warlord—for example—demands payment of a bribe to guarantee employees safe passage to work? Here, it might be easy to say, "no, our values are unwavering"; but this would prompt a critical follow-on question—if we are unwilling to pay the bribe, what lengths are we willing to go to in order to assure safe passage to work for employees?

Read more about it

Apartheid (2010). *History.com*. https://www.history.com/topics/africa/apartheid
Clark, P. A. and O'Brien, K. (2003). Fighting AIDS in Sub-Saharan Africa: Is a public-private partnership a viable paradigm? *Medical Science Monitor*, 9(9), 28–39. https://pubmed.ncbi.nlm.nih.gov/12960920/
Editorial Staff (2020). The history of aids in Africa. *BiM 2020*. https://www.blackhistorymonth.org.uk/article/section/real-stories/the-history-of-aids-in-africa/
South African Breweries website. www.sab.co.za

Case 4.3: Volkswagen Group: Unintended effects of uninhibited ambitions for world dominance?

Case overview

The world was shocked on September 22, 2015, when Volkswagen (VW) admitted to deliberately having installed a defeat device in its turbocharged direct injection

(TDI) diesel engines to bypass the emission controls imposed by the US Environmental Protection Agency (EPA). The largest carmaker in the world had rigged the US emissions tests to circumvent regulations and boost sales using special software to lower emissions during laboratory tests. The day after, CEO Martin Winterkorn resigned.

The VW admission suggests that around half a million diesel cars in the US market and some 11 million cars globally are emitting higher levels of nitrogen oxides (or NO_x) than shown in the official lab tests performed by the environmental authorities. This has obvious implications for human health, although the precise economic implications are somewhat unclear.

The emissions scandal led to significant financial concerns for VW. Initial charges for vehicle recalls of 6.7 billion Euros in the third quarter of 2015 made the company post a loss of 1.7 billion euros. This does not include fines, penalties, or compensation expected to add further costs of tens of billions of euros. The market capitalization of the company dropped by 40% in the following months.

A brief history

Volkswagenwerk was formed by *Deutsche Arbeitsfront* (German Labor Organization) in 1937–1938 sponsored by Hitler as a new state-owned complex (now Wolfsburg) to produce affordable cars for the German people. They adopted a small family car design—*volksauto*—developed by Ferdinand Porsche, featuring an air-cooled rear engine and a beetle-shaped body. The war production changed to a military utility car—*Kübelwagen*—for the German forces. As the war ended, the factory still produced cars despite major disrepair and VW became important in the economic recovery of West Germany.

Sales increased steadily during the 1960s and became increasingly international. Auto Union and NSU were acquired to form Audi. The company eventually diverged from the air-cooled rear-engine toward front-wheel-drive, water-cooled cars. The Passat (or Dasher) was introduced in 1973 and the Golf (or Rabbit) model in 1974 followed by multiple generations. The Volkswagen Group grew to include many known automotive brands, e.g., Volkswagen, Audi, Škoda, SEAT, Bentley, Bugatti, Lamborghini, Porsche, MAN, and Scania. VW has long been Europe's largest automaker and battled over the past decade to retain the title as the world's largest auto manufacturer.

Background

In 2009, the Volkswagen Group was consolidated with Porsche as the tenth brand with the Piëch and Porsche families, descendants of Ferdinand Porsche, in control and Ferdinand Karl Piëch as Chairman of the VW Supervisory Board. (See the Porsche Case in Chapter Five.)

At this point, the Volkswagen group launched an ambitious growth strategy, *Strategy 2018*, with the intent to drive VW to the very top of the global automotive industry becoming a world leader in terms of sales and manufacturing of quality products. This required above-average sales growth in all markets with an operating margin of at least 8% to ensure a solid financial position. The aim was to position the VW group as the global economic and environmental frontrunner. The CEO, Martin Winterkorn, stated the goal as becoming the world's most profitable and sustainable car producer. However, when Toyota released its sales numbers in the fall of 2015, it had actually overtaken Volkswagen, so competition was fierce.

Volkswagen officially focused on environmentally friendly cars with formal initiatives to reduce CO_2 emissions, emphasizing ride-sharing arrangements and electrified vehicles showing social responsibility and ethical leadership echoed in campaigns for eco-friendly driving and green initiatives including clean diesel. VW received the "Green Car of the Year" award in 2009 and 2010.

The economic effects

By fall 2015, Volkswagen had cheated with the diesel engine emissions for about six years—releasing nitrogen oxides that vastly exceed the legal requirements in the EU and the United States. Estimates of the economic costs to public health from 2009 to 2015 can be linked to some nine million vehicles sold in Europe and the United States emitting estimated amounts of nitrogen oxides of 526 ktonnes above the legal limits. This level of emissions can be converted to lost lives at a total value of at least US$39 billion, five times the reserves made to cover the costs of the scandal. Diesel exhaust is a major contributor to air pollution, especially in Europe, where diesel engines are popular. Diesel emissions contain carbon oxides that have serious health effects and cause severe respiratory problems. For example, London attributes more than 3,000 deaths a year to air pollution where diesel traffic accounts for 40% of the NO_x emissions. Across the EU in general, around 20% of the urban population lives in areas where nitrogen oxides exceed the recommended air-quality standards.

The VW stock price suffered significantly in the aftermath, but studies indicate much broader effects on the value of other firms in the automotive industry including suppliers and customers. The evidence shows that direct suppliers to VW suffered a mean stock price reaction of −2.69% in the week after the scandal with European suppliers impacted the most with a mean stock price reaction of −5.52%. The analyses further identify a mean stock price reaction of −5.28% to VW's European customers. Other European motor vehicle manufacturers experienced a mean stock price reaction of −7.60%. VW positioned itself as an environmentally conscious reliable German company promoting high-quality products consistent with—and benefiting from—the positive country image of Germany. Hence, there might be negative network effects where the emissions scandal not only harms the VW brand but also the "made in Germany" label adopted by other German firms. There are signs that the scandal had adverse effects that compromised the positive image of German companies.

The announced installation of defeat devices exposed VW to a corporate scandal of proportions, although total sales bounced back in subsequent years establishing VW as the largest global auto manufacturer due to strong sales in developing economies, such as China and Central and Eastern Europe. All the while, the United States remains one of few countries where VW, so far, has paid significant amounts to consumers and government agencies with over US$23 billion in fines and settlements. In Europe, VW has not really settled with governments or consumers treating court cases as a nuisance and in developing markets—even large countries like Brazil, China, and India—VW has not taken significant actions. Yet, there are indications that VW has remaining issues to be resolved.

The changing VW executives

Hans Dieter Pötsch succeeded Ferdinand Piëch as Chairman of the Volkswagen supervisory board in 2015. Pötsch was the CFO at VW 2003–2015 and became CEO of Porsche Holding in 2015.

Ferdinand Karl Piëch was CEO of the Volkswagen Group 1993–2002 and Chairman of its Supervisory Board 2002–2015. As a grandson of Ferdinand Porsche, he initially worked at Porsche and became CEO of Audi before taking over as CEO at VW where he acquired Bentley, Bugatti, and Lamborghini to complement the Volkswagen, Škoda, SEAT, and Audi brands.

Martin Winterkorn became CEO of VW in 2007 from a position as CEO of subsidiary company Audi and resigned on September 23, 2015. Winterkorn was indicted in the United States in May 2018 with criminal fraud charges over emissions cheating, in March 2019 by the SEC for market misinformation, and in April 2019 for German fraud charges.

Matthias Müller moved from the position of CEO at Porsche to take over the vacant position as CEO of Volkswagen from September 2015 to April 2018.

Herbert Diess became CEO of the Volkswagen Group and VW in 2018 and was named among the "world's best CEOs" by *CEOWORLD* magazine. In September 2019, Herbert Diess and Hans Dieter Pötsch were prosecuted for manipulating Volkswagen's diesel emissions and withholding shareholders from information in violation of German law.

Ralf Brandstaetter became CEO of the VW car brand on July 1, 2020, replacing Herbert Diess, who remains head of Volkswagen Group. Brandstaetter held the position as COO leading the cost-cutting efforts across the largest German VW plants. His appointment followed intense discussions with powerful labor leaders over cost-cutting plans to free resources for electric car manufacturing.

Wolfgang Porsche and Hans-Michel Piech, the family members that control VW on the Supervisory Board, have supported the shift toward electric cars.

How was it found out?

The International Council on Clean Transportation (ICCT) in Washington DC contracted scientists from the Center for Alternative Fuels Engines and Emissions at West Virginia University in Morgantown in 2014 to test emissions from diesel vehicles under realistic conditions. The scientists fitted the cars with a portable emissions measurement system to gather data across different US road types. They found that the levels of NO_x emitted by a VW Jetta were 15–35 times above the US standard and the data for a VW Passat indicated 5–20 times greater emissions. The BMW X5, however, remained at or below the standard except during rural uphill driving. This prompted the EPA to investigate VW's emissions tests threatening to withdraw approval for all VW diesel vehicles in the United States. This caused Volkswagen to admit it had tricked emissions tests using software that senses if the car is in a test.

Diesel vehicles tend to have a lower carbon footprint than petrol-powered cars and the BMW X5 shows that diesel can keep emissions within existing limits. However, the scandal has probably made it difficult to promote the idea that diesel engines can reduce air pollution.

Some implications

The case reveals a type of (irresponsible) greenwashing behavior characterized as deceptive manipulation where the company's sustainability communication promoted pro forma environmental protection projects with the intent of appearing to be a leader in eco-friendly car production. The various press releases, shareholder and investor reports, and transcripts of oral statements issued in response to the crisis show how the information provided during the crisis served to explain the reasons for the company's actions that led to the events while preparing the ground for future mitigating actions. It reveals a priority for actions intended to restore the image of Volkswagen by changing the orientation of the information to reduce the public offensiveness caused by the crisis. The company statements often refer to resolutions for making changes and improving things to enhance a public perception that will strengthen consumer and investor confidence and minimize immediate adverse effects.

This type of corporate behavior provides some good reasons to critique the business ethics presented by the executive leadership acting deceptively to facilitate corporate sovereignty while merely pretending to care about societal concerns and the common good. It displays a form of corporate ethics orchestrated in a self-sufficient manner to enable the business to pursue its self-interests even if it de facto entails deceiving, cheating, and manipulating the truth. Conversely, it also puts into question the efficacy with which society can counter this kind of corporate malfeasance and the court system's ability to hold corporations and their executives responsible.

Volkswagen partnered with Daimler in 2006/2007 to introduce and adopt their clean diesel technology, BlueTec, as a way to boost the sales of their diesel vehicles in the US market. As a key supplier, Bosch was engaged in the development of the software to switch into clean mode during lab tests that was installed in the VW models and the two companies probably collaborated on this as early as 2008. As an outgrowth of this relationship, the pressures of the crisis made VW look into the possibility of claiming damages from Bosch as being partially responsible for the scandal.

Martin Winterkorn and a number of former VW employees have been indicted in the United States for violating environmental laws and committing fraud and some have been convicted. Oliver Schmidt, a German national, who headed VW's environment and engineering office in Michigan, was arrested by FBI agents in 2017 as he traveled in transit through Miami Airport to board a flight to Germany, and subsequently pleaded guilty as charged. And Mr. Liang, an engineer and German national who moved to the United States with his family in 2008 to help VW launch diesel cars, was sentenced to 40 months imprisonment and a US$200,000 fine in 2017 for participating in the emissions cheating. Winterkorn remains a fugitive of justice in the United States, wanted for conspiracy to violate the Clean Air Act.

Volkswagen is planning substantial investment in electric cars over the coming years to retain a dominant global position in the automotive industry. VW announced in early 2021 that sales during 2020 dropped by 23.4% in Western Europe, 17.1% in North America, and 9.9% in China. They further noted that the group "narrowly" failed to meet the new EU emissions targets despite an increase in electric cars. The legislation imposed in 2020 requires that cars sold by manufacturers must not emit more than 95 grams of CO_2 per kilometer on average—potentially sanctioned by hefty fines.

Reflections

Several important points come to life in this case study. Ensuing discussions could be directed to consider at least six of these.

- What role did the extremely ambitious growth and profitability targets imposed by the board and top management play? Did it urge, even force, people to commit or do things they otherwise would/should not find acceptable?
- Are there resemblances to Barings Bank and Société Générale where the leaders liked the earnings (and their own bonuses) and maybe subconsciously accepted flawed behavior out of underlying self-interest? This could indirectly press the employees (traders) to assume positions they otherwise did not have to take.
- Is this an illustrative example of a centralized control-based organization that adopts internal management reporting systems (and enterprise risk management) to achieve strategic objectives and goals at any price?
- Is this another example of leadership that consciously creates a false platform of social responsibility in a cynical conscious attempt to mislead for their own benefit? Another manifestation of discrepancies between espoused values and actual values in action?
- Why did no one attempt to do the right thing and "blow the whistle"? Many people must have known as illustrated by the multiple indictments. Was this an effect of an (assumed) autocratic leadership style unreceptive to critique?
- Has the justice system caught the true wrongdoers?

Read more about it

Aichner, T., Coletti, P., Jacob, F. and Wilken, R. (2020). Did the Volkswagen emissions scandal harm the "made in Germany" image? A cross-cultural, cross-products, cross-time study. *Corporate Reputation Review*. https://doi.org/10.1057/s41299-020-00101-5 published online 15 September 2020.

Bovens, L. (2016). The ethics of dieselgate. *Midwest Studies in Philosophy*, 40, 262–283.

Jacobs, B. W. and Singhal, V. R. (2020). Shareholder value effects of the Volkswagen emissions scandal on the automotive ecosystem. *Production and Operations Management*, 29(10), 2230–2251.

Jung, J. C. and Sharon, E. (2019). The Volkswagen emissions scandal and its aftermath. *Global Business and Organizational Excellence*, 38(4), 6–15.

Oldenkamp, R., van Zelm, R. and Huijbregts, M. A. J. (2016).Valuing the human health damage caused by the fraud of Volkswagen. *Environmental Pollution*, 212, 121–127.

Painter, C. and Martins, J. T. (2017). Organizational communication management during the Volkswagen diesel emissions scandal: A hermeneutic study in attribution, crisis management, and information orientation. *Knowledge and Process Management*, 24(3), 204–218.

Rhodes, C. (2016). Democratic business ethics: Volkswagen's emissions scandal and the disruption of corporate sovereignty. *Organization Studies*, 37(10), 1501–1518.

Schiermeier, Q. (2015). The science behind the Volkswagen emissions scandal. *Nature: International Weekly Journal of Science*. https://www.nature.com/news/the-science-behind-the-volkswagen-emissions-scandal-1.18426 (accessed January 19, 2021).

Siano, A., Vollero, A., Conte, F. and Amabile, S. (2017). More than words: Expanding the taxonomy of greenwashing after the Volkswagen scandal. *Journal of Business Research*, 71, 27–37.

Notes

1 Ardichvili, A. and Jondle, D. (2009). Ethical business cultures: A literature review and implications for HRD. *Human Resource Development Review*, 8(2), 223–244. [This article offers a good overview of thinking about ethical business cultures.]
2 Goodpaster, K. E. (2007). *Conscience and Corporate Culture*. Blackwell Publishing, Malden, MA. [This book provides a reflective work on the origins of the corporate conscience idea.]
3 Ardichvili, A., Mitchell, J., and Jondle, D. (2009). Characteristics of ethical business cultures. *Journal of Business Ethics*, 85, 445–451. [This article addresses the specific characteristics cited in the text.]
4 Ibid.
5 Jacobsen, M., Worm, V. and Li, X. (2017). Navigating a global corporate culture: On the notion of organizational culture in a multinational corporation. In Andersen, T. J. (Ed.), *The Responsive Global Organization: New Insights from Global Strategy and International Business*, Chapter 5, 125–148, Emerald Publishing, Bingley, UK.
6 Trevino, L. K. (1986). Ethical decision making in organizations: A person-situation interactionist model. *Academy of Management Review*, 11(3), 601–617.
7 Bass, B. M. and Steidlmeier, P. (1999). Ethics, character, and authentic transformational leadership behavior. *Leadership Quarterly*, 10(2), 181–217.
8 De Hoogh, A. H. B. and Den Hartog, D. N. (2008). Ethical and despotic leadership, relationships with leader's social responsibility, top management team effectiveness and subordinates' optimism: A multi-method study. *Leadership Quarterly*, 19, 297–311.
9 Deal, T. E. and Kennedy, A. A. (2000). *Corporate Cultures: The Rites and Rituals of Corporate Life*. Perseus Books Publishing, New York.
10 Camerer, C. and Vepsalainen, A. (1988). The economic efficiency of corporate culture. *Strategic Management Journal*, 9, 115–126.
11 Schein, E. H. (2004). *Organizational Culture and Leadership*. Jossey-Bass, San Francisco, CA.
12 Campbell, J. T. (2012). Multinationals and corporate social responsibility in host countries: Does distance matter?, *Journal of International Business Studies*, 43, 84–106; Schaubroeck, J. M., Hannah, S. T., Avolio, B. J., Kozlowski, S. W. J., Lord, R. G., Trevino, L. K., Dimontakis, N. and Peng, A. C. (2012). Embedding ethical leadership within and across organization levels. *Academy of Management Journal*, 55(5), 1053–1078.
13 Maignan, I. and Ralston, D. A. (2002). Corporate social responsibility in Europe and the U.S.: Insights from businesses' self-presentations. *Journal of International Business Studies*, 33(3), 497–514.
14 Witherell, B. and Maher, M. (2001). Responsible corporate behavior for sustainable development. *OECD Observer*, 226/227. http://oecdobserver.org/news/archivestory.php/aid/511/#sthash.XoKL2ann.UMDAvsUv.dpuf
15 Harrison, J. S. and Freeman, R. E. (1999). Stakeholders, social responsibility, and performance: Empirical evidence and theoretical perspectives. *Academy of Management Journal*, 42(5), 479–485.
16 Campbell, J. L. (2007). Why would corporations behave in socially responsible ways? An institutional theory of corporate social responsibility. *Academy of Management Review*, 32(3), 946–967.
17 Anderson, C. (1997). Values-based management. *Academy of Management Executive*, 11(4), 25–46.
18 Freeman, R. E., Harrison, J. S., Wicks, A. C., Parmar, B. L. and De Colle, S. (2010). *Stakeholder Theory—The State of The Art*. Cambridge University Press, Cambridge, UK.
19 Husted, B. W. (2005). Risk management, real options, and corporate social responsibility. *Journal of Business Ethics*, 60, 175–183; Kytle, B. and Ruggie, J. G. (2005). Corporate social responsibility as risk management: A model for multinational. Corporate Social Responsibility Initiative Working Paper No. 10, John F. Kennedy School of Government, Harvard University, Cambridge, MA.
20 Ciulla, J. B. (2014). *Ethics, the Heart of Leadership* (3rd ed.). Praeger, Santa Barbara, CA. [This is the current edition of work that was initiated in the 1990s and reflects some of the earlier efforts to investigate leadership and ethics.]
21 Schein, E. H. (2004). *Organizational Culture and Leadership*. Jossey-Bass, San Francisco, CA.
22 Padilla, A., Hogan, R. and Kaiser, R. B. (2007). The toxic triangle: Destructive leaders, susceptible followers, and conducive environments. *The Leadership Quarterly*, 91(2), 308–325. [This article offers a reasonably rounded argument for bad leadership itself, but also in relation to followers and the context.]

23 Schumann, P. L. (2001). A moral principles framework for human resource management ethics. *Human Resource Management Review*, 11, 93–111. [This article sets out moral principles in an accessible format.]

24 Ciulla, J. B. (2004). Ethics and leadership effectiveness. *The Nature of Leadership*, Chapter 13, 302–327. [This book chapter offers a more recent history of changing views on virtuous leaders in more recent times.]

25 Velasquez, M. G. (1992). *Business Ethics: Concepts and Cases* (3rd ed.). Prentice Hall, Englewood Cliffs, NJ. [This is an older but useful source on basic concepts related to virtue and virtuous leadership and the cases provide helpful illustrations.]

26 Padilla, A., Hogan, R. and Kaiser, R. B. (2007). The toxic triangle: destructive leaders, susceptible followers, and conducive environments. *The Leadership Quarterly*, 91(2), 308–325. [This previously cited article has a particular focus on destructive leadership.]

27 Goodpaster, K. E. (1997). Moral projection, principle of. In Werhane, P. H. and Freeman, R. E. (Eds.), *Blackwell Encyclopedic Dictionary of Business Ethics* (p. 432). Blackwell Publishing, Malden, MN. [This is where the concept of teleopathy was first proposed.]

28 Williams, B. (1981). *Moral Luck*. Cambridge University Press, Cambridge, UK. [Williams is a philosopher credited with the concept of Moral Luck.]

29 Northouse, P. G. (2019). *Leadership*. Sage Publishing, Thousand Oaks, CA. [This is a widely used university level textbook … note particularly the "leader among followers" idea in chapters 8, 9, 10, and 11.]

30 Etzioni, A. (1996). The responsive community: A communitarian Perspective. *American Sociological Review*, 61(2), 1–11. [This is one of the earlier articles credited with advancing the communitarian concept.]

31 Snow, C. P. (2001) [1959]. *The Two Cultures*. Cambridge University Press, London, UK.

32 Young, P. C. (2004). Ethics and risk management: Building a framework. *Risk Management*, 6(3), 23–34. [This article is an early effort to incorporate ethics into risk management thinking and practice.]

33 Young, P. C. (2010). Risk management. In Boatright, J. (Ed.), *Finance Ethics: Critical Issues in Financial Theory and Practice*. Wiley-Blackwell Publishers, New York, Chapter 26, 495–509.

34 Goodpaster, K. E. (2007). *Conscience and Corporate Culture*. Blackwell Publishing, Malden, MA. [The book provides a particularly penetrating look at espoused values and those values in action.]

35 Anderson, H. J., Baur, J. E., Griffith, J. A. and Buckley, M. R. (2017). What works for you may not work for (Gen)me: Limitations of present leadership theories for the new generation. *The Leadership Quarterly*, 28(1), 245–260. [This article presents a topical look at employee values and attitudes with an examination of millennials.]

36 An example of many articles that examine ethics in the face of crises is Sandin, P. (2009). Approaches to ethics for corporate crisis management. *Journal of Business Ethics*, 87, 109–116.

37 Uhl-Bien, M. and Arena, M. (2018). Leadership for organizational adaptability: A theoretical synthesis and integrative framework. *The Leadership Quarterly*, 29, 89–104.

5 Risk leadership as social science

Thinking about thinking

We hold the view that risk management is, in its essence, a *way of thinking*.[1] This may seem confusing to some. To explain this, it may be helpful to separate this way of thinking as representative of a "point of view" in contrast to thinking as an aspect of—say—negotiating retention limits on a general liability insurance policy, where we review actuarial forecasts and decide what to do. We have a very specific image in our minds when we argue that risk management is a way of thinking, so let us try to be a little clearer on this.

First, we do not argue that risk management, or risk leadership, is *only* a way of thinking; insurance policies continue to be evaluated, safety training programs are still implemented, risk leaders continue to advise on strategic choices, and so on. There are things to *do* as well as things to think about. Second, while humans are always thinking—slow or fast as we will later explore—we have to recognize that the *way* we think is influenced by a raft of factors (generalized mental acuity, personal experiences, frames of reference, and we could go on). In our preceding book, we investigated the story of risk management and came to the view that risk management, as currently interpreted, has produced a way of thinking that *may not* be supportable in its fundamentals and may require some reconceptualization. So, how should we think about risk management? The prior book and this book together represent a kind of journey into that new view and in the concluding chapter, we intend to summarize our stance and point to alternative interpretations. But, in terms of explaining where we are at this moment, it is a useful mental exercise to start by describing the essence of the work of risk managers, which is to think critically and act in response to a recognition that we live in a risky, uncertain, significantly unknowable world, which is characterized by its distinct complexity.

Walking out from that initial insight, a new view of risk management begins to emerge. We see that while there is an explanation as to why risk management is described as it is today, it also must be understood to be the result of a path-dependent process—it could have ended differently. Indeed, scholarship on modern risk management is inconclusive in terms of modern risk management's contribution to value and performance. So, is the "way things are" the best we can do?

We extend our reflections to include the nature of the world we live in; as noted, it is complex and features uncertainty and the unknown more so than measurable phenomena. Morality looms as a central feature of how humans think about their world and how values affect the decisions they make to deal with that world. Our values are our decision rules, and embedded beliefs and accepted norms influence the behavior of organizational (and societal) actors. It affects how we work together for common ends, where

DOI: 10.4324/9781003148579-5

collaboration and cooperative efforts are considered, not just as tools or techniques, but as a means for risk managers and leaders to sense impending changes and finding better solutions. This implies a focus on the people that operate the organizations—and how to lead them. Although this may not lead to a conclusion that leaps off the page, we think that these observations mean risk management is a social science first and foremost. Critical thinking may require numeracy (the age-old Trivium and Quadrivium assumes so), but a reorientation in thinking about risk management begins by stating that it is fundamentally about understanding human beings and their behaviors.

This chapter cannot contain the wide sweep of subject matter required to study humans, but an indicative sense of the challenge can be offered in the form of three particular questions that provide a sense of what is entailed in the social science view.

1. Is it possible to develop insights into the role individual people—and particularly executive decision-makers—play as both exposures to risk as well as potential sources of risk—and as possible solutions to risk challenges?
2. By examining bad or destructive leadership, can we gain insights into the human dimension of risk leadership and its relationship to followers?
3. What roles do remembering, forgetting, and openness to imagine play in considering risk management or risk leadership as *a way of thinking*?

To do this, let us first take a closer look at various artifacts that characterize human behavior in order to explore and illuminate aspects of these questions.

People

Human behavior is, of course, a result of a complex range of factors: evolution, genetics, distinct aspects of mental capacity, emotional influences, personal experience, socialization, environment and circumstance, external complexities, and perceptions of the same. Undoubtedly, this is a challenging subject to summarize, and it will not happen here. Rather, the quest is narrowed to allow a focus on thinking and behavior under conditions of uncertainty. To do this, the probe limits itself to three indicative subjects—behavioral psychology, culture, and human relations (leadership-followership).

Behavioral psychology

For most of the early history of risk management, the general analytical frameworks were based on the principle of rational economic behavior; that is, individuals and organizations tend to act in consistent ways to advance their economic interests. Although both theoretical and applied research support economic rationality in a general sense, there are a very large number of observable violations—large enough to have led economists to alternative theories and modifications to classical economic thought. The principal, and notable, result has been the emergence of behavioral economics as a field of study.[2]

Behavioral psychologists have applied considerable effort to understanding human attitudes and responses to risk and uncertainty. Perhaps the most well-known scholars in this field are Daniel Kahneman and Amos Tversky, who explored many of the inconsistencies found when economic rationality is measured against actual human behavior. Many other psychologists have followed their ground-breaking work (as have behavioral economists).[3] Just to illustrate the wide-ranging impact of this line of inquiry, a few notable findings are:

1. Humans tend to ignore the fact that runs of good and bad luck regress to the mean over time
2. Emotion can damage the ability to decide rationally
3. Humans almost never possess all information necessary to decide in an economically rational manner
4. Human choice is often based on inadequate sampling (one's own experience is not representative, though it is accessible—which is another issue in and of itself)
5. Humans tend to be loss averse more than risk-averse
6. Humans tend to overestimate low-probability/high-drama risks and underestimate high frequency/low-drama risks
7. The manner in which risk issues are framed and presented can, or will, influence human attitudes about that risk
8. Obtaining more information on certain risks tends to promote a greater willingness to take on those risks

Taken as a whole, the work of behavioral psychologists and economists is a reminder that other factors influence choice and responses under conditions of uncertainty. Economic rationality is still useful and can be important in business planning, but risk managers and leaders must be conscious of the fact that a different kind of "rationality" may be at work when uncertainty is present. That this different form of rationality does not conform to traditional economic thinking does highlight the presence of influential cognitive biases, but—as it turns out—it does open the door for risk leaders to develop a potentially more useful—realistic?—means of framing risk decision analysis under conditions of extreme uncertainty.

The idea of *risk competence*, raised in earlier chapters, includes conversance with the insights from psychologists. It not only offers a distinct view on how people see and respond to an uncertain world but also—and perhaps mainly—how it impacts our thinking about the substance of those risks and uncertainties. It also helps us understand human responses to risk management itself (a risk management measure is presumed to change how people behave, but sometimes it is change for the worse). Humans are imperfect observers of the world and as a first-order matter, some sound skepticism about our perceptions and judgmental capacities should always be present. We are often correct in our assessments, but often enough our misperceptions lead to risk management mistakes and difficulties.

Culture

Culture as manifested in particular customs and behaviors undoubtedly influences the perception of risk, as sociologists have long understood. Some cultures promote risk-taking, some emphasize risk aversion. Some cultures are flat and respond to risk and uncertainty in ways that protect the interests of the group, while others promote individuality.[4] The present-day highly interconnected global world with many multi-cultural business networks obviously further complicates these cultural influences.

However, it should be emphasized that comparative studies of social cultures is a far from settled field of research. Tools for comparison do exist, but perhaps the question that best typifies the controversies that remain is simply this. Is there actually such a thing as an average Dane, Nigerian, or Vietnamese? Everyone is unique, and so efforts to discern cultural characteristics always run the risk of creating caricatures of cultures and individuals.

Nevertheless, there is most definitely an important value in being attuned to different norms, values, and behaviors as there are—in fact—distinct differences in how cultures define the group (who is in, who is out), the group's relationship with its environment, and its beliefs. These are real and important matters, but difficult to measure, simplify, and reconcile.

What is more, organizational cultures are important too.[5] Often, the organization's own culture is rooted in the social culture in which it operates, or where its headquarters is located. But, importantly here, organizational cultures are changeable in a way that social, or national, cultures are not. Changes in leadership, among other things, can foster cultural change within an organization in a more direct and visceral way than can, say, electing a new national political leader (for good or ill, we might add).[6] Furthermore, organizational cultures are artificial constructs—at least in terms of how cultures are studied—and some of the attributes of social cultures that create structural boundaries are not naturally present in organizations. These insights have relevance for firms with international business relations, including multinational organizations, as well as collaborative network structures where multiple organizational and national cultures may be in play at the same time. Incidentally, subcultures are sometimes important—professional cultures such as medical doctors and lawyers can be influential in some cases.

Human Relations: Followership

Here we tighten the discussion to consider people in an organizational context with specific reference to the leader–follower relationship. The study of followership is a relatively new phenomenon in leadership research. There are a few reasons for its recent arrival, but probably the relevant point here is that models of leadership have evolved over the past 40 years to become more oriented toward inclusive, democratic, fair, and just frames of reference—reflecting general changes in societal values.[7]

There are some inherent weaknesses in the study of followers, owing in large part to the newness of this line of inquiry. However, it is equally important to say that the value of recognizing followers in any understanding of leadership is obvious. There have been indicative findings that provisionally provide some useful insights.

Investigating followership entails the study of how people come to condone the influence of others in the service of a common purpose with acceptable goals. These efforts have led to a better understanding of follower psychological dispositions, how individuals relate to the idea of being led, and, of course, to understand issues that affect being led by a particular person (or type of person). A study has identified a number of follower typologies, which tend to categorize followers relative to their status as individualists, activists, partners, pragmatists, and so on.[8] It has also considered individual propensities of followership as well as the influence of contextual matters such as physical distance, group size, and inter-follower dynamics.[9] The nature of the work itself is also found to influence the follower typology.[10]

All the while, studies of specific leader-follower interactions are the subject of research as well, although less developed than studies on followership characteristics. Some early insights suggest that leader behaviors interact with follower behaviors providing a suggested template for further exploration of leader-follower relationships.[11] However, there are few studies on the evidently important question of outcomes to explain how the leader-follower interaction may lead to fulfilling desired objectives. Other propositions attempt to structure and guide future lines of inquiry including the motivations of follow-ers as they shape their engagement to the work and organizational agenda.[12]

Finally, we note that bad/destructive leaders also are subjects of study with significant importance for our understanding of possible risk leadership effects, as well as leader-follower relationships, or leader-opponent dynamics.

Bad/destructive leadership

What factors contribute to bad leadership? The most benign explanation probably is that a person is just the wrong individual for the job—wrong training, wrong experi-ence, wrong skill set. This might be ascribed to poor recruitment, or promotion, prac-tices rather than to the intrinsic limitations and behaviors of the individual in question. Obviously, more interesting questions relate to the personal attributes that may contrib-ute to bad leadership; or the circumstances that lead to bad behavior; or the unreason-able expectations of those hiring that leader; or the expectations of the followers; or, of course, the actual behaviors that produce destructive results and damage the organization and/or its culture.[13] It would seem obvious to observe here that careful construction and implementation of the recruitment and selection process itself would be the first order of business as it would be the best time to identify and prevent a reasonable number of bad leadership experiences.

Consideration of extreme examples of destructive leadership is, in many ways, not as helpful as might be expected. Hitler, Stalin, and Pol Pot are illustrations of behaviors so extreme that it is hard to scale the lessons to a meaningful application in everyday man-agement and leadership. Nevertheless, even research in this area has provided some useful analysis.

For example, perhaps one of the more interesting and relevant areas of inquiry has focused on leader *hubris*.[14] Initially drawing on lessons from Greek mythology, tragedy, and other ancient sources, current research has advanced the idea that harmful excessive pride can be studied, described, and even predicted. Hubris can affect a leader's percep-tions of risk, uncertainty, and luck, which tend to present particular challenges for organi-zational attitudes toward risk and risk management.[15] It is worth recognizing, though, that the ingredients for hubris also contain elements that can be *positive* attributes for leader-ship, such as self-confidence, charisma, and persuasive communication skills.[16]

Overconfidence, narcissism, and hubris

Overconfidence is a common and widely studied cognitive bias that affects an individual's ability to make rational error-free judgments and the perceived accuracy of the knowl-edge they possess.[17] *Overconfident leaders* are more prone to engage in risky projects. They are less receptive to corrective feedback that can improve forecasts and gain a more accu-rate assessment of environmental conditions. Overconfidence displayed by an executive influences the way feedback is interpreted, for example, when explaining why events might not have unfolded as expected at the time the strategic objectives were set and developed. The individual traits of overconfidence, narcissism, and hubris are often used interchangeably, although they do have some distinct features; nevertheless, the concepts are intrinsically related. Overconfidence, narcissism, and hubris are often attributed to powerful decision-makers including top managers and CEOs, and have been associated with risk-taking and even value-destroying behaviors and decisions.

A *narcissistic leader* thrives on the accolades of others where media recognition has a particular status as a driver of that behavior. However, there are both positive and negative types of *narcissism*. The "constructive" form of narcissism can facilitate optimism and foster successful outcomes whereas the "reactive" (excessive) form of narcissism is the most conspicuous indicator of defective leadership.[18] This also suggests the likely possibility of a dynamic transformation where constructive narcissism over time can turn into an excessive state of narcissism. The self-confidence displayed by a constructive narcissist tends to perceive the environment more in line with reality and is more open to the insights provided by less powerful others. In contrast, the perceptions of a reactive narcissist are of a more pretentious, or pompous, nature and becomes destructive as s/he seeks personal recognition, at the expense of others, and uses the power position to create a grandiose image of the self.

Hubristic, optimistic, and overconfident individuals typically see positive outcomes arising from uncertain contexts, but they also tend to overestimate their own abilities, seeing themselves as superior to most other people; consequently, they display a strong sense of self-sufficiency. Hubris formally differs from narcissism. A narcissist has a strong craving for continuous affirmation and applause, whereas a hubristic individual has little need for external recognition. *Hubris* is used in contemporary research to describe individuals, or executives, that display excessive pride and self-confidence.[19] CEO hubris is typically associated with risk-taking behavior.[20] Similarly, hubristic CEOs are found to be more associated with *socially irresponsible* activities rather than with CSR.[21] *Hubristic leaders* underestimate the importance of stakeholders and are overconfident in their own capabilities to solve problems. If left unchecked, hubris can lead to arrogance and contempt for other views where executives pursue decisions, and strategic objectives, based on their own self-inflated feeling of confidence fueled by flawed convictions.[22] Studies of US presidents and UK prime ministers, for example, illustrate how hubris can arise over time as a personality disorder among powerful individuals.[23] Hubris reflects a personality with narcissistic tendencies that is reinforced by prior success and general recognition.

Followership studies have also focused on what might make followers susceptible to bad leaders. The need for security and certainty is cited frequently as motivation and should be of particular interest to risk leaders. But the relatively common human need for reassurance from leaders, for feeling special or valuable, and sometimes to help distinguish oneself from "others," can be influential factors.[24]

Destructive leadership

Destructive leadership is characterized as a systematic repeated leader behavior that violates the legitimate interests of the organization, undermining the achievement of organizational objectives and effective use of resources by diminishing the motivation and job satisfaction of subordinates.[25] The associated abuse of power has adverse effects on organizational members and the organization itself, including the formal owners, reflecting an internal stakeholder perspective. However, the negative consequences for value creation will also affect various external stakeholders, for example, financiers, customers, suppliers, partners. The destructive leadership features may not be readily observable as explicit leadership behavior but also considers passive and indirect behavioral effects. The two stakeholder dimensions of the leader behavior, (Pro, Anti) the organization, and (Pro, Anti) the subordinates, can frame four distinct types of leadership.

- *Constructive leadership* (Pro-Pro). The leaders behave constructively toward the organization and the subordinates heeding the organization's legitimate interests in support of strategic objectives engaging subordinates in the optimal use of resources.
- *Derailed leadership* (Anti-Anti). The leaders display anti-organization behaviors (shirking, fraud, or theft) and conduct anti-subordinate acts (manipulation, deception, or harassment) that discard operational excellence and hide failed managerial competencies.
- *Tyrannical leadership* (Pro-Anti). The leaders pursue the legitimate strategic objectives and goals of the organization at the expense of the subordinates that are harassed, humiliated, and manipulated to get things done and accomplish the ends/goals.
- *Supportive–disloyal leadership* (Anti-Pro). The leaders violate the legitimate interests and strategic objectives of the organization and divert resources (materials, time, or attention) by granting employees excessive benefits for their general well-being.

It should go without saying that bad leaders are a profound problem for risk management, just as they are in all other contexts. The reason, of course, is that the powerful positions held by the leaders amplify impacts and consequences. Another reason is just as important but presents many additional—and awkward—issues. Who diagnoses the problem; who brings it forward and to whom; how does an organization come to grips with the fact that its "problem" is the boss? How are whistleblowers afforded protection? Corporate governance studies have a lot to say about the role of governance in controlling for such a problem, but the evidence in the public record suggests that bad leadership is difficult to formally trace and address, and despite the research, anticipating bad behavior is demonstrably challenging.[26] Per extension, it should be admitted, there must also be such a thing as bad/destructive *risk* leaders.

Forgetting/remembering/imagining

Controversial though it may sound, forgetting sometimes may be a good thing and remembering could be harmful. In some of the very interesting work in the organization theory field, the notion has been proposed that for organizations it may occasionally be better to forget certain things from the past (a bad experience that has disproportionately influenced a willingness to take future risks); while remembering can sometimes be harmful for similar reasons (obsessing on past glories). Nevertheless, organizational memory— of good and bad experiences—is broadly considered a good thing, one of the reasons *institutional memory* is prized as a valuable asset when possessed, and much lamented when lost.[27]

Here, however, a more historiographical perspective may be of use. Most people think of history as simply a factual story of the past; that it is a highly organized way of *remembering*. Certainly, that is part of the historian's work. But, in fact, historians tend to look quite differently at the work of remembering.[28]

Historiography—the study of the writing of history—offers some illumination on how history is created and used to remember. Consider a simple vignette:

> A historian decides to study the causes of the Civil War in the United States. The first question likely is directed at the motive for conducting this study. Newly unearthed

manuscripts; controversy over particular interpretations; gaps in our knowledge; all can be motives alongside the historian's own specialized interests and previous work. Then, a following question is likely to ask about the ability to complete the work—is there enough source material—and whether the topic can be framed and (always important in the academy) the likelihood of publication. Since a lot has already been written on this topic, the next challenge is to gain access to the source materials, assess the credibility of those materials, and assess the influence of the source of those materials (do those authors or sources have agendas or limited views?). Then, what to do with the remaining gaps where no resources are available?

Also, who is my audience? What are the themes to feature? Are my perspectives influencing my ability to find the "truth"? And how do I control for that?

Where do I start the story? If we acknowledge that part of the cause of the Civil War is slavery, how far back does the historian need to travel to identify the contribution of slavery to the outbreak of hostilities? Also, what aspects of life in the 1860s are in-bounds for my assessment? Where does my story end?

This is a very different view of history than the one the general public even thinks about. It does not mean that there is not an absolute truth about what caused the Civil War, but it does suggest that human perceptions of that subject intrude profoundly in the selection and telling of that story.[29] And, the view means the "absolute truth" may never be attainable.

Such is the case in organizational history as well. Acknowledging that this act of remembering is fraught with sources of risk and uncertainty is extremely helpful for risk leaders and critical thinking generally. Maintenance of institutional memory would seem to have a critical role in the work of risk management and leadership, but it is far more challenging than just collecting and organizing documents.

A second value derived from the historian's perspective is to compel us to think about the *purposes* of history.[30] Of course, it can be just fun and interesting to read stories about historic figures, but what is the "utility" of history? Three answers have been proposed as particularly relevant for organizations: Objective, Interpretative, and Imaginative usage.

Objective use is what might be called fact-finding; to understand the arc of history in a particular industry as well as the organization's own story; to understand how technologies evolved over time, for example. This requires what scholars refer to as *diachronic* historical thinking. This refers to the ability to think over extended periods of time, such as finding the narrative thread of a story of technological developments that unfolded over many decades. *Synchronic* historical thinking is also likely to play a role—it essentially refers to the ability to think across contemporaneous boundaries. Thinking wide/deep/long; an insight with great resonance for risk leadership.

Interpretative use is what might be called *rhetorical* history. Using history to mobilize, motivate, and create a sense of a shared history. This usage, which—by the way—can be used for good or ill, becomes useful when an organization has withstood a turbulent period, a dramatic incident, or has endured in spite of significant disruption. This not only provides the organization with a story it can celebrate, but also can inculcate values like pride, a sense of accomplishment, and loyalty.

Imaginative use is often referred to as *future perfect* history. It is shaping perceptions of change and continuity, imagining an ideal future, and redirecting energies in new directions. Organizations embarking on a particularly arduous period of change may benefit from an imagined happy future.

The idea that leaders need to think like historians is not particularly new in the academic literature, but it did gain traction in the 1980s employing history to construct narratives, think analogously, and propose methods to critically consider precedents in the face of complex challenges.[31] Arguably, while doing such things is an aspiration for all leaders, this idea resonates with the work of risk leadership, particularly as risk leadership possesses a distinct interest in the matter of *time*. Risk management decisions largely have long-term consequences (not just going forward but far into the past as well—consider the asbestosis/mesothelioma crisis of the 1980s and 1990s as a *prima facie* example of "risks from the past").[32] Further, the search for emergent challenges fits well with the methodologies employed by historians for finding answers contained within gaps in the past record.

Leading people in the face of complexity and risk

Summarization of the human dimension is not easily accomplished—and it certainly cannot happen here. Nevertheless, this chapter does plainly declare that risk management and risk leadership are, at their core, centrally down to understanding people. Assessing and addressing risk, uncertainty, and the unknown start with an appreciation of human perception and behavior, human history, the interaction of leaders and followers, and numerous other influences on the human cognition. Risk management has long focused—correctly—on "external" threats, and more recently on opportunities. That continues to be a key focus. But the fact that human perceptions are also sources of risk and complexity has been, perhaps, less prominently featured in traditional risk management literature. Indeed, this chapter argues for a complete inversion of perspective for risk leaders—start with understanding people, then move to the risks.

The cases

This chapter covers a range of issues pertaining to human nature, and correspondingly, the cases represent—perhaps—the most varying set of cases in this book. Here three particular dimensions of the chapter's subject matter are featured (though other topics appear in supporting roles). Human perception and behavior under conditions of uncertainty are explored with an eye on *not seeing* as well as *seeing* risks and uncertainties. Specific cognitive biases, bad faith, and self-dealing serve to illustrate how thinking and not thinking can lead to poor outcomes. And third, can people (leaders in particular) just be fundamentally bad people?

One of the essential underpinnings of this book is that people are the principal unit of measure in risk management; admittedly a point that rarely is forgotten by risk managers, but which often is somewhat pushed to the side by the more technical, clinical aspects of risk management. As such, beyond the essential story contained in each case, more philosophical considerations are prompted by the implications contained therein.

Case 5.1: *The Fukushima Daiichi incident: One of the most devastating natural catastrophes in history—but why?*

Case overview

A 9.0 Richter scale earthquake hit Japan on March 11, 2011, with the epicenter 130 kilometers east of Sendai in North-Eastern Honshû, Japan's main island, where subsequent aftershocks produced a gigantic tsunami. The Tohoku earthquake on the east coast of northern Japan is believed to be one of the largest earthquakes ever recorded. These combined natural incidents had profound impacts on the nuclear power plants located in the region operated by the Tokyo Electric Power Company (TEPCO).

Three of the six boiling water reactors at the Fukushima Daiichi plant were running at the time of the earthquake and power cuts halted the reactor cooling systems causing a release of radioactive material. The subsequent 14-meter tsunami that hit the plant after the earthquake caused major damages to the pumps and stopped the diesel-fueled emergency generators. Subsequent attempts to install mobile emergency generators failed due to a lack of proper cable connections.

Rising temperatures caused an explosion in reactor 1—on March 12—despite a (somewhat) risky attempt to open the valves manually. The cooling system in reactor 3 subsequently failed and made it necessary to use seawater, but the reactor still overheated and exploded on March 13. The reduced cooling capacity also finally caused a meltdown of reactor 2 on March 15, 2011.

The 2011 Tōhoku earthquake and tsunami created the worst nuclear accident since Chernobyl in 1986— classified as a Level 7 nuclear event—the only other incident to reach that elevated status. The impact on the population was severe with more than 150,000 people evacuated. The event disrupted regional economic activity and displaced people while releasing radioactive materials to the surrounding areas causing around 20,000 deaths and direct losses estimated at US$500 billion.

History

The Japanese electricity sector was nationalized in 1939 in preparation for the Pacific War. The energy industry was privatized again in 1951—ordered by the US occupation forces—to form nine private government-mandated regional power companies including TEPCO. The energy companies developed fossil power plants and transmission networks to support economic recovery and growth after World War II. The companies faced challenges of environmental pollution and oil shocks during the 1960s and 1970s and TEPCO expanded its network of LNG fueled power plants and nuclear power stations. The first Fukushima Daiichi nuclear power plant opened on March 26, 1971.

A legacy of prior incidents

TEPCO was accused of false reporting and concealment of safety incidents as part of the government's routine inspections of nuclear plants. In September 2002, TEPCO released the findings from an internal investigation into alleged concealment of cracks and falsified maintenance records at its nuclear plants. They found that of the 29 cases examined, 16 were inappropriate, although not prone to safety problems. They admitted to systematic and inappropriate handling of nuclear power inspections and repair works where employees were required to follow precedents even though something was wrong, thereby placing responsibility with headquarter departments and their managers.

The chairman, president, and advisory board members resigned, and a new board was instated to implement various countermeasures to make sure no similar incidents would happen again. TEPCO committed to impose corporate ethics and compliance rules to ensure transparency on nuclear operations and internal surveillance in a culture of observance. However, unreported events were still uncovered after an investigation in 2007. TEPCO had to close the Kashiwazaki-Kariwa nuclear power plant in 2007 after the Niigata-Chuetsu-Oki earthquake, which occurred at an offshore fault line, imposing the first loss on the company in 28 years that remained until the plant reopened in 2009.

TEPCO implemented a risk management framework as a centerpiece to identify and evaluate all major group-wide risks that could affect group operations and performance. The company president chaired the Risk Management Committee that monitored risk management units at headquarter departments and operating companies as part of the annual planning cycle.

What happened?

The earthquake took place at 2.46 pm on Friday, March 11, 2011, and triggered a tsunami that hit the coastline in several waves 30–45 minutes later. The Fukushima Daiichi nuclear power station was affected by the combined earthquake and tsunami. The safety and emergency electrical power backup systems worked as designed after the earthquake, but the subsequent tsunami caused major damage.

At the time of the event, three of the six power plants at the station (Units 1-6) were operating while the other three were in cold shutdown and outage. Unit 1 tripped due to the high seismic activity and both emergency diesel generators (EDGs) started automatically, and the reactor reached a state of cold shutdown. Unit 2 was in start-up mode and shifted to cold shutdown automatically caused by the seismic effect. The three EDGs started but remained in a standby state. The subsequent tsunami flooded one division of cooling pumps that lost function while two of the EDGs faulted. One cooling water pump was intact, so no degradation of the cooling function occurred. Unit 3 also tripped due to the seismic activity, but off-site power was maintained until the tsunami arrived, causing the cooling seawater pump to fail but it was still possible to lead the reactor to a cold shutdown.

Units 1, 2, and 3 were at the rated power level when the earthquake happened. Unit 4 was in an outage for a periodic inspection with large-scale repairs waiting and fuel relocated to the reactor building. Units 5 and 6 were also undergoing inspection, but with fuel remaining in the reactor core. The tsunami arrived about 45 minutes after with an estimated maximum wave of 15 meters, which was much above the protective seawall around the plant at 5 meters. All EDGs faulted when the tsunami arrived and submerged the seawater cooling systems for the EDGs, causing a loss of power supply at Units 1–5. Units 1–4 were severely damaged; Units 5–6 were not as they were located at a higher elevation.

When the Tōhoku earthquake was detected on March 11, 2011, the active nuclear reactors automatically closed the normal fission process used to generate power. The shutdown combined with problems in the electrical grid cut the electricity supplies to the three active reactors and activated the EDGs installed to safeguard electric power to the cooling pumps that circulate coolant liquids around the core of the reactors, which is vital to remove residual heat after the fission reactions.

The earthquake generated a 14–15-meter tsunami that arrived after sweeping over a protective seawall around the plant and flooded the lower parts of the reactors (Units 1–4), which caused the emergency generators to fail thereby cutting off the power supply to the circulation pumps. The inability to cool the reactor core caused the three nuclear meltdowns with hydrogen explosions that created radioactive contamination from reactor Units 1, 2, and 3 between March 12 and 15.

Implications and assessments

Various analyses concluded that TEPCO and the monitoring government agencies were ill-prepared for a nuclear disaster where the tsunami that caused the disaster should have been anticipated in advance and ambiguous roles between public and private institutions during the emerging crisis led to poor and ineffective responses. Prime Minister Yoshihiko Noda shared the blame and stated that officials were blinded by a belief in technological infallibility. It was further argued that rigid bureaucratic structures and restraints in communicating bad news preserved the wanting state of the nuclear power plants at TEPCO, which was known for a hierarchical management culture.

Could it have been avoided?

A TEPCO report from 2000 had proposed safety measures for seawater flooding from a potential 50-foot (15-meter) tsunami event, but the leadership questioned the technological validity of the proposal and determined that public discussions of this risk should be subdued to avoid excessive anxiety. Another internal study had identified a need to protect the nuclear facility from potential seawater flooding events referring to possible tsunami waves of 10 meters (33 feet), but headquarters officials argued that this was unrealistic and should not be taken seriously. Other warnings made by various government committees including the Cabinet Office in 2004, arguing that tsunamis above the maximum of 6 meters (18 feet) stipulated by TEPCO and government officials were indeed possible, were also not seriously considered.

Scrutiny and learnings

The National Diet of Japan Fukushima Nuclear Accident Independent Investigation Commission (NAIIC) reported in July 2012 that the causes for the disaster were foreseeable and that TEPCO failed to satisfy basic safety requirements to assess the risks and make contingencies to contain potential damages. The preventive measures and disaster preparations were insufficient to deal with a major tsunami with large-scale complex effects including the release of radioactive materials into the environment.

The committee chairman, Kiyoshi Kurokawa, stated that the cataclysmic events following the Tohoku earthquake and tsunami around the accident at the Fukushima Daiichi nuclear power plant "cannot be regarded as a natural disaster. It was a profoundly manmade disaster—that could and should have been foreseen and prevented." He made clear that the incident should—and could—have been mitigated by proper human interventions to reduce exposures and prepare for eventual disaster responses. The report identifies multiple human errors and even willful negligence that made the Fukushima nuclear plants vulnerable to the events in March 2011. It also scrutinizes the influence of cultural factors like reflexive obedience and reluctance to question authority, which— truth be told—is found (equally) in some organizational contexts outside of Japan. While the report identifies individuals and organizational settings as prone to due criticism, "the goal is not—and should not be—to lay blame." Rather, the report suggests that we learn from events that led to disaster, and "reflect deeply on its fundamental causes."

The Japanese government established an Investigation Committee on the Accident at the Fukushima Nuclear Power Stations of Tokyo Electric Power Company in June 2011 to investigate the Fukushima Daiichi nuclear disaster and it issued its final report in July 2012.

The Chairperson of the committee, Yotaro Hatamura, made a number of closing observations in the report interpreted as follows:

1. Things that are possible happen—and things that are not thought possible—also happen. Often the precautions we take only look at (minor) possible incidents but do not consider a situation of extended blackout. A proper mindset should consider all things that possibly can happen, also keeping in mind that events considered impossible can indeed also happen.
2. You cannot see the things you do not wish to see. You can (only) see what you want to see. Humans tend to note only the things they themselves consider agreeable and consistent with the course they aim to take. They cannot see things they do not want to see or things that are inconvenient.
3. We should make assumptions to the extent possible and make full preparations for them. However, we also need to acknowledge the possibility that things can happen that have not (even) been thought of before. We should take precautions so worst-case scenarios do not become reality.
4. Creating a (risk management) framework alone does not mean that things will work. We can construct frameworks, but they are of little avail if the underlying goals and intents are not shared collectively. The operators and regulatory and regional institutions that adopted the formal frameworks for nuclear accident responses found they were partially flawed when the accident actually occurred.
5. Everything changes in a crisis so responses should be flexible and adapted to the changes. When given conditions are seen as predictable and stable, we can develop detailed (but superficial) responses and crisis plans. However, when conditions constantly change and unexpected things happen, the planned responses become inconsistent with the actual circumstances.
6. We should acknowledge that (major) risks exist and create a culture that is able to openly discuss and debate those potential risks. Refusing the possibility to reason and challenge prevailing scenarios is not conducive to sincere thinking but may lead us to deflect an emerging reality.
7. We should be conscious of individual observance, thinking, decisions, and actions to cultivate diverse insights. Dealing with disaster is beyond the scope of predetermined

assumptions and cannot rely on scripted manuals. The people involved must consider various possibilities based on information at hand and use this to decide how to deal with the situation and take action.

Some eight years after the Fukushima nuclear disaster in September 2019, a Japanese court eventually cleared three former TEPCO executives operating the plant of professional negligence.[33] These were the only criminal charges in the aftermath of the disaster that caused a triple meltdown of nuclear reactors at the company's Fukushima Daiichi power plants. The three (former) executives were indicted for failure to implement countermeasures to the tsunami that caused the death of 44 people. No one died directly around the nuclear facilities, although 13 people were injured by the hydrogen explosions, however, more than 40 hospitalized patients died after they were rushed away from the evacuation zone.

Reflections

There are questions that could apply across the full spectrum of risk management. This case could be viewed from the lens of emergency response, disaster recovery, internal controls, planning and loss prevention, risk communication and reporting, strategic risk assessment, ethics, and—possibly—there is a cultural dimension (both organizational and social). Here the recommendation is to consider the following:

• Who were the individuals responsible for this disaster? What specifically was the nature of that "responsibility"? Think about this in terms of both the pre-disaster and post-disaster context.
• Both a technical and leadership perspective might be employed to consider the following questions. Could the disaster have been avoided altogether? What concrete steps might have been taken to avoid such an event?
• Do we see signs of cognitive biases among executive decision-makers and public policy-makers? What are the ethical leadership aspects in this case? Do we see signs of conscious negligence to advance self-interest or are we dealing with subconscious cultural artifacts?

Read more about it

American Nuclear Society (2012). FUKUSHIMA DAIICHI: ANS Committee Report, The American Nuclear Society Special Committee on Fukushima. https://hps.org/documents/ANSFukushimaReport.pdf

Investigation Committee on the Accident at Fukushima Nuclear Power Stations of Tokyo Electric Power Company (2012). *Final Report on the Accident at Fukushima Nuclear Power Stations of Tokyo Electric Power Company.* https://www.cas.go.jp/jp/seisaku/icanps/eng/final-report.html

The Fukushima Nuclear Accident Independent Investigation Commission (NAIIC) (2012). Official Report, *Executive Summary.* https://reliefweb.int/sites/reliefweb.int/files/resources/NAIIC_report_lo_res2.pdf

Tokyo Electric Power Company (2012). Fukushima Nuclear Accident Analysis Report. https://www.tepco.co.jp/en/press/corp-com/release/betu12_e/images/120620e0104.pdf

Case 5.2: Vestas Wind Systems A/S: Ethical aspects of enterprise risk management

Case overview

Vestas designs, manufactures, installs, and services wind turbines around the world and considers itself the choice global partner on sustainable energy solutions. The global wind turbine industry is, yes, turbulent and has at times faced abrupt changes calling for diligent actions to deal with uncertain business conditions.

When the Vestas Group fell on difficult times in the aftermath of the global financial crisis 2007–2008, where the demand for windmills was negatively affected by the generally bleak market outlook, the situation became particularly harsh for firms producing these types of long-term investment goods. The situation was aggravated further by internal operating challenges, characterized by recurring project delays and mounting quality issues. These adverse developments led to dwindling investor confidence, resulting in a dip in the Vestas shares with a stock price almost halved in value over the five-year period 2008–2012 relative to its all-time high in 2007. If challenges were not sufficiently vexing, an internal scandal emerged during this time that cast a critical light on the leadership and—as it turned out—risk management within Vestas.

This case is filled with a number of issues that resonate with Chapter Five and indeed with the book in its entirety. Internally, questions arise regarding leadership, of course, but also behavioral problems, assessment of strategic risks, and perceptions of risk and uncertainty. Externally, the particularities of the alternative energy sector led to specific challenges for strategy and the ability to monitor emerging threats and opportunities.

A historical review

The roots of the Vestas' name date to 1898 when Hand Smith Hansen bought a blacksmith shop in the small town of Lem, close to the Danish west coast in Southern Jutland. His son Peder Hansen formally incorporated the business in 1945 under the name of Vestjysk Stålteknik A/S to produce household appliances and subsequently agricultural equipment, intercoolers, and hydraulic cranes for industrial use. Pronouncing the full name of Vestjysk Stålteknik can be a bit demanding (even in Danish) and therefore the short form, "Vestas," became the preferred name in public use.

The company entered the wind turbine business in 1979—focusing solely on this market from 1989 onwards to eventually becoming a global market leader for onshore turbines. By 2012, Vestas had installed more than 48,000 wind turbines in over 70 countries around the world with production facilities in more than 12 countries including Spain, the United States, and China. In 2015, the company employed around 19,000 people with a global presence. The Vestas stock became listed on the Copenhagen Stock Exchange (NASDAQ Copenhagen) in 1998 and is included in the benchmark OMXC20 stock index.

An accelerating event in Vestas' growth was its merger with another Danish wind turbine manufacturer, NEG Micon, in 2005. At that point, Vestas became the world's largest wind turbine manufacturer under the name of Vestas Wind Systems; headquartered in Randers, Northern Jutland. The company suffered from slumping sales in 2005, posting operating losses but partly recovered in 2006 due to the merger. However, this was followed by a drop in global market share from 28% to 14% by 2009, which was the result of the 2008 financial crisis, but also due to tough competition from major companies like Siemens (Germany), General Electric (USA), Goldwind (China), and Enercon (Germany) among other players.

Between 2009 and 2016, a number of significant top-line events transpired; all warranting a brief mention.

- Vestas' US headquarters had relocated from Palm Springs, California, to Portland, Oregon, in 2002, signaling ambitious expansion plans in North America, which were halted due to difficult economic conditions after 2008.
- Manufacturing operations on the Isle of Wight in England were closed in 2010 as were production activities in Denmark and Sweden due to lower demand in Europe. In contrast, workers were again hired in China, the United States, and Spain due to faster growth in these markets.
- In 2011, the corporate headquarters was moved to Aarhus in Eastern Jutland (the second-largest city in Denmark with a major university) to obtain better facilities and attract skilled staff.
- An increase in competition further strained the economic performance of Vestas and the company posted losses for the period 2011–2013. However, after major restructuring and cost-cutting efforts with employee layoffs, the company returned to a global growth strategy in 2014 of focusing on quality products, operational excellence, and value-adding services.
- The restructuring and turnaround occurred after the Vestas board appointed Anders Runevad (a Swedish citizen with international experience from L. M. Ericsson) as its new CEO in September 2013 to replace Ditlev Engel who had led the company since 2005. Runevad's appointment was marked by an official statement from the Chairman, Bert Nordberg:

  > "Following the recent measures taken, it is now the appropriate time to make this change. The company is now entering a new phase, where we want to realize our growth potential, and I am confident that Mr. Runevad has the right experience to lead the company going forward. The restructuring program has resulted in a more competitive company and we thank Mr. Engel for his leadership over the past eight years" (WindPower Monthly, 2015).

- Vestas added more jobs to the North American operations in 2014–2015 by then counting for almost half the global production.
- Vestas received its largest order ever for the Fosen wind farm project in Norway in 2016 and established manufacturing facilities in India to employ more than 2,500 people. Vestas was seventh on the Clean200 list in 2016 and is currently expanding its offshore wind parks for sustainable energy solutions in collaboration with Mitsubishi Heavy Industries, a leading global manufacturing and engineering firm. The strategic partnership with Mitsubishi reflects a long-term move to expand the offshore wind energy business with the aim of being a leading global player in the industry.

This abbreviated timeline is intriguing in that it appears that Vestas has weathered the storm and emerged in 2016 as having rebounded positively. All true, but the underlying details of this timeline are of particular relevance to this chapter.

Strategic exposures

The global business environment in the alternative energy sector has been rather volatile over the past decades marked by dramatic fluctuations in demand partially influenced by changes in regulatory requirements and economic incentives. Additionally, the global wind energy sector has become highly competitive with large-scale participants in the US market, technology-driven European players, and several cost-efficient entrants in China and India.

In spite of the aforementioned sector volatility and increased competition, the overall industry dynamic has been toward greater interest in, and demand for, renewable energy solutions—with wind turbine technology seen as particularly attractive. Additionally, energy providers (the primary customers for Vestas) have been keen to find ways to reduce costs and prices. Wind farm development has been one particular solution. The development of wind farms has been a means of reducing the installation prices to improve the profitability of wind as a self-sustaining energy source. While this solution has increased demand, it has put high pressures on the turbine manufacturers to reduce costs in order to improve affordability. Additionally, to expand its leading position in wind energy, Vestas also has chosen to focus on other wind energy solutions that create value for the owners of wind power plants and operators of the electricity systems. The expectation is that this move will lever the research capacity and operating experience to deliver reliable and cost-effective wind energy platforms with hybrid solutions that combine wind, storage, and other generation sources in co-developed solutions with advanced grid integration and impeccable cyber-security features.

Enterprise risk management

In 2005, the responsibility for risk management and internal controls rested with the Board of Directors in the Vestas Group but it ultimately rested with the Executive Committee (EC). The EC was constituted by the two-person top management team consisting of Ditlev Engel, President and CEO, and Henrik Nørremark, Deputy CEO, Chief Operating Officer (COO), and acting Chief Financial Officer (CFO). The company officially emphasized adherence to good risk management practices with strong internal controls to minimize international operational errors, ultimately moving to install effective enterprise risk management (ERM) practices throughout the organization. The risk management processes identified, assessed, and addressed major existing (and emergent) risks to reduce potential adverse financial impacts. The ERM processes were integrated across all domestic and overseas operating business units adopting a standardized approach to manage Group risks, which—according to the firm—had provided the basis for significant reductions in commercial insurance premiums.

The integrated risk management function was performed by a central office located in Copenhagen close to the airport in Kastrup and headed by a Group Risk Manager. The office was formally part of the Finance Department and reported to the Group CFO, Henrik Nørremark. Hence, the finance function was instrumental in forming the risk management procedures to ensure the systematic identification and handling of all relevant risks. The Board of Directors and the EC would—as explicitly stated by the company—assess the potential for risks related to fraud in the international organization twice annually. The risk management processes and internal controls were officially imposed to ensure fulfillment of the company's strategic objectives and compliance with corporate policies and procedures. This presented the outside world with a structured ERM approach to identify, assess, and monitor major risks supported by a dedicated risk management function.

Business developments

As referenced previously, the CEO, Ditlev Engel, was appointed to lead the Vestas Group in 2005 at a time when the company was challenged by unsatisfactory quality components from external suppliers and an international supply chain that was stretched by the global reach of corporate activities. Ditlev Engel addressed this successfully by investing heavily to internationalize the production facilities and the supportive value chain forging ahead to win global market share. Consequently, the business expanded, profits soared, and the stock price went to an all-time peak in 2007, earning Ditlev Engel the title of "Mr. Wind Power."

Given the global structure of Vestas, Engel emphasized improvements to the operational performance, minimizing the potential for disruptions in production and delivery while engaging in collaborative arrangements with suppliers and product development efforts incorporating customers, sales, and production units to reduce lead-time and achieve lower costs. However, the global financial crisis of 2008 reversed the international demand for wind-generating hardware. Customers were unable to secure funding to invest in long-term energy infrastructure projects and Vestas' order book began to shrink rapidly. The global expansion strategy had negative effects on financial performance and the stock price nearly halved between 2008 and 2011.

Executive biases

As Lehman Brothers went under and the global economy tumbled in late 2008, severe repercussions for most industries were felt as demand conditions deteriorated dramatically. In this situation, the continued investments in global production created overcapacity and reduced net cash flows, making the company dependent on external financing. However, Ditlev Engel continued to follow the initial strategic plan laid out in 2005 despite the dramatic changes in the global business outlook after the financial crisis. Even with clear signs in 2010 that this strategic path could have serious consequences for the financial standing of the firm, he adhered to the original plan. Why he retained this strategy in these circumstances has never been explained. This is a curiosity as, with hindsight, it seems obvious that the dramatic and extremely negative developments in the global economy would require major adjustments.

The observed phenomenon of sticking to a prior successful strategy may be ascribed to the difficulty of dealing with uncertain conditions that defeat simple linear projections from the past into the future. However, a more plausible explanation may be that the determined adherence to the preset strategic path was an effect of executive over-confidence or hubris created by the previous successes. The executive's views might be reinforced by adherence to ERM with an explicitly stated purpose of ensuring that the set strategic targets and objectives are achieved thereby—possibly—discounting the urgency to change course. This could reflect what cognitive psychology refers to as a *prior hypothesis bias* or *confirmation bias*, where an executive decision-maker overestimates the importance of information that confirms her/his prior beliefs and subconsciously discards contradictory or non-confirmatory information.

Regardless of motives, no adaptive changes were made, and the financial performance continued to deteriorate. Ditlev Engel was awarded stock options as part of the executive pay package, but the options were deeply out-of-the-money. Whatever the motive, this decision, or lack of a decision, seems to imply what is called *escalating commitment bias*, often observed among traders in financial markets where an individual dealer will continue to hold, and even escalate a position based on a strong personal belief or interest in a market reversal, even when the market continues to move against this outcome.

(Un-)ethical behaviors

With the dire outlook at the time in 2011, a concerned Board of Directors attempted to remove Ditlev Engel as CEO. However, for reasons that have never been publicly revealed, the board did not succeed. And yet, this failure triggered an unusual chain of events. The CFO, Henrik Nørremark, was accused of defrauding Vestas for some US$20 million linked to transactions with an Indian business partner. In response, the board dismissed Nørremark in February 2012 after eight years as CFO. With his firing, the Group Risk Manager was discharged as well and the ERM ceased to function as responsible risk leaders and were now gone. Noting the semi-annual board and EC process to monitor potentially fraudulent acts in the Vestas organization, this turn of events seems rather precarious.

It subsequently was revealed that the CEO, Ditlev Engel, and the board believed the Indian business deals had been transacted without due authorization and without their knowledge, and this led to Ditlev Engel recommending that the Board of Directors fire Nørremark. However, this recommendation appears to have served as a distraction to buy Ditlev Engel additional time. He was not officially dismissed by the board until August 2013—at which time he received a separation compensation of two years' salary. Interestingly, Nørremark was never convicted or declared guilty of having committed any wrongdoing and his case has since been withdrawn. In addition, Henrik Nørremark was awarded compensation of around US$7 million in 2017 as the outcome of a private, undisclosed settlement—apparently as compensation for the undue firing.

Reflections

This story could be examined in numerous ways. But—to begin—it is the ERM dimension that first attracts attention. The implementation of a formal ERM framework was presented in all the right ways although some intriguing executive and governance maneuvers made the framework unable to save the company against the biggest strategic risks—which came to include poor judgment and dubious behaviors at the highest levels of the organization. The exposure to a doomed strategic course heading toward disaster continued without anyone being able to challenge the direction, including the risk management function itself, which was sacrificed by the CEO and the board.

The key elements for reflection here include 1) the fact that Ditlev Engel effectively managed strategic risks early in his tenure, but 2) when market conditions worsened after 2008, his determination to maintain that strategy led to serious financial problems. If this were merely an example of the common saying "when you find yourself in a hole, stop digging," this would still be a serious risk management story. Inflexibility in understanding dynamic business conditions and making changes accordingly is serious mismanagement of strategic risk. When the more nefarious aspects of the story are added, matters of illegality and immorality become prominent. Interestingly, since 2013, ERM has been reinstated and a new, highly regarded Group Risk Manager has been appointed. Nevertheless, at least three observations from this case merit discussion.

- It seems apparent that ERM was not picking up on key strategic risks at any point in the story. An obvious question would be to ask, should the ERM process have detected the deterioration of market conditions and adverse economic developments in 2008? But perhaps the broader question attaches to the problem of achieving "tone at the top" regarding a commitment to and understanding of risk management. How does a risk manager/leader get the appropriate level of buy-in and commitment?
- The Board has a critical governance role when it comes to risk management. They seem to be largely missing-in-action in this story (except in their reaction to the discovery of problems). What should be expected of a board in terms of assuring that risk management is meeting its expectations?
- There is an element of "who is watching the watchers?" in this story. Part of this question is related to risk governance, but more broadly it seems that an ethics governance (a term serving only a rhetorical purpose here) was missing. Indeed, it may be as big a strategic issue as any of the legal or financial dimensions of this case. How should managing ethical risks fit into an overall risk management function?

Read more about it

WindPower Monthly (2015). Ten of the biggest and the best manufacturers. https://windpowermon thly.com/article/1352888/ten-biggest-best-manufacturers. Accessed on 01-15-2017.

From press release. https://www.navingocareer.com/vestas-appoints-anders-runevad-as-group-presi dent-ceo/. Accessed on August 23–08-2013.

Vestas and Mitsubishi Heavy Industries strengthen partnership in sustainable energy. https://mhivest asoffshore.com/vestas-and-mitsubishi-heavy-industries-strengthen-partnership-in-sustainable-ene rgy/. Accessed on 28-12-2020.

See, for example, Schwenk, C. R. (1984). Cognitive simplification processes in strategic decision-making. *Strategic Management Journal*, 5(2), 111–128.

Case 5.3: Porsche: Can an epic family feud become a strategic risk?

Case overview

Hollywood could hardly have scripted this. High dramatic encounters involving two opponents related by complicated family ties, gigantic egos colliding, investment banking virtuosity, and, of course, winners and losers. It is a tale of one of the world's most profitable firms driven by ambitious executives and board members. And it involves two business titans; Porsche and Volkswagen (VW), premier global brand names with deep roots in the German automotive industry.

By 2005, Wendelin Wiedeking had very successfully headed Porsche as its CEO for more than a decade, with Holger Härter serving as CFO for most of Wiedeking's tenure. Risk management at Porsche was handled by the treasury department (shaped by Holger Härter) and was particularly engaged in financial hedging on the dollar revenues from the important US market. This financial risk management effort was viewed as a significant contributor to company profitability. It seemed to be smooth sailing for Porsche.

A brief history

Ferdinand Porsche founded Porsche in 1931 with Adolf Rosenberger and Anton Piëch, establishing an office in Stuttgart. The first car "for the people" ordered by the German government resulted in the Volkswagen Beetle in 1939—a forerunner to the Porsche. During the war, the company produced a military version of the Beetle. After the war, Ferdinand lost the Chairmanship of VW. His son, Ferdinand Ernst (Ferry) Porsche, then built what he saw as his own car, designed as he wanted it (this was the Porsche 356) and it was produced by Porsche in Stuttgart in 1950. The Porsche design featured an air-cooled rear-engine—like the Beetle. Fourteen years later in 1964, the company launched a new model, Porsche 911, with a six-cylinder boxer engine designed by Ferdinand Alexander Porsche (Ferry's oldest son). In a side story, Ferdinand Alexander subsequently founded his own company, Porsche Design, known for exclusive sunglasses, watches, and other luxury items.

The company changed its legal form to Aktiengesellschaft (AG)—a public limited company—to accommodate continued growth. This move introduced an "outside" Executive Board without members of the Porsche family, but with a Supervisory Board dominated by the family. As a consequence, both Ferdinand Alexander Porsche and Ferdinand Piëch had to leave the executive ranks.

Louise Piëch was the daughter of Ferdinand Porsche and sister of Ferry. She married Anton Piëch and their son Ferdinand Piëch (Ferry's nephew) ultimately became Chairman of the VW Supervisory Board. Ferdinand Piëch remained the second-largest individual shareholder in Porsche, holding 12.8% of the voting shares whereas his cousin Ferdinand Alexander Porsche held 13.6% of the votes. Both were members of the supervisory board. A key development in this story occurred in 1993 when Wendelin Wiedeking became the CEO of Porsche. He was rapidly recognized as responsible for an effective transformation of business operations and the creation of a very efficient and highly profitable automotive company. Holger Härter joined Porsche as the CFO in 1996—his early accomplishments included a reorganization of company finances.

Enterprise risk management

According to the company annual reports, Porsche proclaimed it had adopted sound risk management principles with clear segregation between functions and prudent use of financial instruments with approved counterparts and set exposure limits. The corporate risks were assessed in the annual planning process and exposures were monitored in the management reporting. As far as possible, the operating exposures were handled through restructurings in a flexible production network and when this proved insufficient, the company engaged in derivative instruments exclusively for financial risk management purposes.

The annual reports classified the risks. *Default risk* was managed through collateral, assessment of credit ratings, and analyzing the financial records of counterparts. *Liquidity risk* by controls on net cash flows from operations, securitizing receivables, a buffer of short-term liquid assets, and standby credit lines. *Market risk* used Value-at-Risk (VaR) calculations to assess the corporate exposure. There were indications from the reports of open communications between the supervisory board and the executive office with the

Porsche and Piëch families holding the voting power in a reassuring (to them) tight ownership with strong governance oversight.

The key players

VW is a European giant in the car manufacturing business and despite some challenges in 2005 the company was able to recover and was among the best performers after the economic crisis of 2007–2008. VW is different from Porsche—Goliath versus David. It is not a typical company; it is protected by a VW law that limits the voting right of individual investors to 20%, with the state of Lower Saxony holding a 20% stake alongside mandated veto power. On top of this, the Porsche and Piëch families owned 100% of the voting and 50% of the non-voting shares.

As noted, after becoming CEO of Porsche, Wendelin Wiedeking revolutionized the company, introducing new lean techniques. While producing results, he was not particularly known for a soft touch in terms of personal relations with staff and colleagues. Further, an early curiosity: he increasingly identified himself with Porsche and spoke about the company using the first person.

Holger Härter, Porsche's CFO, was considered a genius in the use of derivatives—praised in a 48-page Goldman Sachs report describing his hedging strategy. Porsche never suffered from the sliding US dollar despite the importance of the US market. This made Wendelin Wiedeking claim in 2003 that "my CFO can make money even when we're not selling cars."

Wolfgang Porsche, the youngest son of Ferdinand Alexander Porsche, became the family spokesperson to chair the Porsche supervisory board in 2007 and joined the VW supervisory board in 2008. He did not seem to nurture personal ambitions and remained somewhat in the shadows of his cousin, Ferdinand Piëch.

A slow beginning

In September 2005, Porsche bought 5% ownership of VW plus an option to expand to 18%. VW had profit margins under 5% dropping below 2% from 2003 onward and the ROCE at 14.2% in 2000 dropped to 3.6% by 2005. Analysts began questioning the company strategy with a diverse product range from luxury to low-end cars. The market value of VW was €16.5 billion in 2005, but Audi was valued at around €10 billion, Europcar (car hire) and Gedas (information technology) at €1.5 billion each, and VW Financial Services alone produced €1 billion pre-tax profits a year. A hostile takeover could arguably pay handsomely, and it might no longer be impossible as the European Court of Justice challenged the VW law.

This was a concern for Porsche as it relied on VW for price-competitive supplies, sourcing 30% of components from VW. Furthermore, VW's expansion into luxury brands like Audi, Bentley, and Lamborghini could become a threat to the recognition of the Porsche brand. Therefore, Porsche endeavored to become more involved with VW to restore financial health and coordinate brand strategies. Wendelin Wiedeking was aware that VW was very important for Porsche; so, when Porsche took the first steps in acquiring VW shares, the financial analysts interpreted the move as a defensive strategy and the market reacted favorably.

Porsche kept a low profile for almost two years only slowly increasing its stake in VW to ownership of 23% by April 2006, announcing later in the year its intention to acquire a stake just below 30% to avoid a mandatory tender offer. However, on March 26, 2007, Porsche surpassed the 30% threshold and launched a mandatory tender offer at €100.92 per share somewhat below the VW stock price. To back the offer, Porsche arranged the second biggest ever European loan facility in a €35 billion installment with banks eager to commit. Having secured more than 30% of VW, Porsche had defended VW from hostile raiders.

During the fiscal year 2006/2007, Porsche had record profits of €5.7 billion of which €3.6 billion were gains from VW stock options. By late 2007, Porsche had a firm grip on VW, but they had no intention of resting. It has been argued that management attempted a complete takeover of VW encouraged by the huge gains on the option positions on VW stock. Concealing a full takeover avoided a sudden rise in VW shares and made it possible to buy stock options at low premiums. Hence, some observers have argued that executive management acted without involving the supervisory board, although this seems particularly tricky in a tight family controlled company structure.

The European court declared the VW law illegal in October 2007 because it imposed restrictions on the free movement of capital. In the meantime, then-Prime Minister of Lower Saxony, Christian Wulff, had convinced Angela Merkel to redesign the VW law, leaving the state veto power untouched, it seems with the tacit approval of Ferdinand Piëch. Unaware of the informal talks between Wulff and Merkel, Wendelin Wiedeking then disclosed publicly in March 2008 that Porsche wanted to raise its stake in VW to 50% by year-end.

This announcement made various hedge funds take short positions on VW shares thinking that VW stock would not rise any further, based on the assumption that VW's share price immediately would drop to a value more in line with its industry peers once the takeover was completed. The hedge funds went long on Porsche stocks at the same time to pursue a market-neutral strategy. However, the unforeseeable occurred. Lehman Brothers declared bankruptcy on September 15, 2008. Since Lehman Brothers was heavily involved in the short trading, the collapse of the bank forced the hedge funds to dismantle their long-short strategies. They were forced to buy back the VW shares and stock price increased by €100 during the first two weeks of October. On October 26, Porsche announced that it owned 42.6% of VW and had options on another 31.5%.

During the fiscal year 2007/2008, Porsche made €8.6 billion profit before tax with revenues of €7.5 billion, reporting a gain of €19.3 billion in the income statement as a "stock price hedge," which was partly balanced by "other operating expenses" of €12 billion. Hence, only 12% of Porsche's profits came from car manufacturing—the core business—the remaining 88% of profits derived from Holger Härter's stock hedging strategy.

However, the financial resources Porsche spent to establish the stock option positions were substantial, with major drawdowns on loan facilities, which affected the capital structure of the company. In 2007, Porsche was financed 41% by debt which grew to 49% in 2008, substantially increasing the financial leverage. A maturity analysis of Porsche's financial liabilities suggested that 75% of the debt (€13 billion) was due within one year, leaving the company with a net liquidity position of minus €3 billion.

The aftermath

In January 2009, Porsche disclosed that it owned 50.76% of VW and would reach 75% by the end of the year, but Porsche had no resources left to execute the plan—the company ran out of money (and luck). On March 24, Porsche was able to refinance its debt only by the skin of its teeth using VW shares as collateral and committing to repay €3.3 billion within six months. Within a week, Porsche needed another €2.5 billion in cash to reach the 75% threshold, but the money was not available. On May 6, 2009, Porsche announced its intention to drop the takeover of VW and it was agreed to merge the two companies. Soon after, Ferdinand Piëch made clear that he and VW were in the driving seat. Porsche's glorious plan had fallen apart.

Wendelin Wiedeking made final desperate attempts to save the situation by asking the Qatar fund to provide the needed cash, but Qatar wanted to await the situation between the two groups. Hence, Wendelin Wiedeking and Holger Härter stepped down from their positions at Porsche with Piëch leaving them no place in the new group.

To reduce the debt load, VW bought 42% of Porsche's car business for €3.3 billion and Porsche became the tenth brand in the VW group. The Qatar fund bought 10% of Porsche plus some options in VW with the new VW group owned 50% by the Piëch and Porsche families, 20% by the State of Lower Saxony state, and another 20% held by the Qatar fund.

Explaining the story

Porsche had been the most profitable carmaker for years. But the company almost went bust—not because the products were of poor quality, and not because the market suddenly changed tastes—but because the company assumed an excessive level of risk to fulfill the ambitions of the executive management.

This suggests a flaw in the decision-making that leads executives to overlook significant relevant risks and exposures. However, the annual report notes that the main risks are associated with the equity investments in Volkswagen and Porsche. This is also reflected in VaR calculation of €1.8 billion, which compared with annual profits of around €1 billion from the core business, is probably too much. So, there was no seeming lack of transparency, or was there?

We should remember that risk management frameworks and management reports are enablers whereas the people who read them must apply qualitative judgments to interpret them. Here, the decision-makers seemed to have strong biases being victims of mental traps, where the human brain can distort what is seen, and obscure the decisions of otherwise capable people. Wendelin Wiedeking and Holger Härter were both successful executives—considered the best in class.

They might have succumbed to "emotional tagging" where the brain stores emotions associated with prior events and recalls them when similar situations seem to occur. Wendelin Wiedeking spoke about Porsche using the first person, a clear symptom that he saw himself as more than just a CEO—identifying himself with the company—what was good for him, was good for Porsche. Wolfgang Porsche had been in the shadow of Ferdinand Piëch until Wiedeking and Härter proposed the takeover. He might have been grateful for being elevated to fame and he defended his CEO and CFO. They also shared similar views on VW as a company without prestige and maybe they disliked Piëch—powerful shared emotions.

Holger Härter as the architect behind the takeover plan was generally considered a genius with derivatives. So, when Wiedeking discussed the need to secure VW, Härter probably quickly thought of an ingenious plan with complex derivatives and options—this is human nature. We tend to propose solutions we are familiar with. It may not be the best solution, but it falls within our knowledge space and competencies creating a bias toward it.

It seems as if the people involved, with their biases and mental traps, created a self-reinforcing set of behaviors—falling into a "confirming evidence trap." If Wiedeking had doubts about what to do, he would probably speak to Holger Härter, whom he—and others—considered the ingenious craftsman behind the takeover plan. Conversely, Härter would not provide negative feedback about the evolving situation. There was nobody to challenge their embedded views. This could provide a self-reinforcing system where the three most powerful executives united their common beliefs, where it would have been virtually impossible to change their views, even with the best risk governance system.

Leadership theory refers to this situation as shared leadership, which occurs when top executives, say a Chairman, CEO, and CFO, develop tight linkages between them. This may foster a good collaboration but also complicity. The advantage of shared leadership is the ability to pool more relevant knowledge together, but it also makes it difficult, maybe impossible, to move in a different direction than the one already chosen.

Reflections

The case itself spells out a number of theories to explain the underlying causes for the events described. Here, perhaps more so than in the book's other cases, we come close to what might be called aberrant or destructive behavior. Certainly, there were immensely strong and confident personalities at work. Three discussion points are proposed here.

- Beyond those mentioned in the case, what are some of the psychological biases that can be discerned from the conscious or unconscious managerial actions in this case story?
- This story highlights an aspect of risk management that receives only limited treatment. Risk management is assumed to have an effect on an organization's risk profile, and the basic assumption is that risk management results are beneficial to a firm. Employees who are given safety training have fewer accidents. However, risk management measures—unintentionally—can change behavior for the worse. Reflecting on the CFO's approach to financial risk management, do we see adverse leadership behaviors arising from good ERM-based risk management practices? How does an organization deal with this?
- While the story centers on personalities, the governance structure of Porsche and VW serves as an interesting meditation on what constitutes effective governance. What are the fundamental structural concerns that impede good governance? Is there an important role for a risk-aware culture in the case and how should that be imposed on the organization? And finally, did the risk governance and financial market regulations perform as we would expect regarding managing executive and market behaviors?

Read more about it

Porsche Annual Report 2007/2008.
VW deal shows Porsche CFO worth his weight in gold. *Reuters*, November 3, 2008.
Cash and short-term liquid assets minus short-term payables and financial debt (information extracted from the notes of the annual report 2007/2008).
Hammond, J., Keeney, R. and Raiffa, H. (2006). The hidden traps in decision making. *Harvard Business Review*, 83(1), 3–9.

Jackson, B. and Parry, K. (2008). *A Very Short, Fairly Interesting and Reasonably Cheap Book about Studying Leadership*. Sage Publications, London, UK.

Notes

1 Andersen, T. J. and Young, P.C. (2020). *Strategic Risk Leadership: Engaging a World of Risk, Uncertainty, and the Unknown*. Routledge, Abingdon, UK.

2 Thaler, Richard H. (2016). Behavioral economics: Past, present, and future. *American Economic Review*, 106(7), 1577–1600. [This article provides a good overview of the evolution of behavioral economics.]

3 Shefrin, H. and Statman, M. (2003). The contributions of Daniel Kahneman and Amos Tversky. *Journal of Behavioral Finance*, 4(2), 54–58. [This article provides a helpful understanding of the breadth and depth of Kahneman and Tversky's impact. It is additionally noted that Kahneman won the Nobel Prize in Economics despite not being an economist—which reinforces the idea of the connectivity between psychology and economics.]

4 Minkov, M. and Hofstede, G. (2011). The evolution of Hofstede's doctrine. *Cross Cultural Management: An International Journal*, 18(1), 10–20. [This article is a useful reference to a great deal of Hofstede's work, which is not free from controversy but still presents a widely known point of entry into the comparative culture literature.]

5 Alvesson, M. (2013). *Understanding Organizational Culture*. Sage Publications, London, UK. [This book offers a good introductory overview of the subject of culture in organizational settings.]

6 Houmanfar, R. A., Alavosius, M. P., Morford, Z. H., Herbst, S. A. and Reimer, D. (2015). Functions of organizational leaders in cultural change: Financial and social well-being. *Journal of Organizational Behavior Management*, 35(1–2), 4–27. [While there are many older and well-regarded articles on leadership and organizational culture, this is a more recent contribution that has additional relevance here in its focus on effecting cultural change.]

7 Uhl-Bien, M., Riggio, R. E., Lowe, K. B. and Carsten, M. K. (2014). Followership theory: A review and research agenda. *The Leadership Quarterly*, 25, 83–104. [This article provides a good summary of work done on followership.]

8 Kellerman, B. (2008). *Followership: How Followers Are Creating Change and Changing Leaders*. Harvard Business School Press, Boston, MA.

9 Kelly, R. E. (2008). Rethinking followership. In Riggio, R. E., Chaleff, I. and Lipman-Blumen, J. (Eds.), *The Art of Followership: How Great Followers Create Great Leaders and Organizations* (pp. 5–16). Jossey-Bass, San Francisco, CA.

10 Uhl-Bien, M., Riggio, R. E., Lowe, K. B. and Carsten, M. K. (2014). Followership theory: A review and research agenda. *The Leadership Quarterly*, 25, 83–104.

11 Ibid.

12 Kellerman, B. (2008). *Followership: How Followers Are Creating Change and Changing Leaders*. Harvard Business School Press, Boston, MA.

13 Padilla, A. Hogan, R. and Kaiser. R. B. (2007). The toxic triangle: Destructive leaders, susceptible followers, and conducive environments. *The Leadership Quarterly*, 18, 176–194.

14 Petit, V. and Bollaert, H. (2012). Flying too close to the sun? Hubris among CEOs and how to prevent it. *Journal of Business Ethics*, 108, 265–283.

15 Frank, R. H. (2016). *Success and Luck: Good Fortune and the Myth of Meritocracy*. Princeton University Press, Princeton, NJ. [Although Frank is a scholar, this is more of a professional book—but highly readable, personal, and with many insights.]

16 Ibid.

17 Klayman, J., Soll, J. B., Gonzalez-Vallejo, C. and Barlas, S. (1999). Overconfidence: It depends on how, what, and whom you ask. *Organizational Behavior and Human Decision Processes*, 79, 216–247.

18 Kets de Vries, M. (2004). Organizations on the couch: A clinical perspective on organizational dynamics. *European Management Journal*, 22(2), 183–200.

19 See, for example, Hayward, M. and Hambrick, D. C. (1997). Explaining the premiums paid for large acquisitions: Evidence of CEO hubris. *Administrative Science Quarterly*, 42(1), 103–127.

20 Hiller, N. J. and Hambrick, D. C. (2005). Conceptualizing executive hubris: The role of (hyper-) core self-evaluations in strategic decision-making. *Strategic Management Journal*, 26, 297–319.

21 Tang, Y., Qian, C., Chen, G. and Shen, R. (2015). How CEO hubris affects corporate social (ir) responsibility. *Strategic Management Journal*, 36, 1338–1357.

22 Brennan, N. M. and Conroy, J. P. (2013). Executive hubris: The case of a bank CEO. *Accounting, Auditing & Accountability Journal*, 26(2), 172–195.

23 Owen, D. and Davidson, J. (2009). Hubris syndrome: An acquired personality disorder? A study of US Presidents and UK Prime Ministers over the last 100 years. *Brain*, 132(5), 1396–1406.

24 Padilla, A., Hogan, R. and Kaiser. R. B. (2007). The toxic triangle: Destructive leaders, susceptible followers, and conducive environments. *The Leadership Quarterly*, 18, 176–194.

25 Einarsen, S., Aasland, M. S. and Skogstad, A. (2007). Destructive leadership behaviour: A definition and conceptual model. *Leadership Quarterly*, 18, 207–216.

26 Torfing, J. and Ansell, C. (2017). Strengthening political leadership and policy innovation through the expansion of collaborative forms of governance. *Public Management Review*, 19(1), 37–54. [This is one of a number of possible references selected because it covers governance and leadership in a public sector setting and introduces the subject of collaborative governance.]

27 Linde, C. (2009). *Working the Past: Narrative and Institutional Memory*. Oxford University Press, Oxford, UK. [This book covers the subject of institutional memory but includes several case studies illustrating key aspects.]

28 Campbell, P. R. (1998). The new history: The *Annales* School of History and Modern Historiography. In Lamont, W. (Ed.), *Historians and Historical Controversy*, UCL Press, London, UK. [There are many, many books to choose for reference on historiography, but this is probably a good starting point that offers a substantive treatment of the subject.]

29 Ibid.

30 Suddaby, R., Coraiola, D., Harvey, C. and Foster, W. (2019). History and the micro-foundations of dynamic capabilities. *Strategic Management Journal*, 41, 530–556. [This article provides an interesting treatment of history as an organizational dynamic capability while also introducing a framework for approaching and using history.]

31 Neustadt, R. and May, E. R. (1986). *Thinking in Time: The Uses of History for Decision Makers* (1st ed.). Free Press, New York. [This is a classic book on the subject of uses of history for leaders and decision-makers.]

32 Ibid.

33 BBC News, Fukushima disaster: Nuclear executives found not guilty, September 19, 2019. https://www.bbc.com/news/world-asia-49750180

6 Collaborative risk leadership

Collaboration

Collaboration is a working practice whereby individuals work together for a common purpose to achieve business benefit. Collaboration enables individuals to work together to achieve a defined and common business purpose.[1]

Everyone understands collaboration in its most basic sense. However, even within the simple definition offered here, finer points emerge. *Common purpose* suggests that there are shared objectives among all parties or potential parties; that the motive to collaborate is elective and not coerced. A *defined … business purpose* at least implies an initial agreement will have been reached and a process is in place for the work that follows.

What, of course, is not suggested in the definition is any indication of how collaboration is enabled and successfully accomplished—and of course, what role a leader might play. On that last point, it may be just possible to imagine collaboration occurring without detectable leadership.[2] For example, some cultures present characteristics that could influence a more cooperative and consensus-based approach, and to do so in such a way that leadership or leaders is/are not easily seen. In such cases, it might be said that the cooperation/consensus cultural orientation itself *is* leadership, as it may shape how collaborative effort is achieved. This is a useful insight to pocket because previous discussions of Leadership for Organizational Adaptation could be said to embody very much that kind of "leaderless leadership"—that is, hundreds of agents interacting within networks, making decisions, and taking actions in response to challenges to the system. Perhaps just (and only) to put a marker down this could be referenced as a form of *Emergent Leadership*.[3] Leadership as *deus ex machina* might also be suggested, although that could be pushing the point too far. Still, it does convey the sense of leadership without an identifiable leader. Having reflected on this possibility, the wider question still remains as to how collaboration is engaged and enacted in complex environmental settings.

Presume here that a somewhat more conventional view of leadership generally holds, and we are able to identify individual parties (people, groups, organizations, communities, even countries must be included) who exhibit leadership characteristics and behaviors where collaboration is considered or agreed upon. What can be said about this? Leadership research certainly touches upon this subject, but other reference points are also available.[4]

DOI: 10.4324/9781003148579-6

The relevance of collaboration

Collaboration is an essential feature in any exploration of risk leadership. The history of risk management, at least in medium to large organizations, can be characterized as a growing and evolving collection of technical risk management functions that were not particularly seen as connected or related until the early 1990s.[5] At that time, intellectual ferment and emerging regulatory and legal requirements led to an endorsement of a more holistic approach to risk management—ultimately formalized as Enterprise Risk Management (ERM).

As this vision came into sharper focus, the key features included:

• A firmly embedded framework for engaging all employees to be risk managers within the scope of their responsibilities
• Risk assessment and reporting processes and information flows that cascaded up, down, and across the organization
• Risk policies such as identification of risk appetites and tolerances established by executives and supported by the board
• An integrated view (a risk portfolio view) of the organization's risk profile, leading to an assumed sense that all risks are connected
• An argument that somehow these features were key contributors to risk management adding value to the organization

Surveys and other analyses subsequently have revealed that full actualization of the ERM vision has been (often) sought but rarely achieved. Nevertheless, one thing has become apparent—the achievement of anything approaching a fully integrated effort to assess and address risk and uncertainty will necessitate *collaboration* as the means by which different silos of risk activities may be broken down to facilitate coordination and integration.[6]

Perhaps an even more powerful influence in the emergence of the collaborative risk management idea is found outside the context of single organizations—the impact of large-scale, some might say, global risks.[7] While it has long been recognized that phenomena such as pandemics, regional political crises, and major disasters (nuclear power station failures, hurricanes, prolonged droughts) present a particular challenge to adopting large-scale coordinated responses, clearly recent developments have intensified awareness of the need for collaboration. For example, the COVID-19 pandemic experience has featured both positive and negative responses as compelling real-time case studies of the abiding problems of scaling up our collective capacity to respond to large-scale phenomena. Even when recognizing that some of these threats are, almost literally, existential there have been notable failures.

Alongside the naturally occurring global risks like pandemics, we find that many of the large-scale risks are created or caused by humans. The vast and complicated interconnected global financial, technological, and transportation systems—for example—present huge global economic contagion threats not dissimilar from transmittable viruses.

In this chapter, the objective is to provide a basis for describing an idea—collaborative risk leadership—but in doing so to seek out connectivity to the wider leadership literature. Additional important insights will be drawn from research in strategic management, modern cognitive science, political science, international relations, and negotiations.

Responsiveness, adaptation, and collective intelligence

A conventional strategy perspective outlines a purposeful adaptation process where executives reconfigure and adapt the organization in view of ongoing changes to achieve above-average returns.[8] This portrays a linear process with periodic diagnostic controls whereas, alternatively, a more realistic process reflects imperfect organizational learning in a path-dependent (partially stochastic) and largely unpredictable environmental context.

Strategic responsiveness is conceived as the ability to assess the environment and mobilize resources in effective responses that allow the organization to adapt and maintain a "good fit" with the changing context.[9] It relates to the concept of *dynamic capabilities* often described as an ability to sense changes, seize opportunities, and reconfigure the organization in rapidly changing environments influenced by managerial interventions.[10] Heterogeneous strategic response capabilities across firms differentiate performance outcomes and result in inverse risk-return relationships where effective responses generate higher average returns with lower variability in returns over time.

A *dynamic adaptive system* can arise from interacting fast and slow information processes where the organization responds in non-linear meta-stable moves.[11] The human brain, groups of people, organizations, and societies constitute fast-slow information processing systems. The exchanges of fast experiential insights from local activities and slow analytical reasoning in central planning can provide the basis for dynamic adaptive processes.[12] An effective adaptive system exploits the entrepreneurial minds of many while using their current insights to update strategic thinking. However, numerous factors may inhibit information processing, creating distortions and suboptimal filtering mechanisms including, potentially, adverse effects associated with executive power and overconfidence. The distributed knowledge in organizations typically remains untapped and together with information distortions, they can explain why only a few organizations are able to adapt and outperform.

Collective intelligence is defined as distributed group intelligence that resides with many individuals connected within a social system that can, or may plausibly, be mobilized in real time through digitalized computer-based interventions.[13] The collective insights can make better predictions and enhance the ability of groups to perform various tasks more effectively.[14] It reflects the collective capacity of people to engage in intellectual cooperation and create better more innovative solutions and outcomes.[15] And it projects collective ideation processes with open sharing of information and ideas to resolve complex issues that drive human ingenuity.[16]

Good, bad, and misguided leadership

Consideration of collaborative approaches to leadership can take further inspiration from the thin, but thoughtful, book by the Italian economic historian Carlo Cipolla presenting his basic thoughts about "human stupidity."[17] His basic laws stipulate that we tend to underestimate the number of stupid individuals, partly because they are hard to identify, but also because the probability of stupidity appears unrelated to specific personal characteristics. This seems to highlight a general observation, that stupidity can emerge when we least expect it—with or without purposeful intent. Difficult to admit, but we may all be disposed—in varying degrees—to this faculty of human behavior.

According to Cipolla, a stupid person is an individual who imposes losses on other people without receiving any personal gains and possibly even incurring a personal loss.

Such a person does not act out of economic self-interest, as economists often assume, s/he is ignorant about potential consequences and is either oblivious or acting maliciously. Cipolla's "technical interlude" may be illustrative, interpreted here in an adapted form given our specific leadership focus (Figure 6.1).

An *intelligent leader* will attempt to act in ways that benefit her-/himself or the organization while producing positive effects for other people. A *helpless leader* is unable to create benefits for her-/himself (or the organization) but may produce positive effects for or on other people. A *bandit leader* benefits her-/himself at the expense of other people, but the *stupid leader* wreaks havoc for all imposing negative effects on her-/himself as well as other people. Cipolla argues that a stupid person is the most dangerous—more dangerous than a bandit—because at least a bandit acts rationally for own gain (which allows for a prediction of the bandit's actions), whereas a stupid person is irrational and lacks conscious awareness. Furthermore, it seems obvious that the more powerful a stupid person—or leader—is the more havoc s/he can create for everyone. And these actions are hard to predict. Additionally, we can put this insight into the context of hubristic leaders discussed earlier. We may be able to discern and explain how hubris arises and exert its influence, but it still constitutes a "stupid" leadership behavior.

The framework is illuminating, though admittedly simplistic. Still, it may be expanded through additional thought and interpretation. For example, the bandit leader may exemplify organizations that willfully pollute to gain a short-term profit (say, by outsourcing production to developing countries with few environmental restrictions and weak institutional settings). They create *negative* economic externalities imposing costs on other stakeholders. However, this also creates long-term liabilities where those adversely affected eventually may be able to seek compensation for damages. Conversely, a seemingly helpless leader may exemplify a firm that invests in *positive* externalities, so while

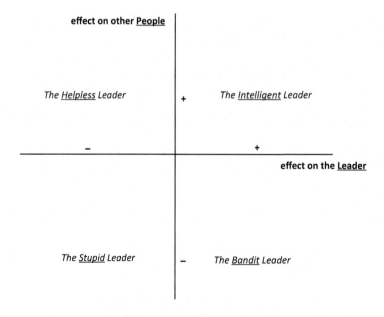

Figure 6.1 Configuring "stupidity" across different leader-follower relationships.

it incurs immediate expenses it may create goodwill that can have longer-term potential collaborative benefits. In other words, there is a time dimension to consider here weighing short-term gains against long-term penalties—and vice versa. Thus, helpless leaders may be intelligent leaders given time, but the opposite is also possible. In any event, however, stupidity has no justification, and yet it likely happens in all organizations to different degrees. This is clearly a major concern for risk management or risk leadership.

Cipolla's insights resonate with the thinking behind good, bad, and misguided leadership introduced by Paul Lawrence.[18] He argues that good (or *intelligent*, as it is) leadership based on a leader-follower relationship of trust and care—where collective as well as individual needs are satisfied—reflects "natural" human behavior as demonstrated through evolution, which enabled humankind to survive and thrive. From that perspective, he also argues that good leadership is, in fact, *moral leadership*. Human beings are arguably motivated by four basic "drivers" stimulated by emotional brain signals: The drives to *acquire, protect, bond,* and *comprehend.*

The first two are drivers for survival—collecting sufficient resources and guarding them. The bonding aspects illustrate that we are a social species that thrives through collaborative acts and actions, while the urge to comprehend is uniquely human, for example, the capacity to interpret the context and project the current into the future and assess potential consequences. Problems arise when future projections are distorted, possibly because they become dominated by hubristic leaders, or fail to be updated by the true experiences encountered by the many doers within and around the organization. And problems can arise when the social contracts break and stupid, or bad, leadership is allowed to prevail and dominate. Organizations depend on cooperation among many individuals, which requires social bonding.

Enactive leadership

A collaborative approach arguably needs a new type of *enactive leadership* where individual leaders, or decision-makers, realize they cannot know everything but must rely on the collective insights from many people within their own organization. This offers a break from conventional views on the leadership role.[19] It adopts the view that human cognition derives from the dynamic interaction between an active organism (a person) and the surroundings where s/he acts and where the changing context is interpreted through updated experiences from the surroundings.[20] Information cannot be collected from a given or predetermined dataset but must be formed by experiences in an evolving system where meaning is generated from ongoing interpretations of the changing environmental context as it evolves.[21]

Understanding, or the human drive for comprehension, is entangled with updated information from physical interactions with the environment as ongoing actions are triggered by changing circumstances and they add new important cognitive components to the perceived context. So, enactive cognition consists of perceptually guided actions and cognitive structures that are formed on the basis of the observed reactive patterns—all of which update current perceptions and, in turn, guide subsequent perceptual actions.

Enactive leadership is foremost an executive recognition that one single individual, no matter how smart, intelligent, or powerful, cannot know everything and is unable to solely understand the complexity of contemporary business environments. Contrast this to an overconfident hubristic CEO. In an organizational setting, this reflects the close connection between forward-looking analytic planning and the responsive actions taken by employees in the operating entities as they fend the daily business that provides new insights. These experiential insights contain important information that can update the ongoing planning considerations including the need for strategic initiatives and adjusted action plans. However, in most organizations, this updating does not really take place.

An enactive leader sees forward-looking planning and objective setting, the daily execution of organizational activities, and the evolving changes in the business environment as a coherent whole, where one seeks to use the many insights of employees—their collective intelligence—to inform ongoing strategic deliberations (we are reminded here of the historian's capacity for synchronic thinking). This breaks with the linear view of strategic objective setting—prevailing thinking behind the ERM frameworks—that assumes we can think through future events and predict the conditions that allow us to implement planned activities and realize the set objectives. However, this will never happen in dynamic complex environments. These contexts require a willingness to experiment and thereby identify what works under uncertain and unpredictable conditions—a form of ongoing trial-and-learning process.

Uncertain and unknowable conditions with potentially extreme effects put demands on the ability to innovate and explore to identify opportunities that enhance the ability to respond and maneuver through the changing risk landscape. Uncertainties tend to encourage adoption of formal control-based approaches in a belief they will secure effective processes that can guarantee planned outcomes. However, this is not a viable approach as most assumptions will fail to materialize and tight controls constrain the flexibility to experiment and search for creative responses. That is, if we prioritize operational savings and the efficiency of existing processes, it most likely happens at the expense of an ability to take innovative initiatives that generate the long-term value potential of the organization.

Human thinking is formed by experiences that can help us understand effects and consequences where the ongoing feedback from the surroundings enriches and updates our comprehension. Thinking helps determine a way forward and the current experiences advance our understanding of evolving developments so we can update the planned course of action. Hence, there must be a balance between rationality at the corporate center and empiricism in the operating periphery in ongoing interactions between central thinking and peripheral sensing. This makes it possible to adapt strategic activities—as we go along—based on current updated experiential insights. So, enactive leadership emphasizes rational analyses but it can be seen as part of a dynamic interaction between conscious forward-looking thinking and (unconscious) experiential processes of responding, acting, and learning from ongoing activities.

Enactive leadership shifts the focus from individual, that is—executive—superiority to a more collaborative approach that promotes an organizational ability to think together and generate viable solutions to complex problems by combining the collective creativity and insights from many stakeholders. We as humans are fundamentally social beings where the biggest organizational and societal advances are generated from joint social efforts. The social brain of a human differs from animals—we assume—by our ability to think together and build on the power of our collective intelligence. This is not a new revelation but is often overlooked as we tend to praise individual leadership traits. However, in increasingly complex surroundings, collective intelligence outperforms individual intelligence in dealing with complex problems that are best resolved through collaborative efforts.

Collaboration and leadership

We turn to other source materials here to try to establish some reasonably stable observations about the Collaborative Leader. While this literature is similar in its general findings to business leadership research, it acknowledges that many of the global risks can only be engaged by multilateral public and public/private involvement. For example, there is a robust literature focused on international relations and negotiations that offers some selected insights. One particular focus is on predicting and explaining who exercises what kind(s) of leadership in different settings of multilateral negotiation; and, of course, tracing the effects of various leadership approaches on outcomes. [22] Scholars have had some positive results in predicting and explaining the "who," whereas efforts to understand the effects and outcomes have been a less fruitful exercise.

For our purposes, we propose two categories of collaborative structures as a means of framing the following discussion. One category is internal to the organization including its adjacent stakeholder agents (suppliers, buyers, lenders). The other category is comprised of structures that are partly, or fully, defined by the presence of public or quasi-public agents alongside private sector agents.

There is a general view that the presence of governmental bodies has a significant effect on the nature of collaboration as well as the leadership tools and strategies employed (and, of course, who may employ them).[23] Broadly speaking, the presence of a governmental body introduces possibilities of leadership by *coercion* or *unilateral action*, and, of course, by *legal fiat*. While versions of these tools may sometimes be employed by powerful private organizations, the main reason for mentioning this here is that there has been significant investigative work done on what enables or permits coercion and unilateral action. The power to coerce or act unilaterally derives from several possible sources: legal/constitutional authority; influence and reputation and willingness and capacity to apply force.[24] So, one issue in understanding "who leads" is the need to clarify the potential standing of the leader. However, as noted, capacity is important. In some situations, the capacity to lead is not commensurate with the standing to lead. For example, the government of a developing nation may have the standing to respond to a natural disaster but may not possess the capacity—means and resources—to do so.

Most of the major global risks present particular difficulties both in standing and in capacity. There are, potentially, a number of leaders with standing on—for example—responses to global climate change. Selection of a leader could further bring to bear the capacity to respond (others falling in line behind the selected leader). The issue, or obstacle, in this case could be—and often is—willingness to lead. Political contentiousness, not surprisingly, is an obvious impediment to a willingness to engage something like climate change. So, here must be added the idea that adjunct to having standing and capacity, a potential leader must also be willing (including political will) to become that leader. The *standing, willingness*, and *capacity* to lead—all three aspects are necessary.

Questions of standing, willingness, and capacity are relevant in any context, so to bring this discussion to an organizational level, consider risk leadership in an organization—particularly the Chief Risk Officer role. As noted elsewhere, CROs often face the challenge of establishing their standing. In most organizational leadership positions, standing is often developed around leadership being *assigned*. This means that standing is inherent in the position, in the job title, and perhaps in the perceptions of that individual's qualifications prior to recruitment for the position.

Most new executive-level individuals recruited from outside an organization can be expected to have work to do to solidify any assigned standing—to become known, demonstrate competence, and develop relationships. This is a common challenge for all potential leaders. So, to argue that CROs are distinctly different in this regard would be misleading. However, the limited research on CROs does suggest that there is something of an obstacle, which is the gap between the perception of a formally assigned standing and the actual standing in practice. In other words, the title CRO conveys executive standing, but the authorizations granted (and to be fair, some aspects of the nature of the work) tend to not quite align with what one might normally expect. The reasons for this are interesting but appear to revolve around how the organization decided to recruit a CRO in the first place.[25] As noted previously, the most common motives are that the organization is required to have a CRO by regulation or law, and/or that the recruitment is prompted by a disastrous event—a crisis situation. Much less commonly recruitment is the result of a considered executive or board decision to meet strategic objectives or creating a more responsive organization. But the common motives are not ideal for putting the wind behind the CRO's sails.[26] Thus, collaborative leadership presents the question of the capability or capacity to lead, of establishing leadership standing (and on what basis), enacting leadership in moving toward a decision, and then acting upon that decision.

Instruments of collaborative leadership

Without question, the most comprehensive effort to address collaborative risk leadership is represented in the work of the International Risk Governance Council (IRGC). Since 2003, the IRGC has set out a framework and an ambitious research agenda for better understanding what it labels *Risk Governance*, which:

> Includes the totality of actors, rules, conventions, processes, and mechanisms concerned with how relevant risk information is collected, analysed and communicated and management decisions are taken. Encompassing the combined risk-relevant decisions and actions of both governmental and private actors, risk governance is of particular importance in, but not restricted to, situations where there is no single authority to take a binding risk management decision but where instead the nature of the risk requires the collaboration and co-ordination between a range of different stakeholders. Risk governance however not only includes a multifaceted, multi-actor risk process but also calls for the consideration of contextual factors such as institutional arrangements (e.g. the regulatory and legal framework that determines the relationship, roles and responsibilities of the actors and co-ordination mechanisms such as markets, incentives or self-imposed norms) and political culture including different perceptions of risk.[27]

The work of the IRGC is admirable, and not only centers its attention on collaboration with respect to risk, uncertainty, and complexity but provides a detailed framework for understanding and employing methods and measures for assessing and addressing important global risks. Further, the initiative on which IRGC rests is an effort to collaborate across fields of study, adopting an integrated approach to understanding the multi-dimensionality of context. It in no way is a criticism of IRGC's ongoing work to note the distinction between this book and the IRGC's efforts, which is to say that we are focused mainly on the individuals operating within such a system or structure, in an effort to understand how they think, act, and lead.[28]

It may be that internal organizational collaboration presents situations where coercion or unilateral actions are employed (or are attempted to be employed), and direct commands from or intervention by the executive may sometimes serve a similar function. Other possibilities exist, obviously. Charismatic leadership is, probably, a self-evident version of collaborative leadership.[29] Charisma has its uses, but a more meaningful concept here might be Instrumental Leadership—a multi-purpose term that broadly refers to skills, knowledge, and abilities at negotiation and influencing other participants. This capability includes intangible elements like charisma, yes, but more commonly derives from standing, intellectual leadership, reputation/authority/power, understanding "the game," specific technical expertise, and—well—other capacities that may pertain in specific cases.[30]

An effort to clarify requisite or relevant capabilities to lead collaboratively would seem to be important for at least two reasons: obviously to identify possible leaders in a given situation, but also to be able to develop collaborative leaders for the future.[31] Considerable work has been done to better understand what this might entail. The University Network for Collaborative Governance (UNCG) has developed a Collaborative Competencies framework, which sets forward a frequently used (although far from the only) model, or program, for identifying and acquiring capabilities that support collaborative leadership:[32] The structure of this development program is outlined as:

Leadership and management

- Strengthening collaborative leadership (e.g., collaborative leadership styles, entrepreneurialism, and risk-taking)
- Planning, organizing, and managing for collaboration (e.g., process design, designing governance structures, engaging stakeholders)

Process

- Communicating effectively
- Working in teams and facilitating groups
- Negotiating agreement and managing conflict

Analytical

- Applying analytic skills and strategic thinking (e.g., situation assessment, understanding political and legal context of collaboration)
- Evaluating and adapting processes

Knowledge management

- Integrating technical and scientific information
- Using information and communication technology

Professional accountability

- Maintaining personal integrity and professional ethics

This framework is one part of understanding the requisites for collaborative leaders, but this list does not particularly differentiate collaborative leadership competence from any other leadership context; nor does it provide much insight into how these competencies are developed. Other work in this area may get a bit closer in providing substance, though also with limitations. One alternative considers competencies across phases of collaborative action: Assessment, Initiation, Deliberation, and Implementation. Using this framework, more substantive detail is presented on particular skills such as strategic thinking, stakeholder engagement, consensus building, network management, and more. This framework also highlights and details what are called Meta Competencies for effective collaborative leadership. They are a collaborative mindset, openness, and humility.[33]

Collaborative risk leadership

There seem to be at least three relevant risk leadership ideas unfolding from the preceding discussion.

1. The aforementioned Meta Competencies (collaborative mindset, openness, and humility) are the differentiating factors when comparing different forms of collaborative leadership. While they are plainly important in collaborative contexts, they also pinpoint "a sensibility" to think collaboratively and engage in collaborative action and diverse *ways of thinking* that complement the previous discussion on risk competencies.[34]
2. Echoes of the historiographic approach are evident, and most certainly might be nearly fully overlaid on initial Assessment phases, serving subsequently to organize the Initiation phase.[35]
3. Evidence of potential connectivity with Adaptation and Innovation leadership frameworks is present. There is something of a gap in the Leadership for Organizational Adaptability concept in terms of how activities within networks are initiated, how interactions are facilitated, and how different networks support ongoing interactions. There is a good chance that the collaborative model might be testable in practice.[36]

The cases

This chapter presents an idea that might not seem to warrant individualized attention— collaboration within risk management. However, as the chapter presents it, the emergence of collaboration as a subject within risk management and leadership is important because the impetus for heightened attention comes from several, mainly, independent forces—forces impacting individual organizations, organizations and their stakeholders, and larger multi-organization efforts to respond to risks held in common. Beyond that, there is a more clinical matter, which pertains to how collaboration is achieved. Often, an individual encountering a large(er) scale challenge may not possess the standing to lead a response, which presents a challenge. But even beyond that, the book argues that collaboration also represents a *sensibility* that represents much of what risk leadership entails.

Here, the three cases present illustrations of collaborative risk management and leadership; the first focusing on an individual organization and the second looking at a specific project but then expands to consider collaboration in a wider setting that engages an entire nation as stakeholders. The final case also presents a wide-ranging and complex setting, but here the collaborative risk leadership occurs within an emotionally intense, even life-and-death, story. Collaborative risk management and leadership exist in a variety of forms, as well as wide variations in scale and scope. Nevertheless, the cases set forward the idea that there are common and distinct features that are relevant in all settings.

Case 6.1: Collaborative risk leadership: Scandinavian Airlines and Copenhagen Airports

Case overview

In 2012, Scandinavian Airlines (SAS) publicly announced that the company would declare bankruptcy if it could not succeed in settling critical union contracts and address other expense concerns. Subsequently, SAS entered into intense union negotiations to meet its cost reduction objectives. By 2016, the airline was again profitable after following a demanding restructuring process, though a dramatic decline in fuel prices was a significant factor in the turnaround. Throughout this period of time, the European airline industry remained highly competitive and legacy carriers like SAS continued to struggle with a higher cost structure relative to the increasing number of low-cost carriers. Regulations imposed by governments as well as restrictions imposed by government investment contributed to complicated tightrope conditions. It was in the aftermath of this situation that Copenhagen Airports (CPH) set out to evaluate prospects for strategic growth, assess the impact of possible airline industry alliances, and identify other danger signals across all business sectors.

Crisis at SAS

The 2012 SAS announcement followed several years that were characterized by a severe drop in demand, expanding operating costs, high jet-fuel prices, and increasing low-cost carrier competition. Overall air travel demand dropped due to the global economic downturn (2008–2009), which led to a more competitive consumer and business travel market. Many European carriers responded to the downturn with low-cost options and extended routes. SAS, however, resisted market conditions and maintained an operating plan and cost basis that resulted in declining unit revenue and profitability.

SAS initially reported trouble in the first quarter of 2012, giving indications to investors and employees that significant structural changes would be necessary to address longer-term challenges. Later that year, as SAS announced restructuring details and its third-quarter results — the leadership considered a planned response. By this time, the external pressure to address its problems had become intense. The potential failure of this major airline would shake not only the airline and its employees but have a regional impact and clearly would affect other industry participants. Reactions from consumers, industry watchers, and social media quickly turned hostile. While SAS had long been recognized as providing good service at a fair price, various observers had commented critically on leadership, the culture, and lack of innovation as factors that were driving SAS toward potential bankruptcy. SAS employees joined the fray and became increasingly vocal about the 2009–2012 performance.

National governments in the region also voiced their concerns. Holding a 50% owner-ship share, Scandinavian national governments were demanding cost restructuring, which employees—not surprisingly—rejected as the SAS plan included cutting their salaries by up to 25%. Correspondingly, with significant operating cost constraints being considered, public observers and employees also questioned top management salaries, especially the CEO's, whose fixed salary was greater than the combined salaries for the seven-person management team at the low-cost competitor, Norwegian Air.

SAS's plan was approved by its Board of Directors. Extensive and complex negotia-tions followed, and as part of the plan, SAS was able to establish new credit lines with major banks as well as from the Swedish, Norwegian, and Danish governments. SAS's executives then entered negotiations with the unions in order to obtain major changes to employment terms, conditions, union labor agreements, and pension schemes—all agree-ments to be in line with banking requirements. During this period, the sense of urgency was heightened when the European Union's (EU) decided to cut credit lines unless its own terms and conditions were met.

SAS negotiations with unions opened with the airline's declared intention of reduc-ing salaries and eliminating 800 jobs. As part of the cost reduction plan, SAS also sold Wideroe, a regional airline, its ground handling services, and a number of other assets. In marathon negotiating sessions, SAS and union executives debated the options, understanding the fate of the firm rested on cost reduction measures that could posi-tively impact credit ratings and investor confidence. Ultimately, the airline achieved an agreement with multiple unions to introduce wage cuts of up to 15%. Following the announcement of the union agreements, SAS stock rose 3%. Banks and shareholder governments also responded to the new working contracts by offering additional credit facilities totaling US$519 million.

Copenhagen Airports

CPH business

Hosting over 26.6 million passengers in 2015, CPH reported a continuing rise in annual passenger volume, with 3.8% growth compared with 2014. CPH competes with a num-ber of airports in central and northern Europe, including Stockholm, Oslo, Brussels, Zurich, Berlin, Amsterdam, Munich, and Frankfurt, with over 254,000 flights annually routing through CPH. Business and leisure travelers utilize CPH for mainly international travel, making CPH a regional hub for global destinations.

CPH has been an international airport since its inception in 1925, and at the time this case study examines, passengers were able to travel to 156 global destinations, 32 being intercontinental. The international consumer and cargo business was an important con-sideration in CPH's strategy. Ongoing investment in the structure, technology, services, and logistics would be required to sustain this growth. CPH invested more than 1 billion Danish Kroner, approximately US$155 million, in 2015, into airport operations. CPH ranks among the top 25 international airports, closest to New York's LaGuardia in terms of 2014 passenger volume. Of the top-ranked, busiest European airports, only Istanbul outpaces CPH's annualized growth pattern with 10.7% in 2014. CPH supports 23,000 jobs in 700 businesses while declaring its intention to deliver a "seamless airport" experi-ence. A one roof, one terminal airport hosts a major shopping mall featuring specialty retail, food and beverage, and tax-free stores.

Approximately 70 different airlines utilize Copenhagen Airport's facility. In 2015, the top five airlines, respectively, were SAS, Norwegian, EasyJet, Ryanair, and Lufthansa, accounting for 67% of the total passenger count. With SAS the significant market leader, business continuity of the major partner was evident by virtue of its market share.

Short-haul routes from Scandinavia, the Baltics, Poland, Northern Germany, and the UK feed passengers to long-haul routes. Low-cost carriers (LCC) have focused on point-to-point traffic in Europe with no transfer options with other airlines. New fast-growing LCCs have gained the highest growth rates in the last ten years based on a lean business model compared with the legacy carriers. To the LCCs, costs and efficient operations are the most important factors. Airlines such as EasyJet and Norwegian Air gained market share at CPH reaching 28% in 2015. Since 2015, Ryanair presented a new important source of growth in this segment. As a result of their lower average ticket prices, this has boosted demand significantly, especially leisure travel.

Today, roadway, metro, and railway connections provide easy access to the airport. Trains from Malmö, Stockholm, and Gothenburg in Sweden, and the major Danish cities in CPH's catchment area deliver passengers to the airport's train platform situated less than 100 meters from check-in counters. Amenities at the airport include a five-star hotel, duty-free shopping, a central security checkpoint, and Metro station service to Copenhagen city center only 12 minutes away. CPH's declared strategic intention is to become the preferred international airport for all of Northern Europe.

Organization structure and governance

Copenhagen Airports' organizational model is influenced by its ownership. In 1990, the company was converted into a public limited company, Københavns Lufthavne A/S (Copenhagen Airports A/S), with the government as the sole shareholder. Subsequently, in 1994, it was decided to reduce the Danish government ownership stake and to have the company's shares listed on the Copenhagen Stock Exchange. Currently, the Danish Government owns 39.2% while Ontario Teachers' Pension Plan (OTPP) and Macquarie European Infrastructure Fund III (MEIF3) through a joint holding company own 57.6%. The remaining ownership is constituted of international (1.8%) and Danish (1.4%) private investors. The company is based in Kastrup, Denmark.

Copenhagen Airports owns and operates Kastrup, the international airport in Copenhagen and Roskilde airport, situated 41 kilometers west of Copenhagen. Kastrup is also the site of CPH's corporate headquarters. The company provides traffic management, maintenance, and security services, as well as managing the Copenhagen Airport Shopping Center (CASC) and airport projects. CPH also owns the hotel site occupied in 2015–2016 by a Hilton Hotel. Operating in two segments, aeronautical and non-aeronautical, the aeronautical segment includes all airport flight operation functions, while the non-aeronautical segment provides facilities and services to passengers. This segment leases CPH owned buildings, premises, and land that are used for hotel, parking, and the CASC. Professional and consulting services concerning airport operation and related services are also part of the non-aeronautical segment.

CPH and the SAS crisis

CPH's attentiveness to the SAS crisis was particularly keen, given recent memories of similar situations in the European airline industry. Two particular prior bankruptcy events lingered in CPH leaders' minds. First, in a story that also featured Brussels Airport (BRU), Sabena Airlines declared bankruptcy in 2001, one year after reaching a peak in passenger air travel in 2000. This event served to highlight the interdependencies between a carrier and the airports themselves. And indeed, it was only after many years of extensive recovery efforts that total passenger counts began to approach 2000 levels at BRU. The second involved Zurich's (ZRH) airport, where Swissair declared bankruptcy in 2002—also following on from a record-breaking total passenger count in 2000. In this case, it took almost ten years before the prior level of passenger volume was achieved again at ZRH.

A more pointed third example was the 2012 collapse of Barcelona-based carrier, Spanair. Among more general causes for concern, Spanair's former owner, Scandinavian Airlines (SAS), still held 10.9% of shares in Spanair at the time, further complicating the crisis at SAS. At that time trading on the Stockholm Exchange, SAS stock tumbled (during the 2011–2012 period), marking a record low in the stock's history—clearly a contributing factor in SAS's own bankruptcy threat.

Despite the improvement in SAS's situation by 2015–2016, Copenhagen Airports became increasingly mindful of the need to incorporate the risks of key organizations more clearly and fully—such as SAS—into its own risk assessments. And, owing to the significance of SAS to CPH, particular attention would need to be paid to the connectivity of SAS's risks to CPH's own strategic objectives. To be sure, attentiveness to key stakeholders had always been part of CPH's worldview, but the idea of incorporating risks to stakeholders into CPH's own risk assessment fit logically into the airport's internal intentions to create a more holistic and integrated risk management structure.

In the second quarter of 2014, and as part of the new thinking about risk management at CPH, a newly hired member of the executive leadership team, Group Risk Manager Kristine Raffel, attended her first offsite executive briefing where leaders presented a business contingency management plan related to the SAS bankruptcy. During this dramatic introduction to CPH's largest—and most serious—risk concern, she saw that the owners, the board of directors, and the leadership team would be expecting her to take on responsibilities for this specific plan. In Kristine's mind, this particular exercise—focused as it was on SAS—offered a possible gateway or pilot project for her wider responsibilities to establish a new risk management structure at CPH; a structure that would be expected to include an ongoing, formal dialog across CPH business sectors to assess risks, refine the growth strategy, and directly initiate measures to address the risks to all airport operations.

As she began to work on the SAS issue, Kristine learned that Lufthansa, SAS, and other European Union airlines were strongly arguing that government regulation throughout Europe, as well as rising taxes, damaged the European airline sector. CPH was aware that rising fuel costs and slow growth in the sector both impacted the entire, and highly competitive, industry—directly imposing stress on CPH's revenue. Little could be done about taxes and regulations, not just because of the industry, but also because Scandinavian Airlines and Copenhagen Airports were both partially owned by governments. Thus, there were additional important reasons for adhering to regulations, paying required taxes, and addressing these key stakeholder needs (political as well as economic), further adding complications to any risk management plans that would emerge.

Initial actions

CPH declared its intention to expand an "engaged" approach to addressing its network of partners in the aftermath of the SAS crisis. Given the strategic importance of SAS to CPH, leadership from both firms set out a plan for a more cohesive working partnership to address mutual interests. Among the features of this new partnership, the airport set up a monitoring process for examining SAS and other airlines' financial health situation that included evaluating all publicly shared reporting and privately held information. A regular meeting schedule between CPH and SAS was established, and more informal dialog and information exchanges were encouraged; with the understanding that both CPH and SAS may choose to hold some aspects of operations and financial health confidential, CPH leaders expected to review facts and observations (flight booking trends, cost of fuel, payroll) quarterly, in line with intended overall (regular) risk updates. Moving forward, CPH reported these findings internally and compiled a risk report that addressed important points including liquidity and financing, activity and operations, profitability, solidity and risks, danger signals, and an overall CPH management viewpoint.

Reflections

The case directly or indirectly suggests at least three important risk leadership questions:

- One aspect of risk leadership is the need to understand the context of particular risk management issues. The challenge in understanding context, as historians note, is to think diachronically (thinking over extended periods of time) and synchronically (across extended boundaries). Realistically, however, how comprehensively can this ever be done? The question for the Group Risk Manager here is this: How does a risk leader set out the parameters for creating "the context" of this situation? That is, what is in bounds and out of bounds when seeking to develop an understanding of the context of the SAS situation and CPH's exposure to it?
- Think about Kristine Raffel's initial insight that the SAS situation might be a proving ground for the larger task of moving CPH toward an ERM-style structure. Why would she think that; and how should she go about using this particular undertaking to build her own credibility and prove the value of risk management to CPH?
- The "substance" of the partnering idea formulated between SAS and CPH will likely be the quality of the information that is shared between the two parties. What are the issues that surround information sharing, and how might the two organizations establish a relationship where meaningful and useful information is willingly shared?

Read more about it

Amankwah-Amoah, J., Ottosson, J. and Sjögren, H. (2017). United we stand, divided we fall: historical trajectory of strategic renewal activities at the Scandinavian Airlines System, 1946–2012. *Business History*, 59(4), 572–606.

Christiansen, S. (2017). *The Future of SAS*. Copenhagen Business School. https://research-api.cbs.dk/ws/portalfiles/portal/60759112/309767_Simon_Christiansen_without_personal_data.pdf

Copenhagen Airport Website. https://www.cph.dk/en

SAS Website. https://www.flysas.com/us-en/

Case 6.2: Collaborative risk leadership: The LIFFT-Cashew project

Case overview

Shelter For Life International (SFL) and its partner Connexus have undertaken a five-year program in Senegal, the Gambia, and Guinea-Bissau (SeGaBi) with the goal of developing and upgrading value chain linkages necessary to support an integrated regional trade network for the cashew value chain. As such, the project's objectives are to 1) increase outturn quality of raw cashew nuts (RCN), 2) increase processing of RCN in the SeGaBi region, and 3) promote the collective sale of RCN (by developing and upgrading value-chain linkages).

The proposed program has been framed around four components: (1) market infrastructure; (2) financial services; (3) market access and linkages; and (4) on-farm practices. The Linking Infrastructure, Finance, and Farms to Cashew (shortened to LIFFT-Cashew) program targets creating a durable trade infrastructure, increasing access to financial services, organizing and training smallholder farmers to increase production and bargaining power, and building the capacity of local processors to add value to cashew kernels in the SeGaBi cashew production zone of West Africa. The projected outcomes are expected to benefit smallholder farmers, a range of processors, and a variety of other businesses along the cashew value chain. This six-year program was forecasted to directly benefit 21,300 individuals (producers, processors, SMEs owners and employees, and other value chain actors) across all three countries. The project is ongoing as this case is being prepared, but its original budget projection was US$38,000,000—funded by the United States Department of Agriculture (USDA).

Program structure

As noted, the program structure is built upon four key components: Infrastructure; Financial Services; Market Access and Linkages; and On-Farm Practices. In addition, a fifth linking-function activity is proposed to span the components and integrate overall program management.

Component 1: Infrastructure

Activity 1: Infrastructure: Feeder and connector roads

SFL has set out to build or rehabilitate agricultural feeder and connector roads. All roads are intended to be designed and constructed or rehabilitated according to local standards for tertiary roads. SFL is overseeing the design and construction of appropriate drainage for each road according to topographical surveys. A combination of heavy equipment and manual labor will be used for construction and rehabilitation. Manual laborers were/ are paid as Cash for Work laborers and are chosen from the local communities along the selected roads.

In addition, the SFL infrastructure team is training local communities on basic labor-based maintenance that would improve the longevity of the roads, and particular focus will be on maintaining proper drainage. This is being done with a pictorial maintenance manual. At the completion of each road, SFL intends to formally hand over responsibility for the road to local government authorities. This is to be done according to agreements signed between SFL and the local authorities prior to rehabilitation or construction. These legal documents formalize each government's commitment to providing ongoing maintenance past the life of the program.

Activity 2: Infrastructure: Post-harvest handling and storage

SFL will provide technical assistance and consultation to Cashew Market Associations (CMAs) for the construction, rehabilitation, and management of cashew storage and post-harvest handling. Storage units will be designed according to the topography of the land and the needs of the producer groups. Construction and rehabilitation work will be done in coordination with associations.

Component 2: Financial services

Activity 3: Financial services: Facilitate agricultural lending

SFL will facilitate and encourage agricultural lending from local and regional financial institutions (FIs) to CMAs, cashew farmers, and related businesses. This will be done by assessing the current needs and constraints in agricultural financing, vetting, and partnering with FIs in the region, and providing training and technical assistance to FIs as well as potential borrowers. In addition, SFL expects to be working with FIs to identify risk mitigation options for lending to encourage lending within the cashew value chain.

Activity 4: Financial services: Cashew Fund

SFL is establishing a *Cashew Fund* to provide a mechanism for investment in small and medium cashew businesses, a process that includes establishment of the governance structure and management requirements, the qualifications for borrowers, and procedures setting out how funds will be triggered and disbursed. Once established, the Cashew Fund will provide equity investments as well as other structured financial instruments to cashew-related businesses, with an early emphasis on local cashew kernel processors. The terms of the investment will be driven by the specific needs and risk profile of each recipient. Access to the fund will be for investment-ready cashew value chain actors that can demonstrate impact across the value chain or the potential to link to regional and international markets, projected cash flows to cover operational costs, and a clear strategy toward a return on investment over time.

Component 3: Market access and linkages

Activity 5: Capacity building: Cashew Marketing Associations

SFL will strengthen existing Cashew Marketing Associations (CMAs), and provide capacity building, technical assistance, and training opportunities in order to improve bargaining power and strengthen value chain linkages On an ongoing basis, SFL expects to provide technical assistance in areas that include competitiveness strategies, collective bargaining power, improved market information, post-harvest handling practices, management of storage facilities, and grading and aggregating RCN. Grants will be available as needed by the CMAs.

Activity 6: Market access: Facilitate buyer–seller relationships

SFL will develop and strengthen buyer–seller relationships in target countries. The program aims to build the capacity of CMAs and strengthen their relationship with international buyers, which includes bringing regional and international buyers and CMA members together, facilitating communication between them, and promoting bulk purchase/sale of RCN through associations, instead of individual interactions between buyers and farmers. SFL will also work with producers, buyers, and processors to improve their approach to marketing, branding, and selling their products. Where necessary and appropriate, SFL will provide training and research requirements for attaining USDA organic certifications.

Activity 7: Capacity building: Trade associations

SFL intends to provide capacity building and networking support to various local trade associations. Acknowledging each organization's strengths and weaknesses, the project expects to be engaged with new and existing groups and to include them in the design of activities, collection of market data, and evaluation of results. This will involve supporting and encouraging the inclusion of these activities in all project-related training and workshops relevant to their area of expertise. SFL will also facilitate relevant cashew stakeholders to attend ComCashew Master Training Program by partially underwriting the cost of training.

Component 4: On-farm practices

Activity 8: Agricultural development: Demonstration plots and nurseries

SFL has committed to encouraging the application of Good Agricultural Practices (GAP) by working through partner producer associations and groups. SFL will build the capacity of its partner associations to provide training and support for cashew producers through the use of demonstration plots, in-kind grants, and the development of cashew nurseries.

Cross-functional component

Activity 9: Management of information systems

A key part of the program is the development and management of a scalable database platform that can store and disseminate cashew production data, market information, and the identity and asset information of farmers and enterprises who may become borrowers. The platform will have the capacity to analyze data and create reports, all of which should be accessible on a single website to local government, USDA, and other key stakeholders in the cashew value chain. The platform will also collect and store information about potential borrowers utilizing biometric data. This information includes the identity of farmers and other value chain actors and the registration of their physical and intellectual assets. It will be available to the Cashew Fund.

Program intended results

These nine activities support the program's overall goals and objectives and each one is applicable to multiple results streams. The activities are designed to be complementary and coordinated. The following objectives support the overall goal:

- *Increase cashew production and value* by organizing and building capacity of farmers to improve on-farm practices, improve post-harvest practices, and increase bargaining power.
- *Increase local cashew processing* by increasing access to financial services, capacity building, and upgrading value chain linkages.
- *Expand the trade of cashews* by developing and upgrading value chain linkages necessary to support an integrated regional trade network, which includes creating durable market infrastructure and improving access to markets for value chain actors.

Target beneficiaries

SFL will target enterprises and individuals in the following regions:

- *Senegal*: Fatick, Ziguinchor, Sedhiou, Kolda
- *The Gambia*: North Bank, Western, Lower River
- *Guinea-Bissau*: Cacheu, Biombo, Oio

The program is expected to engage a wide range of beneficiaries including both individuals and groups, as outlined below. In each beneficiary group, SFL will purposely target women and youth to increase their level of engagement in the value chain. This includes working with enterprises and financial institutions that are committed to the support of women's engagement and participation.

CFW laborers: selected from among the communities along the targeted road and prior to the start of work. Each laborer must register with the department of labor and SFL selects the required number of laborers, primarily based on their ability to participate in demanding physical labor.

Financial institutions: a range of financial institutions providing services to the agriculture sector will be targeted for training and technical assistance designed to encourage inclusive financial services to cashew farmers and other value chain actors, including a wide range of enterprises.

Cashew kernel processors: SFL will contact every processor or individual planning to process via phone, email, and in-person meetings. Engagement in the program will be voluntary, and because the number of processors is low at this time all will be invited to participate. Processors will benefit from a range of activities including financial services, market linkages, and training.

Cashew-related enterprises: to include input providers, farmers, processors, warehouse managers, transporters, and traders, as well as cashew nurseries. Enterprises will benefit from a range of activities including financial services, market linkages, and training.

Cashew farmers: the team will identify and contact each of the preexisting cashew producer groups in Gambia and Senegal and identify villages in those countries as well as in Guinea-Bissau that do not yet have producer groups. The team will seek to have as wide of a geographic and population coverage as possible. Farmers are expected to benefit from inclusion in the CMAs, agricultural best practice training, and training in post-harvest handling, as well as financial services.

Reflections

This chapter provides an analysis of Collaborative Risk Management/Leadership, and it is obvious by its appearance here that the LIFFT-Cashew Program provides an extremely useful context for thinking about issues relevant to collaboration. Three directed questions are offered.

- Shelter For Life (SFL), in proposing to undertake this program, has set out its goals and objectives in response to a Request for Proposal released by the United States Department of Agriculture's Foreign Agricultural Service—which funds internationally oriented programs like LIFFT-Cashew. What are the likely goals and objectives of the USDA's FAS body for a program like this? One would expect that its goals would be similar to LIFFT-Cashew's, but it is worth considering how USDA/FAS views its overarching goals and objectives for the entirety of its portfolio of funded projects? Should SFL really care about these broader goals? Thinking about other key stakeholder goals, can we imagine what the objectives would be for the national, regional, and local governments, as well as the farmers and others (present and future) affiliated with the cashew value chain? Here a central issue with programs similar to LIFFT-Cashew comes to light. This is a discrete program with a beginning, middle, and end. However, there is a long-term implication—that the cashew sector will be properly structured in a way that will stabilize this sector of the economy for long-term benefit to the region. How is this continuity issue planned for and addressed? The fixed-term nature of programs tends to lead to framing central concerns as *crisis* conditions, whereas the better term probably should be *chronic* conditions.
- The post-conflict "temperature" with this program is lower than similar projects in—say—Afghanistan, but the fact remains that key stakeholders may have been on opposing sides in previous conflicts, meaning there is an added dimension in efforts to achieve collaborative participation. Here it seems that understanding the region's history may play a critical role in understanding the program context. However, it is worth reflecting on the leadership measures necessary to construct a context that could be seen as acceptable to all. How would a collaborative risk leader set about getting all stakeholders to an agreement? And what specific issues need to be considered with the specific issue of getting participants on the same page with respect to the perception of risk and uncertainty?
- A close reading of this case suggests that cultural considerations shape (or should shape) the way the program is designed. Examining the evidence that suggests those considerations, it is helpful to think about cultural impacts on multi-cultural collaborations in general. A story from SFL's early work on LIFFT-Cashew is telling and illustrative here. The development of storage facilities was initially seen as introducing a practical, cost-effective, and efficient way to protect cashews from degradation after harvest. However, the program team initially met with significant resistance

by the farmers as a common general storage area would allow all farmers to see one another's harvest, which may in turn create rivalrous relationships. Further, identifying the successful farmers could lead to those farmers becoming targets for unsolicited loan requests and other unwanted interactions. Measures were taken to restore anonymity in the storage process—but a lesson learned was to create greater sensitivity to historic and cultural influences on the relationships of participants. How does the risk leader ferret out these issues in advance?

Read more about it

Ag4Impact.org. (n.d.). *Agriculture for Impact Building Social Capital.* Retrieved from Ag4Impact: http://ag4impact.org/sid/socio-economic-intensification/building-social-capital/

Bromley, D. W. (2011). *Exports, Employment and Incomes in West Africa.* West Africa Trade Hub. Retrieved from http://www.africancashewalliance.com/sites/default/files/documents/th_-_multiplier_effects_-_exports_employment_and_incomes_in_wa_2011.pdf

Ludwig, C., Nagarajan, G. and Zaman, L. (2016). *Systematic Review of the Effects of Rural Roads on Expanding Agricultural Markets in Developing Countries.* Social Impact, Inc., Arlington, VA.

RONGEAD (2015). *The African Cashew Sector in 2015.* Retrieved from http://www.rongead.org/IMG/pdf/african_cashew:market_review:rongead_ica_2015.pdf

Case 6.3: Adaptation in complex settings: Responding to the humanitarian crisis in Kosovo

Case overview

The Balkans region of Europe has a long history of conflict and instability, a history that can be traced as far back as 2,500 years. Why this is the case (and remains so today) sits as a provocative question for historians. It probably is worth noting that the Balkans serves as a geographical crossroads for cultures from the East, West, North, and South. Different peoples entering the arena inevitably were bound to collide and contest for the right to remain there.

In the region's more recent history, the ongoing political temperature has been frequently subjected to additional incitement, notably including conflicts with the Ottoman Empire, the immense disruption of two World Wars, the disintegration of the Warsaw Pact in the late 1980s, and then the particular dynamics associated with the break-up of Yugoslavia. All these events introduced what in retrospect can be seen as a century-long escalation of tensions that became super-heated in the 1990s—to a point where a rolling region-wide series of conflicts (small and large) propelled the Balkans into a highly volatile state of affairs. And, it must be admitted, this state of affairs has not been meaningfully resolved even in the two decades that have passed since that time.

In this case study, the story takes place in 1998–1999. Here the central focus is fixed on a NATO peacekeeping initiative in Kosovo. At this time, a serious crisis broke into armed violence between Serbia and Albanian separatists, both of whom had staked a claim to the province of Kosovo. Dramatic swings in the fortunes of each side had occurred, and—critically here—outside powers had begun to take sides in supporting the antagonists. Into this situation NATO controversially made decisions to intervene in an effort to stabilize Kosovo and, in doing so, it was hoped to create a breathing space for nego-tiations. As the case unfolded, a combination of unintended consequences, random bad luck, close-run events, malevolent intentions, and outside meddling all congealed into a situation where the NATO peacekeeping effort, which had a narrowly defined mission, suddenly confronted a situation it was not expecting to address.

In this story, we see matters emerge related to collaborative risk management and lead-ership, but issues pertaining to adaptation are prominently featured, as are distinguishing elements that differentiate management from leadership, and then—of course—decision-making under conditions of extreme uncertainty. This mantra *Everything is Connected* provides a notable "shaping" role in the telling of this story.

Setting the context

One of the most notable challenges of developing this short case study—and indeed, in any effort by risk leaders to understand a situation's Context—is settling on an answer to the question, "When does the story begin?" It is not an overstatement to say that a case for understanding the present-day situation could be made to start with the Ancient World, but here perhaps the point needs only be made that roiling waters run very deep and there is profound density to the motivations and factors that undergird present dynamics.

Here the choice is to focus on the propulsive influence of the disintegration of, first, the Warsaw Pact followed by the disintegration of Yugoslavia. It is in these two suc-cessive events that nationalist, racial, and religious movements that had heretofore been suppressed by the Soviet Union generally, and Marshall Tito (the leader of Yugoslavia) specifically, sprang back to life and provided fuel for the turbulence that swept through the region.

Kosovo, a province within Yugoslavia, which by this time consisted only of Serbia and Montenegro, presents a distilled but acute illustration of the general problems that emerged in the 1990s. Map-making and racial/social demarcations frequently do not align, and this is definitely the case for the province of Kosovo. A distinct Serbian popu-lation existed alongside an Albanian population. Deep resentments and hostilities were particularly sharp. The Serbian government that emerged after Tito's death, while nomi-nally communist, moved toward a more purely authoritarian form. The unsettled state of affairs in Kosovo was troubling in its own right, but Serbian president Milošević is said to have seized on the situation as a means to further promote his Greater Serbia ambitions. Various efforts to ameliorate the tensions failed to prevent or disrupt the armed violence that erupted in the mid-1990s.

An Albanian separatist movement in Kosovo was linked to similar Albanian efforts in Macedonia, Montenegro, and Southern Serbia—what collectively was referred to as the Greater Albania movement. Alongside this particular conflict, of course, numerous other flashpoints existed in the former Yugoslavia. Serbians, Bosnians, Croatians, and Slovenians all participated in serious armed conflicts during the early 1990s. The inten-sity and complexity of these conflicts eventually became issues of concern for countries outside the region and—notably the "great powers" of the United States, the European Union, and Russia and former Soviet nations, as well as varied interests in the Middle East. All began to interpret the events in the Balkans as threats to the interests of the wider world. Here the case study accelerates toward its specific moment of focus.

Kosovo: 1999

If this were a story of a conflict between the Serbian government and the Albanian separatist movement (which mainly was personified by the Kosovan Liberation Army—KLA), the narrative would be horrific enough. Kidnappings, civilian massacres, military confrontations, terrorist attacks, assassinations, and bombings all featured prominently in the conflict between the two sides. However, this story involves the intervention of outside interests and led to a "taking of sides" dynamic that did not fully align with the actual arbitrating interests of these outside interests. For example, the United States both declared the KLA a terrorist organization, but in many respects found itself aligned with Albanian interests. The European Union and NATO interests did not neatly overlay regional interests, nor could that be said of Russia, nor indeed of the United Nations.

One of the most controversial actions in this particular conflict was the NATO decision to place bombing Serbian forces and locations on the table (and ultimately to employ that tool). Among the many ramifications of that decision, this placed NATO (and somewhat less directly, the United Nations) in the position of being a belligerent while at the same time intending to be an arbiter of conciliation between regional opponents. This inconsistency is worth a moment's reflection as it highlights what is often considered a first-order risk—lack of clarity or consistency in mission (goals, objectives, strategy). Plainly put, decisions are particularly difficult to make when there is no consistent identification of purpose.

Into this situation in late 1998 entered the NATO authorized Kosovo Verification Mission (KVM). The KVM was a contingent of unarmed Organization for Security and Co-operation in Europe (OSCE) peace monitors that moved into Kosovo. As a monitoring mission, its arrival had virtually no effect on the violence and, in fact, acts of aggression increased. The pivot point during the first month of 1999 was the Račak massacre of 45 Kosovan-Albanian civilians. International outrage at this event led directly to the NATO decision to insert forces to establish some level of stability. (Note: while this move was described as a peacekeeping effort in the media, this is technically not accurate as peacekeeping requires an agreement from both sides of a conflict; "peace enforcement" or "peace support" have been suggested as more accurate terms.) The Račak incident indirectly led to later war crime charges against the Serbian leadership, including President Milošević.

The Spring of 1999 saw the bombing of Serbian forces and locations in an effort to drive Serbia toward an agreement to cease fire. This remains a hugely controversial decision and is still a subject of heated debate. Numerous mistakes in bombing targets remain particular flashpoints in this controversy. Nevertheless, in late Spring, Yugoslavia agreed to a cessation of hostilities, and shortly thereafter, Milošević and the parliament accepted the terms of an international peace plan to end the fighting. Following that, the North Atlantic Council ratified the agreement and suspended air operations.

On 12 June, the NATO-led peacekeeping Kosovo Force (KFOR) of 30,000 soldiers began entering Kosovo. KFOR had been preparing to conduct combat operations, but in the end, its mission was only peacekeeping. The force was based upon the Allied Rapid Reaction Corps headquarters commanded by then Lieutenant General Mike Jackson of the British Army. It consisted of British forces (101 Logistic Brigade and 4 Armoured Brigade), a French Army Brigade, and a German Army brigade, which entered from the west, while other forces advanced from the south, including the Italian Army and United States Army brigades.

The humanitarian crisis

Alongside the preceding narrative, the specific subject of this case begins in January of 1999 when the then Brigadier Tim Cross, Commander of 101 Logistic Brigade (UK) arrived in the region as part of KFOR's "receive, stage, onward move, and integrate" logistics effort. The staging area was Macedonia, which shares a border with Kosovo, with the intention of eventually moving into Kosovo. The arrival of supplies that anticipated a more active role for KFOR in Kosovo began to mount and accumulate in Greece and Macedonia, all the while the situation in Kosovo was quickly deteriorating. As noted previously, this deterioration led to the bombing campaign in the Spring of 1999, but relevant here, the main implication is that Brigadier Cross's mission (supporting a peace support force quickly became irrelevant to the situation.

Indeed, a very new mission began to take shape in mid-March when it was reported that over 200,000 displaced persons were on the move, mainly to the borders of Albania and Macedonia. Suddenly, 101 Logistic Brigade was faced with a refugee crisis—in fact, a very large and dire crisis. Here the case study reaches its essential moment. Brigadier Cross found himself in a situation where his mission no longer aligned with the facts on the ground. The new mission, though still not crystallized at that moment, evolved to respond to a rapidly developing refugee crisis. The question forefront in his mind was this; can the various units of his brigade—engineer, medical, logistical, and other units— be quickly repurposed to serve a very different role?

Several critical elements became evident to Brigadier Cross.

1. The command-and-control structure of the military would be useful, but some limitations existed in as much as other organizations—particularly non-government organizations and aid agencies, as well as governments—would need to be involved.
2. There were capable individuals and useful resources in 101 Logistical Brigade, but it was only somewhat constituted to deal with a humanitarian crisis of this scale. How possible was a rapid reconfiguration of the Brigade to serve a different purpose?
3. The Brigade leadership was positioned to provide structure and to lead in finding adaptive solutions, but it would require a dramatically different way of thinking about the task at hand.

It was, perhaps, an "if not now, when; if not us, who" moment for Brigadier Cross. Here is what next happened, in his own words:

> There could be no doubt that the refugee crisis would get worse, so we produced contingency plans; as usual, of the 3 options we planned for it was the fourth that actually happened. On Thursday 1st April, I drove out to look at several sites that the Macedonian Government were intending to develop as refugee camps. They were small and in poor locations, very close to the border with Kosovo. The government-led reconnaissance was badly organised and chaotic, but I was able to meet with some UN officials, in particular the head of the UNHCR mission to Kosovo, Jo Hegenauer, and a representative from the U.S. State Department, David Scheffer, an Ambassador at Large for War Crimes Issues.

The result of these discussions was an outline of intentions, which can be summarized as follows:

1. Construct major camps around an airfield and range complex near the Macedonian/ Kosovo border. The ultimate site was selected based upon space, proximity to water, and ease of access. A smaller camp was also constructed to respond to immediate needs and meet contingencies that might arise (quarantining, for example).
2. In the face of rapidly increasing numbers of refugees, shelter/food/medical services became an immediate concern. UNHCR should have had a primary role, but Brigadier Cross would be prepared to put 101 at the disposal of this effort, establishing a tactical headquarters. The intention was to provide a logistical focal point for the delivery of necessary supplies of food, blankets, and medical supplies.
3. Immediately on the heels of #2, field kitchens were set up and food preparations began and were ongoing thereafter. (Note: the temperatures were near freezing with rain and sleet, adding to the urgency of the situation.)
4. All of this to be done while continuing to support 4 Armoured Brigade in its training and preparation for potential war-fighting operations in Kosovo itself.

Brigadier Cross continued:

> Pressure was mounting on the Macedonian Government, and on the UNHCR, whose small team was self-evidently going to be overwhelmed. Various government officials visited Tac HQ during the following day, Saturday 3rd April; most importantly, in retrospect, Julia Taft from the U.S. State Department. The U.S. was putting real pressure on the Macedonian government, who clearly needed convincing that the situation…could not be allowed to continue. There was inevitably a great deal of uncertainty but I was convinced that the dam at the border would break at short notice, and when it did we had to be able to deal with the torrent of refugees that would be released. No other organisation was in a position to help and we could not stand idle; apart from the human needs it was clear to me that the Macedonian Government needed KFORs strength, and we needed them to maintain their resolve. After a night of detailed planning I ordered construction work to start.

The complexity of the task at hand should not be underemphasized. Among the numerous tasks in constructing refugee locations, 101 Tactical Headquarters undertook to build a bridge over a river, clearing and shaping the airfield for regularized and frequent traffic, setting the logistics for moving supplies into the refugee camps, preparing reception centers, setting up tents, building water purification and pumping stations, sanitation, and more. All this was done with no particular orders from relevant governments, agencies, and organizations—including HQ KFOR. However, apparent pressure from the US government seemed to lead to the Macedonian government stepping in to offer official support and endorsement.

The following day, refugees began flooding into the camps. Within 24 hours, nearly 20,000 refugees had arrived. It is important to keep in mind that the building of the refugee camps was occurring exactly at the time refugees were arriving—a situation that remained manageable, although the possibility of chaos was never far away.

Ultimately, over the next few days, nearly 40,000 refugees arrived. And as inevitably happens, an improvised community began to emerge with all the issues common to communities everywhere—births, deaths, illnesses, small reunions and celebrations, neighborhood squabbles, efforts to provide schooling and supervision of children, crime and corruption, and even a continuation of the armed conflict within the camps. Policing, transportation, communication support, and other infrastructural needs quickly became important.

Brigadier Cross summarized these intense days of crisis response. By the end of the week:

> In one sense the worst was over. Initially the NGO presence on the ground had been minimal. OXFAM arrived first and quickly became effective, playing a key role in the development of the water and sanitation systems. Other organisations began to arrive, but slowly. The UN became more effective as the week progressed. Various senior officials arrived and were briefed, the UNHCR and WFP teams were strengthened, and several key individuals emerged as real "players." For a few days the flow of refugees slowed and the various NGOs began to get organised. On Sunday 11th April, we were able to hand over most of the medical support to Médecins Sans Frontières and the Red Cross. Although we began to plan the hand-over of all aspects of the camps, the following week was still a demanding one. The camps had to be extended as more refugees arrived, policing and security became a problem, and the temperatures began to soar. Rubbish clearance, sanitation and the threat of disease became key issues; once again our military resources had to lead the way. Further influxes of refugees continued and thunder storms flooded the camps. The ability of the various agencies to cope remained suspect and we were asked, by the UNHCR, to stay on for a few more days. Finally, we withdrew over the period of the 17th-19th April, leaving behind a military liaison team.

This was far from the end of the story, however. Refugees continued to arrive in Macedonia and in similar camps in Albania. The search for additional camp locations was complicated by political considerations and the general chaos of the situation. While a semblance of order did begin to emerge over the ensuing weeks, ongoing issues persisted: political corruption, criminality, the continuation of the conflict itself, and the continuing challenge of retrofitting and integrating a redefined mission and improving the collaboration across a host of humanitarian agencies and organizations.

As the case overview case spells out, the intense heat of the refugee crisis was lowered through the remainder of 1999, but it remains a sad testimony to the overall situation in the Balkans that many political, social, and economic issues are unsatisfactorily resolved even two decades after the events described here.

Reflections

For purposes of providing attachment points to the book, return to the first moments when Brigadier Cross begins to see that his brigade's initial mission is quickly becoming irrelevant.

- One important tool of risk leadership is the capacity to assess risks, uncertainties, the unknowns, and complex interconnectivities. Although intentionally not spelled out in the case, it is evident that Brigadier Cross undertook a quick, but sharply focused, risk assessment. The steps he initiated are described here, but a broader question remains. Can we detect the logic of his view of the risks? In other words, can we see how he assessed, prioritized, and made his early decisions to respond to the unfolding situation?

- Collaboration was vitally required to respond to the humanitarian crisis, but at the exact moment, the crisis became real no formalized structure existed to permit risk leadership to be effected (indeed, no overarching leadership was fully present). This presents a very important moment for reflecting on the issue of *emergent leadership*. What were the "assets" Brigadier Cross possessed that may have assisted him in emerging as a situational leader/risk leader? What were the limitations, obstacles, and constraints to him doing so?

- Clearly, a major theme of this case is adaptation in the face of complexity. However, one of the interesting inconsistencies—when this story is set alongside broader thinking about adaptive organizations—is that "agents" and "networks" are tools of adaptation, but leadership involves more than just serving a supporting and maintaining role. It is active and adaptive in its own right. This insight is an echo of the book's reference to Command as a distinct form of leadership ("We will do this NOW!"). It may be that the central presence of military organizations made this more possible, logical, or familiar as a means of initiating a response, but it does raise a more general question as to 1) whether any alternative to a Command-based response is even imaginable, and 2) if military organizations were not present, who would have the positioning to be able to lead an organized response? And what would that look like?

Read more about it

BBC (2016). *Balkans War: A Brief Guide.* https://www.bbc.com/news/world-europe-17632399

Jackson, M. (2007). *Soldier: The Autobiography.* Bantam Press, London, UK.

Judah, T. (2000). *Kosovo: War and Revenge.* Yale University Press, New Haven, CT. https://doi.org/10.2307/j.ctt1xp3spk

YouTube (1999). *Kosovo War and Ethnic Cleansing.* https://www.youtube.com/watch?v=ulPsNrMMZ3E

Notes

1 https://www.aiim.org/What-is-Collaboration

2 Uhl-Bien, M., Riggio, R. E., Lowe, K. B. and Carsten, M. K. (2014). Followership theory: A review and research agenda. *The Leadership Quarterly*, 25, 83–104. [This article contains a discussion of the leadership co-created process idea, which contains elements of "difficult to detect" leadership.]

3 Lord, R. and Maher, K. J. (1991). *Leadership and Information Processing: Linking Perceptions and Performance.* Unwin-Everyman, Boston, MA. [This book poses the idea a bit differently, referring to Implicit Leadership.]

4 Bingham, L. B, Sandfort, J. and O'Leary, R. (2008). Learning to do and doing to learn: Teaching managers to collaborate in networks. In Bingham, L. B. and O'Leary, R. (Eds.), *Big Ideas in Collaborative Public Management* (pp. 270–285), ME Sharp, Armonk, NY. [This article offers one example of sourced from literature outside Leadership.]

5 Haimes, Y.Y. (1992). Toward a holistic approach to total risk management. *Geneva Papers on Risk and Insurance*, 17(64), 314–321. [This article serves as a record of a point in time in the development of risk management when discussion and study began to introduce the idea of integrating various technical risk management practices.]

6 Andersen, T. J. and Young, P. C. (2020). *Strategic Risk Leadership: Engaging a World of Risk, Uncertainty, and the Unknown.* Routledge, Abingdon, UK. [This book spells out the story of ERM adoptions.]

7 World Economic Forum (2020). *Global Risk Report.* Geneva, Switzerland. [These reports provide ongoing and comprehensive reviews of global risks and responses.]

8 Andersen, T. J. and Bettis, R. A. (2015). Exploring longitudinal risk-return relationships. *Strategic Management Journal*, 36(8), 1135–1145.

9 Andersen, T.J., Denrell, J. and Bettis, R.A. (2007). Strategic responsiveness and Bowman's risk–return paradox. *Strategic Management Journal*, 28(4), 407–429.

10 Teece, D. J., Pisano, G. and Shuen, A. (1997). Dynamic capabilities and strategic management. *Strategic Management Journal*, 18(7), 509–533; Teece, D. J. (2007). Explicating dynamic capabilities: the nature and microfoundations of (sustainable) enterprise performance. *Strategic Management Journal*, 28(13), 1319–1350; Teece, D. J., Peteraf, M. and Leih, S. (2016). Dynamic capabilities and organizational agility: Risk, uncertainty, and strategy in the innovation economy. *California Management Review*, 58(4), 13–35.

11 Kelso, J. A. S. and Engstrøm, D. A. (2006). *The Complementary Nature*. MIT Press, Cambridge, MA; Pfeifer, R. and Bongard, J. (2009). *How the Body Shapes the Way We Think: A New View of Intelligence*. MIT Press, Cambridge, MA.

12 Andersen, T. J. (2017). *The Responsive Global Organization*. Emerald Studies in Global Strategic Responsiveness. Emerald Publishing, Bingley, UK; Andersen, T. J., and Fredens, K. (2013). The responsive organization: Understanding the dual processes of the human mind and human interaction in strategy making. CGSR Working Paper Series No. 1, Copenhagen Business School; Andersen, T. J., and Hallin, C. A. (2016). The adaptive organization and fast-slow systems. In Aldag, R. J. (Ed.), *Oxford Research Encyclopedias: Business and Management*. Oxford University Press, Oxford, UK.

13 Hong, L. and Page, S. E. (2004). Groups of diverse problem solvers can outperform groups of high-ability problem solvers. *Proceedings of the National Academy of Sciences of the United States of America*, 101(46), 16385–16389; Page, S. E. (2007). *The Difference: How the Power of Diversity Creates Better Groups, Firms, Schools, and Societies*. Princeton University Press, Princeton, NJ.

14 Woolley, A. W., Chabris, C. F., Pentland, A., Hashmi, N. and Malone, T. W. (2010). Evidence for a collective intelligence factor in the performance of human groups. *Science*, 330, 686–688.

15 Lévy, P. (1999). *Collective Intelligence: Mankind's Emerging World in Cyberspace*. Basic Books, New York, NY.

16 Malone, T. W. (2018). *Superminds: The Surprising Power of People and Computers Thinking Together*. Little, Brown, New York.

17 Cipolla, C. M. (2019). *The Basic Laws of Human Stupidity*. WH Allen, London, UK. (Published in Italian in 1988 by Società editrice il Mulino, Bologna.)

18 Lawrence, P. R. (2010). *Driven to Lead: Good, Bad, and Misguided Leadership*. Jossey-Bass, San Francisco, CA.

19 Andersen, T. J., Hallin, C. A. and Fredens, K. (2018). *Et Netværk af Hjerner: Tænk Med Dine Medarbejdere og Led Med Succes*. Gyldendal Business, Copenhagen, Denmark. [Translation: *A Network of Brains: Think with Your Employees and Lead with Success*.]

20 See, for example, Varela, F. J., Thompson, E. and Rosch, E. (1992). *The Embodied Mind: Cognitive Science and Human Experience*. MIT Press, Cambridge, MA; Thompson, E. (2007). *Mind in Life: Biology, Phenomenology, and the Sciences of Mind*. Harvard University Press, Cambridge, ME.

21 De Jaegher, H. and Di Paolo, E. (2007). Participatory sense-making: An enactive approach to social cognition. *Phenomenology and the Cognitive Sciences*, 6(4), 485–507.

22 Bonham, G. M. (1993). Cognitive mapping as a technique for supporting international negotiation. *Theory and Decision*, 34(3), 214–232.

23 Underdal, A. (1994). Leadership theory: Rediscovering the arts of management. In Rubin, J. Z. (Ed.), *International Multilateral Negotiation: Approaches to the Management of Complexity*, Chapter 8. Jossey-Bass, San Francisco, CA.

24 Ibid.

25 Liebenberg, A. P. and Hoyt, R. E. (2003). The determinants of enterprise risk management: Evidence from the appointment of Chief Risk Officers. *Risk Management and Insurance Review*, 6, 37–52. [This is an early effort to identify factors that influence the adoption of ERM.]

26 Beasley, M. S., Clune, R. and Hermanson, D. R. (2005). Enterprise risk management: An empirical analysis of factors associated with the extent of implementation. *Journal of Accounting and Public Policy*, 24, 521–531. [This provides an early assessment of implementation.]

27 Renn, O. (2003). *Risk Governance: Towards an Integrative Approach*. White Paper, International Risk Governance Council, Lausanne, Switzerland.

28 A brief illustration of work referenced by the IRGC could include: Renn, O. (2014). *Stakeholder Involvement in Risk Governance*. Ark Publications, London; Renn, O. (2014). Emerging risks: Methodology, classification and policy implications. *Journal of Risk Analysis and Crisis Response*, 4(3), 114–132; Renn, O. and Klinke, A. (2014). Risk governance and resilience: New approaches to cope with uncertainty and ambiguity. In U. Fra Paleo (Ed.), *Risk Governance: The Articulation of Hazard, Politics and Ecology* (pp. 19–42). Springer, Heidelberg.

29 Boehm, S. A., Dwertmann, D. J. G., Bruch, J. and Shamir, B. (2015). The missing link? Investigating organizational identity strength and transformational leadership climate as mechanisms that connect CEO charisma with firm performance. *The Leadership Quarterly*, 26(2), 156–171. [This is a relatively recent example of the study of charisma.]

30 Getha-Taylor, H. and Morse, R. S. (2013). Collaborative leadership development for local government officials: exploring competencies and program impact. *Public Administration Quarterly*, Spring, 71–102.

31 Ibid.

32 Emerson, K. and Smutko, L. S. (2011). *UNCG Guide to Collaborative Competencies*. Policy. Consensus Initiative and University Network for Collaborative Governance. Portland, OR.

33 Morse, R. S. and Stephens, J. B. (2012). Teaching collaborative governance: Phases, competencies, and case-based learning. *Journal of Public Affairs Education,* 18(3), 565–584.

34 Andersen, T. J. and Young, P. C. (2020). *Strategic Risk Leadership: Engaging a World of Risk, Uncertainty, and the Unknown*. Routledge, Abingdon, UK.

35 Campbell, P. R. (1998). The new history: The *Annales* School of History and Modern Historiography. In Lamont, W. M. (Ed.), *Historians and Historical Controversy*. UCL Press, London, UK.

36 Uhl-Bien, M. and Arena, M. (2018). Leadership for organizational adaptability: A theoretical synthesis and integrative framework. *The Leadership Quarterly*, 29, 89–104.

7 The case for risk leadership

A restatement

The structure of this book has been to first outline what we think we know about so-called "modern" risk management (primarily ERM but including other current forms), and then describe what the evidence reveals about risk management in action—that is, its performance and actual value contribution. So, Chapter One provided a short history of risk management—as we understand it today—and then Chapter Two looked at the evidence of its effectiveness. Three particular things were established:

1. The story of risk management starts with a collection of specific ideas and practices that all were responses to particular issues, problems, and challenges arising in organizational management over the course of the past 60 years. From this sequence of events and developments emerged a broader idea that these efforts were really different versions of the same thing and that it would be more productive to think about this larger thing as risk management playing out in a wider-ranging, interconnected context. In the terminology of this book, therefore, risk management revealed itself as an *emergent* practice, more so than a practice advancing from any fully formed theory. Although we want to be careful to acknowledge the merits of where risk management has ended up today, we do hold on to the idea that risk management as a field could have ended up differently if its history and construction had not unfolded exactly as it did.

2. Although not a rarity in the world of ideas, the theoretical argument for risk management appears much more persuasive than can presently be shown from practice. In other words, research has not been able to establish clearly that risk management practices produce the benefits that the theory argues should derive from it. There is something of a closed-loop aspect to this, we think. Theories work until they no longer work. Our Earth was assumed to be the center of the universe and centuries of efforts sought to interpret all evidence in light of that central belief—that is, until the weight of inconsistent evidence made that original belief untenable. Perhaps this analogy is overly dramatic, but we suspect something like this may be going on with risk management. This is to say, there is something of a "fitting the evidence to the theory" feel to the risk management literature. We search for evidence to justify the ERM idea, and we do succeed in finding some. But, exceptions, inconsistencies, and inconclusive evidence are mounting to a point where it is reasonable to ask, is the prevalent conceptualization of risk management actually the correct, or the only, way to think about it or do we need to extend our views?

3. Risk management as it is seen and practiced today is not wrong in its particulars. Things that risk managers do, by and large, need doing (buying insurance, hedging

DOI: 10.4324/9781003148579-7

financial risks, preventing accidents), but here we simply think that risk management has not been properly scoped. In focusing on the "doing" of things, the wider world of uncertainties, emergent phenomenon, and human perceptions sit as sidebar issues despite the fact that they seem to be the central issues in an increasingly complex world. So, we do not doubt that were we able to impose our way of thinking about risk management, it would still embrace and include the various technical practices we see today. They would just be contained within a much bigger idea.

Chapters Three to Six establish what might be seen as the basic pillars on which our bigger idea rests. In sum, the pillars are these. First, we need to reorient our thinking to look at the world through the lens of *complexity*. In employing that lens, we end up thinking differently about risk, uncertainty, and the unknown. Second, we observe, and believe, that risk management largely is a *moral exercise*, and all the technical aspects of risk management are instruments to support that morality and enhance critical thinking for the common good. Third, it has been said over the years that risk management is as much an art as a science, which we believe but—owing to the phrasing of the statement—it is usually interpreted as "risk management is as much an art as a science … but is mainly a science." In that light, we suggest a clarification. If risk management is science, it is primarily a *social science*. And fourth, risk management is increasingly about *collaborative effort*, partially as complex solutions benefit from collective inputs but also because many emergent exposures have community-wide (even worldwide) implications that cannot be resolved solely through individual efforts.

Oh yes, this book is obviously about risk leadership too—indeed, mainly so. Here we believe we have opened doors to making more firm research connections with the larger leadership literature, which may end up being the most useful outcome. Although academic noodling sometimes receives short shrift in the professional world, it still remains true that research generates new insights and ideas, and it can validate the relevance of those ideas to practice. In our view, if ideas such as risk leaders and risk leadership are allowed to float untethered from the larger scholarly sphere, they are ideas that are going nowhere.

We also believe—or hope—that our illustrative cases have served a constructive or revealing purpose, though we would be the first to admit that frequently (well, almost always) the cases leave us with more questions than answers. Still, if they have provoked fruitful discussion and provided some impetus for further investigation this may be the best one could hope for: to fuel critical thinking and learn from it.

Still, something is missing. In the Preface we conjured a picture of a risk manager/ leader, sitting alone in an office, with all the tools, ideas, techniques, and methods that are understood as comprising modern risk management. And our question to ourselves was really this: How does that person proceed in this leadership function? How is it all organized to address the things that need to be done? How is everything assembled? What is the game plan? And then, how are things operationalized in a specific organizational and/or environmental setting? Finally, what is this person's sensibility in organizing an approach to work? Well, let us talk a bit about this.

The reflective risk leader

We include risk managers in our thinking here but let us focus on risk leaders and risk leadership. And to begin, recall the provisional definition of risk leadership:

Risk Leadership, consistent with all Leadership, anticipates a moral relationship between leaders, followers, and other stakeholders that recognizes and accounts for the presence of contextual factors. Key characteristics of that relationship are that it is trust-based, attuned to rights and responsibilities, and includes a recognition of the emotional dimension and a commitment to the common good. It differs from other Leadership concepts in the technical focus, which is to thoughtfully engage the challenges driven by the presence of complexity, risk, uncertainty, and the unknown.

Ultimately, we will have some slight amendments to this definition, but here we want to consider those parts of the definition that connect with the book's chapters:

- Complexity is risk leadership's conceptual context
- Risk leadership is fundamentally a moral endeavor
- Risk leadership is a social science, and risk competence is its hallmark
- Humans are social beings and collaboration is the natural order of things
- This all implies a case for certain types of leadership

In discussing each point in turn, the intention is not just to restate the previous chapters but also to suggest ideas that might be considered and employed.

Complexity is risk leadership's conceptual context

There is one thing to say immediately about framing a professional view around the idea of complexity. It is humbling. Further, we will go out on a limb here and say that *humility*, in fact, may be a most useful attribute possessed by a risk or any type of leader. This version of humility, however, is not characterized by a lack of confidence in one's own abilities. Rather, it simply refers to a natural respect and regard for our human capabilities and limitations—particularly here with respect to our ability to truly understand our world. This is a prerequisite for an *enactive* approach to leadership that recognizes the limitations of executive decision-makers and invites the views and insights of many to derive more effective risk responses.

More clinically, we see humility as the root of our view that the purpose of risk management is to seek *sustainable resilience*. Others have noted this as an objective, but we want to be clear how utterly fundamental this is to our view of the risk leader's *sensibility* and work. Yes, preventing bad things from happening is important, but it is important in the sense that it supports the quest for resilience. Yes, capitalizing on opportunities is important too, but it is also important in the sense that it supports the quest for sustainability.

Beyond these clinical observations, focusing on sustainable resilience is supported by two basic motives. First, it signals our commitment to playing a long game—we want to win, whatever that may mean, but we want to be here for the long term and the long-run view must be central to our orientation and our work. Second, our sensibility is structured synchronically and diachronically (thinking across time and over time). In other words, we strive for the big picture view and—realizing that this is always just outside our grasp—we respect our limitations.

So, how do we acquire humility? This is a question of philosophy that is deserving of more attention than we can provide. It is also influenced by human psychological artifacts that can affect successful people such as executives and drive them toward hubristic behaviors. So, perhaps the better way to address this is to ask what we can do that presents opportunities to enhance and experience humility. There is a multitude of answers to this, but something simple or mundane like volunteering at a food bank or a homeless shelter or showing compassion and a willingness to do good for other less fortunate individuals might be a good start. However, let us try to be as concrete as we can about what humility means in the specific context of risk leadership.

Humility is a core attribute of leadership as we argue, but to focus only on it might forestall a more textured way of thinking about leadership in a complex and uncertain world. Perhaps the obvious first thing to suggest that understanding complexity (as a theoretical construct and as an empirically observable thing) seems to be a logical building block of humility. The essential impact of thinking about complexity is to shake one's mind free from linear, deterministic thinking. There are times, of course, when B follows A, but we always should be a bit surprised (and delighted and appreciative) when that is the case. For the most part, we are faced with uncertainty. Therefore, the sensibility of the reflective risk leader is shaped by an awareness that our main concerns should be focused on what we do not know, things we cannot say with confidence.

The immediate response to the preceding observation might be to wonder how we focus on the things we do not know. A revealing and relevant anecdote, strange though it may sound, is drawn from Martin Kemp's fascinating research on Leonardo da Vinci, highlighting alternative ways of critical thinking.[1] One of the world's leading scholars on da Vinci, Kemp has devoted many years to studying how da Vinci thought and reasoned. Through, among other things, an examination of the artist/scientist's notebooks, Kemp argues that *analogous thinking* was a key feature of the way he approached problem-solving. In da Vinci's case, his artistic genius was complemented by his methodical (though highly imaginative) scientific reasoning. Simplifying Kemp's view is not an easy thing, but one way to describe the da Vinci method is to see his scientific mind and his artistic mind as resources for one another. When struggling with an engineering problem, he might resort to his painting to work through the aspects of that problem. The reverse seemed true as well. Consider his work on perspective in his paintings.

Very, very few of us are Leonardos, but the more general observation is that there are ways of reasoning that do not particularly rely on strictly structured, modern research methodologies. Perhaps being widely read as a means of breaking down our own mental silos can help us—which actually leads to our second response.

Thinking Through Time, a book written by Richard Neustadt and Ernest May (1986) initiated a particular line of inquiry into how the study of history might benefit decision-makers.[2] Their work is referenced in Chapter Five, and one piece of advice would be to read it. Interestingly, Neustadt and May also highlight the importance of *analogous reasoning* as a central insight into how historians think. Beyond this capability, the authors focus on what we elsewhere call *synchronic* and *diachronic* thinking, among other tools and techniques, to help improve the ability to develop a capacity to think over long periods of time and across time as well.

What suggests itself here is a specific approach to critical thinking that is formed around:

- A familiarity with the concept of complexity
- A wider exposure to different ways of thinking and the interconnectivity of things
- An ability to have the longer-term view of "how things work"
- A basic understanding of the fundamental principles of logic
- An understanding of human nature/behavior and the influence of culture

These five elements would seem to at least heighten an appreciation of the centrality of humility and skepticism in our approach to leading on risk (uncertainty, etc.). But here we must acknowledge that managers and leaders do not just *think* about things; they are expected to *do* things too. There is plenty of reason to believe the elements above might guide one to a hermetic or—dare we say it—academic existence. Always contemplating; rarely doing. We are talking about managers and leaders here, so failure to consider the "doing" would be a fundamental omission.

Striking a balance between thought and action has been a preoccupation of philosophers since ancient times. Reflection is a benefit in its own right, but—importantly—also as a means of fortifying oneself for engagement. While bending the point just a bit, the emphasis of thinker/practitioners like Seneca might be said to strive for cheerfulness (read this, perhaps, as *optimism*) in the pursuit of self-knowledge and for *bravery* in engaging the uncertain and the unknown.[3] For Seneca, who—after all—was an advisor to Nero, of all people, the consolations of philosophy are found in the uses of reflection for finding one's way in the world.

Trawling the world of the ancient Romans may not be every reader's cup of tea, but the point to take away is that finding a balance in reflection and action has never been fully solved, but simply recognizing that *both* matter, and that struggling with that balance requires serious effort may be a step forward for most of us.

Risk leadership is fundamentally a moral endeavor

Possessing and maintaining virtue within an organization is not an easy thing. Behaving ourselves has—and will always be—as much an aspiration as an achievement. Societies and organizations have sought to control bad behavior by diktat, by moral suasion, and by every alternative in between—all with varying results. Having noted this, we were intrigued some time back by a comment made regarding the COSO guidance. An anonymous observer commented that "risk management should be an expression of an organization's values." We not only thought this was an interesting observation, but it has prompted an ongoing discussion to better understand exactly what that means or might mean. We began with a simple thought experiment: how could buying property insurance be interpreted as an expression of values?

While at first it seemed difficult to offer a credible answer, further consideration revealed that the question actually might be a quite useful way to think about the decision to employ risk management tools. For example, buying property insurance arguably might be motivated by the firm's need to affirm the importance of stewardship of resources, affirm a commitment to follow the laws of the land (since some insurance might be legally required), it might also signal a commitment to the long run, and it may also demonstrate managerial seriousness and competence to key stakeholders.

Still, the point stands that it is not always obvious what it means to see risk management as an expression of values. We will have a bit more to say below, but here recall the discussion of *teleopathy* and note that one way to support a values-based discussion of risk management might be through thinking about the Goals–Means–Values triad. Is risk management serving to secure the connection between these three things, or is it placing stress on, or breaking, the connections? Is the way in which we manage IT security demonstrating our values in terms of supporting the means by which we pursue our organizational goals? If risk management is an expression of values, then consideration of teleopathy very well might be a starting point for risk-related decision-making.

Consideration of the moral dimension of risk management shines a light on one particular aspect of what might be called the *duality* of risk management and the risk leadership role. While this is not precisely an exclusive feature of risk management, it is nevertheless true that the Risk Leader is conceived as both a trusted member of the leadership team and as an independent monitor of how decisions are made and implemented. We might specifically say the same of some others, internal auditors come to mind, but there is a difference in terms of the scope of responsibility. A vivid illustration of this duality is found in Risk Leaders being expected to contribute to the development of strategy while also possessing the capacity to be able to step back, objectively observe, and critique the process and the actors. For example, in this book, we offer a rather pointed discussion about human behavior and particularly the behavior of "bad leaders." Does a CRO have the ability to advise that CEO on some particular decision, but also have the bandwidth (is that a useful euphemism?) to be able to call out that same CEO for deceitful or illegal behavior? We wonder.

Let us try to be as clear as possible here.

Several of the case studies have highlighted that while virtuous behavior may be assumed to be the norm in general—and we tend to think that view is more often correct than incorrect—examples of egregious violations of that norm abound. Values and virtuous behavior matter, but they both are in constant need of attention. This does not mean that legislating morality alone is the answer, nor is self-regulation a singular solution. The realistic response is to note that human weakness will often lead to bad behavior and that some controls are necessary, but that most people strive to be virtuous and so strict rules and regulations can send a signal to employees and managers of low trust and can be overly constraining. And constraints can interfere with supporting an organization's capacity to adapt and innovate. This is precisely why the importance of organizational *culture* features so prominently as a "third" vehicle for virtue.

Later, the discussion turns to risk leadership as a social science, and one implication of this view is to first understand human morality as a central feature of culture. It is a feature of other things too (the entirety of human nature, for example), but since leadership requires leaders and followers, it may be useful to consider immorality first in a cultural context. How does culture (through its values, beliefs, etc.) establish what is moral and immoral? And then, second, what does culture "do" about immorality? This does seem to suggest a rather cumbersome way of responding to a specific illegal action, for example, but for the *reflective* risk leader, consideration of immorality, illegality, and bad behavior in light of the culture seems to be a first-order issue. In any event, this appears to be a sounder footing for then considering what may be done from a rules and controls standpoint, what may be expected from self-regulation, and what may be signaled through other cultural means to address bad behavior.

Clearly, this is an issue for societies as a whole, but it leads to a very different line of investigation. Here, in the context of organizations, the possibility of addressing the cultural roots of virtue seems to present itself at a smaller scale with—perhaps—a more realistic opportunity for improvement.

Two related issues warrant a mention here—one of which, we concede, may simply not be resolvable. First, the view that risk management is—or should be—an expression of organizational values needs further consideration and study. Even if that view is correct, it is difficult to offer a complete and orderly argument at present. The beginning of such a supporting argument does seem simple enough. Risk managers tend to deal with the consequences of decisions and actions in their organization, which almost by definition have moral consequences (sometimes amoral motives). Further, an organization's values are reflected in its reputation, the loss of which most executives continue to believe is a top strategic concern. Beyond this, however, it becomes quite difficult to work out how we determine that something is an expression of values—except in the most obvious or abstract situations. The teleopathy concept provides some footing for this, but more thought is necessary.

The more practical issue, which may have no easy solution, is the *duality* of the Risk Leader role. Risk Leaders are part of the decision-making management team, but there is an assumption that they are also auditors, monitors, and regulators of the organization's decisions and actions. Can a CRO be both in the team and not in the team? This is not a unique aspect of risk management and leadership, as noted. Ideally and presumably the risk leader would exhibit consistent virtue in all aspects of life, so the issue here probably is not so much the difficulty in personal constancy. Rather, it is the external stresses, pressures, and differences between the two roles where issues arise. The perceptions of others matter too. Is "auditing" executive performance seen as "not being a team player?" Earlier, the observation was made that the emergence of the CRO role has largely been the result of outside forces (new rules and regulations); motives that have been shown to raise the question in c-suites "are you or are you not with us?" Further, because that perception exists, many CROs cite the development of a working relationship with the c-suite (in both roles) to be the first—and often the most critical—thing they have to address. And, in some situations, it is the only thing they can focus on in the early days.

Risk leadership is a social science and risk competence is its hallmark

This is a challenging proposition to summarize. We suppose the glib answer is to encourage hiring liberal arts majors (good ones, that is). As business professors, this is a rather unsettling argument to make—unsettling to us because we would lose students—but there is a substantive point here. The idea of an educated individual was, for hundreds of years, conceived as involving knowledge of grammar, logic, and rhetoric. Logic, by the way, would include logic with numbers, so this concept in no way slights numeracy. These are the liberal arts in their essence, the mastery of critical thinking.

We have discussed whether our view is just a rhetorical device or whether it actually means something to say that risk management and leadership are social sciences, rather than, say, a technical-scientific function. Perhaps not surprisingly, we do think it means something. It is a dramatic change of perspective—and effort—to say that a foundation knowledge of risk management is to understand people. All the technical things we do to assess and address risk and uncertainty are important to know, but this is putting things the wrong way around. Those are things we do, informed by our knowledge of our fellow humans. What can be done about that?

First, acknowledge that this issue is significantly related to the discussion of complexity. It would seem probable that the sensibility described in the analysis of complexity would lead to an understanding of the centrality of the human dimension of risk management. The difficulty in making the distinction we seek here is that risk management has always paid attention to the impact of risk on humans, notably employees. Workplace safety, worker safety, employee benefits, and wellness programs—all have a long-distinguished history in the array of risk management concerns.

Still, the argument that the core focus on risk management has always been on humans and human behavior derives from a limited framing of the issue. Traditionally, we have been primarily concerned with harm that might befall our employees (decidedly a good thing to focus on), but we tend to short-change the myriad ways in which humans are exposed to risk but also produce interactive effects with the risk management measures we employ and—importantly—are a source of risk themselves for good or ill. Some might say that fidelity or surety bonds provide examples of anticipation of humans as a source of risk, and that is true enough. But there we are talking about humans as a source of specific legal risks.

Employee and manager underperformance (and overperformance, for that matter) includes various behaviors that do not rise to the level of illegality but affect outcomes for good or bad. Some of those are handled through Human Relations, or Ethics Offices, or other areas of management. But only rarely are those activities integrated with risk management (or *vice versa*). To state our argument as simply as possible, risk management requires a 360-degree view of people as the complicated bundle of opportunities, exposures to risk and uncertainty, sources of risk, producers of adaptations and innovations, conveyors of virtue, and—it must be included here—threats.

Humans are social beings and collaboration is the natural order of things

This insight might seem secondary to our other essential points. Here we seem to be talking about a methodology rather than a matter of philosophy. However, our view of collaboration is not that it is only a method for responding to risk and uncertainty (though it certainly is that). Rather, that collaborative endeavor is fundamental to human nature.

It is true that the dynamic life of risk management has led us to a greater awareness of the importance of collaboration in ERM, but also in meeting the global risk challenges we face today. But taking a step back, we have to say that the rediscovery of the centrality of that fact remains incomplete. In modern times—we would suggest—politics, society, economics, and modernity have tended to view collaboration as an option, especially in a 21st century, Western, democratic/free market world. Setting up such a separation of the common good from individual freedom is unhelpful—indeed, we think it is wrong—in denying the basic nature of human beings. We are all for individualism and individual effort and rewards, but they are a *feature* existing within the context of connectivity and collaboration, not its alternative. Or, at least, it should not be seen that way.

What are present and future risk leaders supposed to make of this?

To begin, dispense with the idea of risk managers and leaders having the power of *command*. Occasionally, an emergency or a disaster may put a risk leader in a position of issuing orders, and there may be certain job responsibilities that give risk managers authority to direct particular things. But, for the most part, the risk leader's or manager's influence comes from the power to persuade, collaborate, build partnerships, and encourage cooperation—while at the same time showing humility, recognizing the limits of what is known, and shaping the broad insights that emerge from dispersed organizational stakeholders. This is an approach to forming comprehension under complex circumstances and getting things done; something historically noted as important, but often lauded more in the breach than in the observance. Further, it is sad to say, such an approach is often interpreted evidence of managerial failure, which is to say, persuading comes to be seen as pleading, needling, and pestering employees.

It is in this sense that any discussion of risk leadership also applies to almost all technical risk managers. Virtually all in the field have to rely on skills and abilities that do not rest on express authority or the ability to direct or command. Persuasion is the name of the game, and it is interesting to note that the aforementioned Richard Neustadt actually is better known for his study of the US presidency, arguing in his work that the essential power of a president is the power to *persuade*.[4]

This all implies a case for certain types of leadership

We certainly must allow for the fact that organizations and other settings will always have specific features that require different forms of leadership. We say so in this book. Still, the preceding discussions in this and prior chapters are suggestive of a certain set of attributes *likely* to be most often relevant in a risk leadership context. In Chapter Three, for example, the concept of Leadership for Organizational Adaptability was introduced and considered as a possible "connecting idea" in the Leadership literature. In that discussion, the description of a leader for adaptability was:

> (Facilitating) … (b)oundary spanning, organizing and implementing aligned actions, promoting cross-functional training, joint planning and decision-making, deploying resources across units to foster interconnectivity.[5]

This seems a reasonable start to thinking about leadership in Risk Leadership. It does pertain to actions more so than sensibilities (or knowledge, skills, abilities, attributes in combination), but the essence of leading in complex environments is relevant. Taken as a whole, the book has visited several characteristics that probably sit just below the actions described earlier:

- Risk competence, of course. Adjunct to this, knowledge of the "business" (not just a company but the sector) would be a feature
- Emotional intelligence/self-awareness
- Humility
- Openness to other views/insights
- Eclectic interests–intellectual curiosity
- Seeking personal virtue
- Abstract reasoning/logic
- Brave and optimistic
- Exceptional interpersonal skills

Here, we step aside to reflect on risk management education, training, and professional development more generally. And in reflecting, we observe that the insertion of risk leadership into the range of careers/functions within the field of risk management ends up requiring a reconsideration of all aspects of training and development. This is something beyond the ambitions of this book, but some comments may be useful.

A number of professional certification programs exist to support the development of risk managers. It would feel good to say that colleges and universities around the world offer undergraduate and graduate degrees in the field, but honestly, there are not that many. This may be suggestive of a couple of things—one is business school politics, which is barely worth discussing. The second is the rather technical school orientation of risk management's past, meaning the holder of any undergraduate degree might be prepared through the addition of a professional certification. Frankly, there is nothing wrong with this. The only limitation here is that in the absence of a "major" in risk management within a business school commonly means business students in general get no exposure to the subject, which to our way of thinking is a critical problem for the field.

At the graduate level, someone already in the field is probably better off getting a more generalist MBA or MPA, which by the way was the original intention of MBA programs. The inclusion of a risk *leadership* emphasis/concentration/major might warrant consideration, given demographics in such programs, but most MBA students would not be far enough along in their careers to be looking at, say, a CRO position as their next step.

This leads us to the realm of Executive Development, and that seems to be about the right placement for individuals seeking to become a Risk Leader. However, this book has also described risk leadership as occurring—potentially—at all levels of an organization, and in other settings. This is where we return to the sad omission of risk management and leadership perspectives from general business education at the undergraduate and graduate levels. The orientation of such a course would be different from a standard Introduction to Risk Management and Insurance course, but even a standard introductory course would be something to applaud.

So here we find ourselves at the end of this book—except for the final cases!—concluding on a rather unsettled point. We think it is conceivable to imagine a program of study for risk leadership (and Risk Leaders), but such a thing does not exist at present, and there are some practical obstacles. Still, one of the oldest sayings in risk management is that "nothing sells risk management like a disaster." Returning to our very opening sentences in this book, 2020 has certainly served as a motive for an interest in risk management and, particularly, leadership. The time may be right for some useful advancements in both studying and practicing risk leadership.

The cases

This chapter provides a summarizing assessment of risk leadership, speculating on implications, but it is also focused on particular insights that might guide individuals in that role. The chapter provides not merely a summary but goes some way toward setting out specific ways to apply the subject matter throughout the book. The objective of securing risk leadership within the wider Leadership research field is revisited and future steps are set out. However, the main focus is on the professional practitioner and so the discussion of next steps is more fully addressed to this audience. Two somewhat longer cases, both presenting a specific risk leadership issue, are broad enough to cover a spectrum of risk leadership points for discussion.

Case 7.1: How do organizations and leaders learn? The shuttles Challenger and Columbia

Case overview

While the majority of case studies covering NASA's two most notable disasters tend to focus on one or the other, the story of the relationship of the two events has emerged as a distinctly specific category of examination. Is there a story that directly connects the two events? Of course, it is possible to suspect a connection without examining the details. Both disasters befell space shuttles, both were NASA endeavors, and superficially both were failures of engineering. But in attempting to dig more deeply, the question becomes, not "what" happened, but "why." And how does this help us learn?

However, begin with the "what."

Space shuttle Challenger

On January 28, 1986, the space shuttle Challenger disintegrated 73 seconds after launch, killing its entire crew of seven. The flight was the tenth for the Challenger itself. The technical explanation of the event is summarized as follows:

> Shortly after launch, a joint in its right solid rocket booster failed. This failure was attributed to the specific inability of an O-ring (a seal for the joint) to respond to the unusually cold weather conditions at launch. In simplest terms, the cold temperatures did not allow the O-ring to expand and seal the joint. This allowed pressurized burning gas within the booster to escape and damage hardware attached to an external fuel tank. This led to a structural failure of that tank, which in turn influenced specific aerodynamic forces that broke apart the shuttle.

A number of features of the Challenger disaster added a particular poignancy to the events that day. One feature of note is that the launch was witnessed in classrooms around the United States. The crew included a teacher, and this flight was intended in part to promote science education and include live "lessons from space." Thus—though far from the worst aspect of the incident—the launch was watched by many, many more people than would ordinarily have done so at this stage of the shuttle program's life.

Space shuttle Columbia

The Columbia incident occurred on February 1, 2003, just over 17 years after the Challenger disaster. In this case, the accident occurred at the end of the shuttle's voyage (however, events were set in motion by an incident at launch), with the orbiter disintegrating as it reentered the atmosphere. Again, all seven crew members were killed. The technical description of the event is summarized as follows:

> During launch, a piece of foam insulation broke off an external tank and struck the orbiter's left wing. The damage sustained at that time was to the protective tiles allowing super-heated atmospheric gases to penetrate the shuttle's heat shield. Consequently, the orbiter suffered significant damage with the internal wing structure, which in turn led to the shuttle becoming unstable and breaking apart.

To the general public, the loss of the Columbia appeared to be quite similar to the Challenger disaster. Both events could be traced to a specific engineering failure. However, in addition to the subsequent discovery of deeper "root cause" factors, the story of the Columbia was significantly influenced by the fact that this was the second of two disasters to befall NASA, which introduced a new dimension of analysis. How did this happen *again*?

The search for root causes

Risk analysis may involve a wide-ranging number of methodologies and structural approaches. Beyond the surface issues of likelihood and potential impacts, most analysis endeavors to address underlying factors with the rarely attained Holy Grail being the ultimate *root cause*. It is rarely attained not because analysis methods are not powerful or useful, but rather because complexity is present. Complexity suggests many things, but the key here is the absolute difficulty (impossibility) of having complete confidence in our perceptions and evidence. Even when the outcome is known with certainty, the ability to retrofit a story that explains the causes of that outcome we discover that complexity exists in the past too and the ability to make absolute pronouncements is difficult-to-impossible.

Such is the case with the stories of Challenger and Columbia. We do know a lot, and we do have a persuasive grasp of the factors leading to both disasters, but we have also lost what might be called the "emotional essence" of the story. That is, at any given moment where key decisions were made or not made, or actions were or were not taken, can we fully capture the mind of the decision-maker at those moments? We can imagine bureaucratic, political, even scientific pressures that affect the decision-maker at that moment, but it is just beyond our grasp to say, "This is exactly how a manager saw the situation, saw the choices, managed the emotional dimension, and processed the many considerations that would go into a decision."

So, risk analysis starts with an awareness that there are things we cannot, will not, are unable to know about a given situation. And this happens with assessments of past events as well as the future. So, it must be with the story of the Challenger and Columbia disasters. And yet—there is much that can be gained from what we can find. In brief here is what we can understand about the two stories that may help clarify why a disaster happened *again*.

The analysis of the Challenger disaster was conducted through a formally authorized inquiry, what came to be called the Rogers Commission. In the initial phases, the commission focused on the *immediate proximate cause*, the O-ring failure. Here the science was found to be clear. O-rings harden in cold temperatures preventing a full seal of the joints. Temperatures on the day of the launch were in the range where hardening would occur. Therefore, the question arose, was the decision to launch the true *immediate proximate cause*? A telling quote within the Commission's report contains the essence of that moment. The report indicates that the decision to launch was the product of:

> a conflict between engineering data and management judgments, and a NASA management structure that permitted internal flight safety problems to bypass key Shuttle managers.

Here risk analysis methods turn to consider the "causes of causes." What had produced the conflict that led to the decision to launch? The Commission broadened the scope of its inquiry to examine, yes, the engineering data in more detail, but also managerial judgments and the management structure—and to understand the longer story that leads to the disasters.

For purposes of brevity here, the story of both the shuttle program disasters might be said to begin with the triumph of the moon landings. In very short order, NASA had achieved its strategic purpose—to put a man on the moon by the end of the 1960s. While President Kennedy's directive stands as an example of how a clear, direct, and simple objective can—in itself—serve to propel the work necessary to achieve that goal, in this story it also meant that the achievement of that goal left NASA, and indeed, the United States as a whole, bereft of a clear vision for the future. Political will and commitments of resources began to diminish, and NASA found itself in a position of having to discover a new or longer-term ambition to justify its existence. In some senses NASA never did. What it did do narrows the narrative leading to the disasters.

The response to changes in the political and public support was to conceive of an initiative that was based on routine and economic ventures in space. Certainly understandable as a choice, but also nowhere as clear as the "any cost, any burden" ethos of Kennedy's vision. The manifestation of this new direction—it is difficult to call it a strategy—was the introduction of the Space Shuttle program. The language of this new direction was built around the number of missions per year (24 was the goal), seeking greater economies, and reducing average costs through repeated use of hardware. Tellingly, the design of the shuttle itself revealed this language in action. Some basic safety features were excluded (a launch escape tower, ejection seats). Further, the funding process quickly devolved into a yearly hat-in-hand exercise that—owing to the emphasis on economics and the routinizing of a heretofore glamorous and heroic venture—led to ongoing underfunding, at least in the judgment of the Rogers Commission.

Beyond these underlying factors, issues pertaining to managerial structure and performance, and individual leadership emerged. The Commission sought to recommend a number of measures to improve lines of communication—interactions between the engineers and scientists and managers. Career management issues were discussed. The Commission's essential takeaway was an organizational structure adrift with a lack of clarity in terms of understanding mission, purpose, lines of authority, decision rules, and more. Indeed, the organizational culture of NASA came into focus as an issue influencing almost all aspects of management and leadership.

The Commission's report was released with great fanfare in 1989 and this led to a resumption of the shuttle program, which—to the general public—was interpreted as evidence that the causes of the disaster had been fully identified and, if not fully addressed, were on their way to being addressed. In fact, that general sensibility of "problems solved" remained up to at least 2002. In an interview with NASA's then-Chief Administrator, Sean O'Keefe, he indicated that the safety culture was strong and that NASA managers kept a copy of the Rogers Report in their desks. This view, seemingly, was offered in response to criticisms at the time that echoed the concerns raised in that Rogers report.

Thus, when the Columbia accident took place in 2003, the investigative body (the Columbia Accident Investigation Board—CAIB), followed the pathway set out by the Rogers Commission 16 years earlier, which is to say, the search for proximate, systematic, and root causes commenced again. As noted, the proximate causes were vaguely similar though quite different in technical substance. However, when attention turned to management, leadership, culture, funding, and governance, the story was horrifyingly in line with the Rogers' findings. Such was the consistency in the CAIB findings that it chose to include special analysis on similarities of the two disasters.

Notable in CAIB's assessment of the common features of Challenger and Columbia were three key observations. First, despite numerous technical changes made after Challenger, there was little evidence of institutional change. This was interpreted as meaning that the organization's structure, systems and processes, and management (and leadership) had not been changed in any fundamental ways since Challenger. Second, if institutional change did not take place, accidents like Challenger and Columbia will continue to occur. And third, individual responsibility and accountability are not exempt from the concerns about institutional defects. This was meant to suggest that the personal qualities of managers, engineers, and others were key factors in both accidents. Embedded in that third point was a concern about the institutional *culture*.

Postscript

As just a point of reference, the post-Columbia story for NASA has provided evidence of a significantly different look for the organization; a change characterized by, initially, the Constellation Program, which set goals for the future (including decommissioning the shuttle program, which was completed in 2011). Since 2010, a Commercial Crew Program introduced many features involving human space travel, but significantly—and expressly—involved partnerships with private organizations (Boeing, SpaceX), and international collaborations (Soyuz).

Various initiatives have been proposed, even initiated since Columbia. These include—in no particular order—travel to Mars, a permanent Moon base, a Space Force (part of the US Armed Forces), a Lunar Gateway (a permanent base orbiting the Moon), and a number of commercial collaborations. All in all, while initiatives have been greatly influenced by the political leadership changes since 2003, some general themes seem to have emerged and continued to persist. These include a vision of NASA as an initiator of or catalyst for collaborative ventures, a leader in the identification of new space-related projects, and NASA seems to have recognized that it is a repository of a wide range of knowledge, skill, and experience that may be applied in new ways—education being an obvious example—but also using those assets to collaborate with researchers to test new theories and insights. It is, in fact, a portfolio approach to its mission.

Does this represent "learning from the past," and an adaptive response?

Reflections

In this concluding chapter, an effort is made to consider the implications of the views we set out in the preceding six chapters (and, indeed, in our previous book). We have attempted to apply these views to real uses, but it is nevertheless true that many of our ideas are intended just to prompt thought—that is, thought about the real nature, purpose, and value of risk management and leadership. In the case of Challenger and Columbia, we see a large number of things to reflect on, and a number of things that might be done to bring value to an organization or in other settings. The following sets out three prominent issues deserving reflection, but it is hoped that readers will be able to identify other ideas from this short story. For example, the "Postscript" suggests a story where both *adaptation* has occurred, and where NASA has recognized *collaboration* as a model for future growth.

- To many, culture seems to be an abstract concept and difficult to observe in action. However, in both post-mortem studies of the disasters, cultural problems are identified as critical causal factors. Culture has many definitions, but here we think of it as ways in which a group of people believe, think, and behave. It is, we might say, learned behavior. Perhaps it is slightly more precise to say it is a pattern of learned behavior as well as a product of that learned behavior. The product is our attitudes, values, and knowledge, of course, but also including music, art, language, and other means of communication. And it is important to add that it must be—more or less—shared by the entire group, however, defined.

- Given this imagery, what does it mean to say that "cultural problems" were very much at the heart of NASA's two catastrophes? It is notable that organizational cultures are more mutable than social/national cultures, and this suggests that change, modification, and adaptation can be—perhaps—more quickly and dramatically achieved in organizations. So, beyond acknowledging the influences of culture in these disasters, what specifically might we imagine doing to remedy the problem?
- The risk analysis "journey" from proximate cause to root cause is a particularly interesting aspect of the Challenger and Columbia stories. And it seems to be interesting that though the proximate causes were technically distinct and different, the analysis led to a similar conclusion about root causes—serving as a modest validation of the analytical processes employed.
  - Is it possible to develop a general description of the process of risk analysis? This question seeks to encourage a principles-based, rather than technical reflection. How does a risk leader think about "getting to the bottom" of a risk issue—especially something as complicated as an institutional failure?
- Institutional memory/institutional learning—how is it inculcated into an organization? Remembering and adapting are presented in this book as fundamental risk management/leadership tools. They are, to employ another concept, *dynamic capabilities* that contribute to sustainably resilient organizations. Beyond introducing or developing the ideas, how are they managed and maintained, and how do we know when they are working?

Read more about it

Boin, A. and Fishbacher-Smith, D. (2011). The importance of failure theories in assessing crisis management: The *Columbia* space shuttle disaster revisited. *Policy and Society*, 30(2), 77–87.
Garrett, T. M. (2004). Whither challenger, whither Columbia: Management decision making and the knowledge analytic. *The American Review of Public Administration*, 34(4), 389–402.
Mason, R. O. (2004). Can a culture be lethal? Lessons in organizational ethics from the Columbia disaster. *Organizational Dynamics*, 33(2), 128–142.
Seife, C. (2003). Columbia disaster underscores the risky nature of risk analysis. *Science*, 299(5609), 1001–1002.

Case 7.2: British Petroleum (BP): From "beyond petroleum" to "net zero" and between

Case overview

John Browne, (then) CEO of British Petroleum (BP), was close to UK Prime Minister, Tony Blair, and was on the record endorsing government regulations to reduce carbon emissions. In a speech held at Stanford University in May 1997, he stated:

> There is now an effective consensus among the world's leading scientists and serious and well informed people outside the scientific community that there is a discernible

human influence on the climate…it would be unwise and potentially dangerous to ignore the mounting concern…if we are to take responsibility for the future of our planet, then it falls to us to begin to take precautionary action now.[6]

Browne committed BP to take "five steps" to tackle the climate challenge: reduce CO_2 emissions; support research and development; collaborate on new technologies; invest in alternative energy; and contribute to the search for global solutions.

John Browne argued it was time to act rather than debate.[7] He rebranded BP as "Beyond Petroleum" with a new green-white-yellow logo suggesting a look past oil and gas toward eco-friendly solar and renewable energy. It also symbolized a corporation dedicated to a vision of "*better people, better products, beyond petroleum.*" The urge to take environmental responsibility challenged the industry and earned him the nickname: "Sun King of the oil industry." Browne was knighted for his services to industry in 1998 and was appointed to the House of Lords in 2001 on Blair's recommendation.

Bernard Looney, who spent his career at BP including production and drilling in the North Sea, Vietnam, and Mexico, became CEO in February 2020. One of his first deeds was to set a new ambition for BP: "To become a net zero company by 2050 or sooner."[8]

This established "five aims" for BP: reach net zero CO_2 emissions across operations; achieve net zero carbon effect in oil and gas production; a 50% cut in the carbon intensity of products; reduce methane intensity in operations by 50%; and investing in non-oil and gas businesses.

In Bernard Looney's words:

> The world's carbon budget is finite and running out fast; we need a rapid transition to net zero. We all want energy that is reliable and affordable, but that is no longer enough. It must also be cleaner. This will certainly be a challenge, but also a tremendous opportunity. It is clear to me, and to our stakeholders, that for BP to play our part and serve our purpose, we have to change. And we want to change—this is the right thing.

To deliver on this ambition, BP must undertake major changes:

> We need to reinvent BP. To keep up with rapidly-evolving customer demands and society's expectations, we need to become more integrated and more focused. So we are undertaking a major reorganisation, introducing a new structure, a new leadership team and new ways of working for all of us. [Bernard Looney]

So, what are the prospects of succeeding with the proposed climate-conscious initiatives this time around, and what actually happened in the interim period?

History

The Anglo-Persian Oil Company was founded in 1908 after eight years of search for oil in a remote area of Persia (now Iran). It was renamed the Anglo-Iranian Oil Company in 1935 and became the British Petroleum Company in 1954. The company continued to grow exploration and development of new oil fields under demanding geopolitical and physical conditions. After the 1973 oil crisis, BP started exploration in new locations including Prudhoe Bay, Alaska, and the North Sea. This reduced dependency on the Middle East but also introduced new technical challenges. BP worked with Standard Oil of Ohio that was subsequently acquired followed by mergers with Amoco and ARCO and the acquisition of Castrol. BP grew into a global enterprise with over 100,000 people employed in more than 100 countries.

BP had worldwide operations with headquarters in London, England. North America was the largest division and the second-largest producer of oil and gas in the United States. By 2005, the company was the largest energy company in the world measured by revenues ahead of Exxon and Shell.[9] The company had business operations in all parts of the value-chain in the oil and gas industry ranging from exploration, extraction, refining, petrochemicals, and power generation to energy distribution, marketing, and trading.

John Browne became CEO in 1995 and was instrumental in BP's expansion toward global dominance. He called for a better balance between economic development and environmental protection considering sustainable energy sources to address climate change. He was also mindful of the dependence on oil to source the global energy needs engaging in major exploration projects in Alaska, the Gulf of Mexico, Russia, Azerbaijan, Indonesia, and elsewhere.

When Tony Hayward was appointed CEO of BP in 2007, he identified safety, recruitment for talent, and performance to restore revenues and reduce costs as key challenges for the company going forward. There was some focus on biofuel investments, but the emphasis was changing from environmental concerns to safety and protection of investments.

Shifts in leadership

Tony Hayward took over from John Browne during spring 2007 and Tony Hayward was replaced by Bob Dudley in the fall of 2010. These executive changes happened under two different chairmen. Peter Sutherland was appointed Chairman of BP in 1997, after serving as non-executive director 1990–1993 and 1995–1997. Sutherland retired in December 2009. Carl-Henric Svanberg joined the board as non-executive director in September 2009 from a prior position as CEO of LM Ericsson and became Chairman in January 2010.

John Browne was credited for turning BP into a successful global energy company and the first oil producer to acknowledge a link between the use of fossil fuels and global warming. Hence, Landor Associates survey found that 21% of consumers perceived BP as the greenest among the major oil companies.[10] Lord Browne was known for his willingness to think big and accept risks. It was under his leadership the Amoco merger went through in 1998, as one of the largest M&A transactions ever, valued at US$48.2 billion and making BP the world's largest multinational oil company.[11] The merger combined BP's exploration competencies with Amoco's activities in oil refining and chemicals. The merger was planned to deliver substantial synergies with operational savings of at least US$2 billion annually and another US$1 billion cost reductions in administration.[12]

The Texas City explosion

On March 23, 2005, a hydrocarbon vapor cloud exploded at the ISOM isomerization process unit at BP's Texas City refinery in Texas City, Texas, killing 15 workers and injuring more than 170 others. It was the third-largest US refinery incorporated through the Amoco merger. The incident was caused by numerous technical and organizational shortcomings at the plant and in BP's continued use of an outdated blowdown drum, lack of safety-critical systems, inoperative alarms, and so on. This reflected ongoing cost-cutting exercises, inadequate training, poor communication between operations and managers, failure to invest in equipment, and an inadequate corporate safety culture. The US Chemical Safety and Hazard Investigation Board investigated the incident (led by James Baker III) with its report due July 2007.[13] This prompted the premature resignation of Lord Browne on May 1, 2007.

The report provided a less than flattering picture of the practices in BP stating, "that BP has not provided effective process safety leadership and has not adequately established process safety as a core value across all its five U.S. refineries." Furthermore, the panel found "a lack of operating discipline, tolerance of serious deviations from safe operating practices, and apparent complacency toward serious process safety risks at each refinery." BP was later charged with criminal violations of federal environmental laws with many lawsuits requesting compensation for damages. The US District Court fined BP US$50 million for environmental violations and BP made payments of more than US$1.6 billion to the victims and their families.

Lord Browne stepped down earlier than originally planned. It was already announced in January 2007 that Tony Hayward would replace him in July 2007 (coinciding with the release of the Baker Report). The process was advanced by 18 months from the official executive retirement age of 60 by late 2008. The creeping safety and environmental issues related to the Alaska pipeline, start-up delays at the Thunder Horse project in the Gulf of Mexico, and not least the Texas City explosion seemed to accelerate his retirement. What further prompted the abrupt resignation in May 2007 was the fact that he was caught lying in court about an intimate partnership with another man.[14]

John Browne had asked the High Court to prevent reporting by the *Mail on Sunday* on his male partner, taking the legal battle all the way to the House of Lords, which refused his appeal. The judges ruled that the newspaper could write about alleged misuse of BP resources by his partner including use of computers, support staff, and involving personnel in setting up a company run by the male partner [Mr. Chevalier].[15] This situation forced John Browne to resign with immediate effect and BP accepted his resignation with the "deepest regret."

The shift at the helm

Hayward had joined BP in 1982 and assumed various technical and commercial roles in exploration in London, Aberdeen, Glasgow, France, and China. He became president of BP Venezuela in 1995, returned to London in 1997 as director of exploration, became Group Treasurer in 2000, and Chief Executive of Exploration and Production in 2003. As Tony Hayward replaced John Browne, the corporate emphasis shifted from sustainable energy to focus on safety as a premier priority after the Texas City refinery accident.

Despite this focus on safety, the company had to pay US$13 million in fines for over 400 safety violations at the Texas City refinery during an inspection in 2009 by the Occupational Safety and Health Administration (OSHA).[16] In fact, the Texas City refinery together with another BP facility in Toledo, Ohio, accounted for the vast majority of flagrant violations in the US refining industry over the three years following the explosion. All the while, the competition for global sourcing of crude oil increased due to powerful entrants from various transition economies including firms like Kuwait Petroleum, Lukoil (Russia), Petrobras (Brazil), and Petronas (Malaysia).

Deepwater Horizon

The Thunder Horse oil field was developed by BP with ExxonMobil as a 25% partner from 1999 onwards. It was the largest offshore platform in the Mexican Gulf and an important element of BP's global oil exploration strategy. The development of the field was also a technological challenge because drilling took place on the seabed under 1,500 meters of water. The Mexican Gulf also exposed the seaborne oil rigs to tropical hurricanes.

BP started drilling the Macondo prospect on October 21, 2009. This was initially carried out by a semi-submersible drilling rig, the *Marianas*, leased from Swiss-based Transocean. However, the oil rig was damaged by Hurricane Ida, which passed through the northern part of the Mexican Gulf in late November 2009 as an extra-tropical cyclone. This halted the drilling as the *Marianas* had to undergo repairs, so BP leased another rig from Transocean, the *Deepwater Horizon*, to continue work in February 2010.

BP had encountered problems during the initial installation of the well that led to some alterations on the well abandonment procedure on April 19, 2010, including so-called centralizers to stabilize and hold the installation intact. The reason for this was that a more extensive solution would cost US$7 to $10 million more and take longer. Halliburton, the contractor hired by BP to manage the rig, warned BP about potentially severe gas flow problem if the casing only had six centralizers.

On April 20, 2010, BP was six weeks behind schedule and more than US$58 million over budget on the project. The project advanced to pump cement into the well to stabilize it. A first test showed too high pressures urging a second test, which the site leaders found satisfactory, but as they continued, no one noticed that the pressure started to rise. At this point, the system had reached overpressure and spewed mud across the rig floor. As mud and gas continued to stream onto the rig it triggered several explosions, causing a firestorm.

Of the 126 people on board the rig, only seven were official BP employees, another 79 crew members worked for Transocean, and the remaining 40 people worked for engaged oil services companies including Anadarko and Halliburton. Eleven people were killed by the explosion before the rig was evacuated and 18 injured crew members were airlifted. *Deepwater Horizon* sank on April 22, 2010, after burning for 36 hours with the remains of the rig dropping to the seafloor 400 meters northwest of the initial well.

The oil leaking from the open drilling hole spread and polluted miles of sensitive coastline causing extensive damage to the marine and wildlife with major adverse economic effects on fishing and tourism. After several failed efforts, the well was finally declared sealed on September 19, 2010.

Consequences for BP

Eventually, the environmental and economic realities surfaced, and it became clear that the rig explosion and the enormity of the related oil spill had catastrophic proportions. BP faced hundreds of lawsuits in federal court. The potential costs were substantial, and a survey estimated the median expected cost of the disaster to be around US$33 billion. As a consequence, Tony Hayward was discharged as CEO and replaced by Bob Dudley on October 1, 2010.

At the time of the dismissal, BP chairman Carl-Henric Svanberg stated:

> the BP board is deeply saddened to lose a CEO whose success over some three years in driving the performance of the company was so widely and deservedly admired ... the tragedy of the Macondo well explosion and subsequent environmental damage has been a watershed incident.[17]

Ultimately, BP came to see some of the unintended or unexpected consequences and attempted to contain the payouts. They announced a hotline where people could report fraudulent claims from affected businesses and residents on the Gulf Coast. It was triggered by an increase in claims where "attorneys for BP argued before a three-judge panel of the 5th U.S. Circuit Court of Appeals that the company has been forced to pay out 'fictitious, exaggerated, and excessive awards.'"[18]

According to Robert Dudley: "It was a terrible accident. We are still committed to make sure that legitimate claimants and people who were true victims of the spill are paid."[19] But, he also argued that BP could become a victim:

> Quite frankly, the results have been really strange. The claims going through a claims facility have resulted in absurd results, and millions of dollars are going out to pay people who suffered, in many cases, no losses from the spill. And this is just not right. I don't think it's right for America. We're a big investor in the United States, and we've challenged this really strongly.

Reflections

This case offers a very wide range of possible discussion topics, from moral issues to practical technical risk management questions.

- Reflecting on the leadership dimension of this story, there seems to be an issue of espoused values and values in action. Are we able to say that John Browne was a serious proponent of sustainable energy or was he caught by the requirement for financial returns? How might we determine which is true? More broadly, what can we learn about leadership—in general terms—from this story?
- Organizational cultures are powerful things; famously, management scholar, Peter Drucker, said "Culture eats strategy for breakfast," which might offer a pithy explanation for key parts of this story. But to be more focused, why was it not possible for Tony Hayward to change the operating risk management culture during his reign?
- Historiography plays a role in defining how risk leaders think about the future. Relying on that discussion in the book, what approach is Bernard Looney employing to look forward. On what basis will it be possible to say that BP will be successful in pursuing a corporate strategy toward "net zero"?
- Regarding the preceding question, what would Looney need to do to be successful?

Read more about it

Browne, J. (2011). *Beyond Business: An Inspirational Memoir from a Remarkable Leader*. Orion Publishing, London, UK.

Heller, N. A. (2012). Leadership in crisis: An exploration of the British petroleum case. *International Journal of Business and Social Science*, 3(18), 21–32.

Hilde, J. B., Trannum, C., Bakke, T., Hodson, V. and Collier, T. K. (2016). Environmental effects of the deepwater horizon oil spill: A review. *Marine Pollution Bulletin*, 110(1), 28–51.

Khan, F. I. and Amyotte, P. R. (2007). Modeling of BP Texas City refinery incident. *Journal of Loss Prevention in the Process Industries*, 20(4–6), 387–395.

MacKenzie, C., Holmstrom, D. and Kaszniak, M. (2007). Human factors analysis of the BP Texas City refinery explosion. In Proceedings of the Human Factors and Ergonomics Society 51st Annual Meeting, 1444–1448.

Pranesh, V., Palanichamy, K., Saidat, O. and Peter, N. (2017). Lack of dynamic leadership skills and human failure contribution analysis to manage risk in deep water horizon oil platform. *Safety Science*, 92, 85–93.

Notes

1 Kemp, M. (2004). *Leonardo*. Oxford University Press, Oxford, UK, is just one of several books Kemp has written on da Vinci, but this book focuses more on Leonardo's approach to work.

2 Neustadt, R. and May, E. R. (1986). *Thinking in Time: The Uses of History for Decision Makers* (1st ed.). Free Press, New York.

3 Titus Lucretius Carus, *On the Nature of Things*. Lucius Annaeus Seneca, *Letters from a Stoic,* are two ancient sources reflecting, in this order, the Epicurean and the Stoic views, on balance.

4 Neustadt, R. E. (1990). *Presidential Power: The Politics of Leadership from FDR to Reagan*. MacMillan Publishing Company, New York.

5 Uhl-Bien, M. and Arena, M. (2018). Leadership for organizational adaptability: A theoretical synthesis and integrative framework. *The Leadership Quarterly*, 29, 89–104. [This is the foundational paper on the Leadership for Organizational Adaptability concept.]

6 Brendan Montague, this is what happened when former BP boss Lord Browne called for action on climate change, DesmogUK—*Clearing the PR Pollution*, March 21, 2015. https://www.desmog.co.uk/2015/03/21/what-happened-when-former-bp-boss-lord-browne-called-action-climate-change

7 Lowe, E. A. and Harris, R. J. 1998. Taking climate change seriously: British Petroleum's business strategy. *Corporate Environmental Strategy*, 5(2), 22–31.

8 British Petroleum, Press release, February 12, 2020. https://www.bp.com/en/global/corporate/news-and-insights/press-releases/bernard-looney-announces-new-ambition-for-bp.html

9 CNNMoney: Fortune Global 500 Annual Ranking, July 25, 2005.

10 Environmental Leader. "Beyond Petroleum" Pays Off for BP, Environmental and Energy Management News, January 15, 2008.

11 Youssef M. Ibrahim, British Petroleum is buying Amoco in $48.2 billion deal, *New York Times*, August 12, 1998.

12 Oil & Gas Journal. BP/Amoco merger creates third "supermajor," August 17, 1998.

13 Investigation Report. Refinery Explosion and Fire, U.S. Chemical Safety and Hazard Investigation Board, Report No. 2005-04-I-TX, March 2007.

14 Ian Cobain and Clare Dyer, BP's Browne quits over lie to court about private life. *The Guardian*, May 1, 2007.

15 Joshua Rozenberg, Lord Browne resigns after revelations he lied in court about gay lover. *The Telegraph*, May 1, 2007.

16 The Center for Public Integrity. BP to pay $13 million for safety violations at Texas refinery, Washington, DC, July 12, 2012.

17 From public statement by Carl-Henric Svanberg, BP Chairman, July 27, 2010.

18 Richard Thompson, BP launches hotline for reporting allegations of fraudulent Gulf of Mexico oil spill claims. *The Times-Picayune,* July 15, 2013.

19 Paul M. Barrett, BP's Robert Dudley on the Gulf Oil Spill's Legal Aftermath. *Bloomberg Businessweek*, August 8, 2013.

Index

Printed in the United States
by Baker & Taylor Publisher Services